DERAILED

ALSO BY JOSEPH VRANICH

Supertrains:
Solutions to America's Transportation Gridlock

DERAILED

What Went Wrong and What to Do
About America's Passenger Trains

Joseph Vranich

St. Martin's Press New York

Design by Richard Oriolo

Library of Congress Cataloging-in-Publication Data

Vranich, Joseph.
    Derailed : what went wrong and what to do about
America's passenger trains / Joseph Vranich.
        p.   cm.
    ISBN 0-312-17182-X
    Includes bibliographical references and index.
    1. Railroads—United States.   2. Railroads and state—United
States. 3. Amtrak. I. Title.
    HE2741.V734   1997
    385'.22'0973—dc21   97-13786
                                                          CIP

First Edition: October 1997

10   9   8   7   6   5   4   3   2   1

To Gene and John Feola,
two of the world's finest uncles

CONTENTS

Preface / ix

ONE: Riding Amtrak: An Adventure / 1

TWO: Amtrak's Structural Problems / 27

THREE: New Long-Distance and Regional Trains / 48

FOUR: Sidetracking High-Speed Trains / 74

FIVE: Big Future for Commuter Rail / 104

SIX: Who Will Run Tomorrow's Trains? / 117

SEVEN: America's Booming Freight Railroads / 136

EIGHT: Washington Spins Its Wheels / 154

NINE: Should Amtrak Be Privatized? / 172

TEN: An Amtrak Transition and Dissolution Plan / 208

Acknowledgments / 243

Bibliography / 247

Index / 251

P R E F A C E

T his book is written for mainstream America—people who travel and wonder why America doesn't have better trains, taxpayers who question how their money is spent, and business leaders who can visualize opportunities to replace Amtrak with something better.

Convinced that America must have a passenger train system, I worked to create Amtrak when it was but a legislative proposal in 1970, and for a long time I believed it held promise. After all, America needs good rail passenger service for environmental, economic, and mobility reasons. But the law of unintended consequences took over, and Amtrak became but a shadow of its promise.

Washington is wringing its hands over Amtrak. In early 1997

Amtrak president Thomas M. Downs said, "I do not believe that enough people realize or understand how close to extinction intercity rail passenger service is in the United States." The problem is not so much with passenger trains, it's with Amtrak.

We can develop sensible rail passenger services while reducing public subsidies that total billions of dollars. Syndicated columnist Robert J. Samuelson, an economist, has said Amtrak symbolizes a root cause of the government's budget problems. He points to Amtrak as proof that "programs tied to the past will fail the future." Some train advocates scorn Samuelson's arguments, but he has a point. With the problem of the federal debt hanging over this and future generations, Washington must find ways to provide public services while reducing the bite on the Treasury.

I hope that this book will serve as the blueprint for a restructured rail system—a manifesto for *improved and relevant* train service in America. Not the kinds of trains that Amtrak runs but useful trains that will come about in a post-Amtrak world. Restructuring would include more commuter trains in big cities, regional trains that Amtrak has disfavored, all-new high-speed systems that Amtrak will never build, and specialized long-distance trains that could run at a profit.

The belief is growing that other organizations should run America's passenger trains. In a speech to the New York chapter of the National Railway Historical Society, I asked, "How many think federal law should be changed to remove Amtrak's monopoly on passenger service and to establish a franchise system where others would be allowed to run trains?" I was stunned when the majority of the audience raised their hands—no, *shot* their hands into the air. That event, several years ago, helped give birth to this book.

I worked for Amtrak in its Public Affairs Department through most of the 1970s. I later spent a decade in the aerospace industry, exposed to forward thinking unlike anything I had witnessed in Amtrak's management. I returned to the railroad community as president of the High Speed Rail Association (now known as the High Speed Ground Transportation Association) and wrestled with incongruous attitudes about Amtrak. Publicly, individuals who were Amtrak contractors would support it. Privately, however, these same people held contempt for Amtrak's ineptitude. A major complaint was that Amtrak, through its own actions, was losing opportunities to build for the future.

Such anger at Amtrak surprised me because I had not, in more than a decade in aerospace, witnessed such bitterness between suppliers and their airline customers. Although I could understand why Amtrak would be criticized by passengers, it nagged me that Amtrak's business relationships were so bad. Surely Amtrak's buying power should serve to sooth its suppliers. Then I was reminded that Amtrak is not a customer in the same manner that America's private freight railroads are— Amtrak fails to operate like a business.

That's the point—too often Amtrak eschews businesslike reasoning and strategic planning. Thus, Amtrak's troubles today mirror the problems it had throughout the 1970s and 1980s and portend the difficulties it will have in the future. I often pick up a newspaper to read about Amtrak's latest failure, only to read that a spokesperson has defended Amtrak using nearly identical language as I used in defending Amtrak in the 1970s. I felt that my comments were justified then because Amtrak was a struggling new entity and needed time to straighten out its problems. Seeing the same arguments today to explain why trains are late, or why other service deficiencies occur, means that Amtrak's words have become empty. The public was patient in the 1970s and 1980s, but I believe that patience has run out.

I admit to some change in thinking since I wrote *Supertrains: Solutions to America's Transportation Gridlock.* That book focused on high-speed trains, and because such proposals came not from Amtrak but from other institutions, I was ambivalent about Amtrak. I remain convinced about the promise of fast trains, but I now believe it will be *easier* for high-speed rail planners if Amtrak weren't around to interfere with visionary projects. This book outlines how Amtrak has indeed undermined imaginative rail passenger proposals.

For those who worry about a few inconsistencies between the books, remember that seven years have transpired between the writing of the first book and this one. I recall words of advice from Brenda

Ueland, author of *If You Want to Write*: "Do not try to be consistent, for what is true to you today may not be true at all tomorrow, because you see a better truth." Well, this book deals with the truths about Amtrak as I see them today. Other Amtrak observers also have revised their views, so I feel I'm in good company.

This book summarizes domestic and international developments regarding public services like Amtrak. Why and how, for example, are countries as diverse as Japan, Great Britain, and Argentina privatizing their railways? What lessons do their actions have for the United States? While this book does not promise that privatization is the exclusive answer to restructuring Amtrak, it explains how it is a partial solution.

This work is not a financial plan. It explores existing policies and proposes new ones to help establish a useful framework for future rail services. Only when we better understand what the new policy context might be can those with more expertise—investment bankers, planners, railroad executives, legislators, and others—begin to shape train services for a post-Amtrak era.

This book provides an action plan that involves creating a federal Amtrak Transition Board to carry out Amtrak's liquidation and dissolution. The plan came about only after I had taken a firsthand look at other railways in the world and their new organizational structures. Despite the data contained here, I'll be criticized by those in industry, labor, and government who prefer the status quo. I can only comfort myself by recalling the words of the late Chief Justice Earl Warren: "Everything I did in my life that was worthwhile I caught hell for."

Although I prefer to travel by train, my dissatisfaction with riding Amtrak is such that I travel by air virtually everywhere on domestic trips. Yet, when I'm in Europe or Japan, I ride trains without question. If I—a longtime rail travel promoter—avoid Amtrak, is it any wonder that millions of others do, too?

In the interest of disclosure, I at times write in the first person. It would be unnatural to do otherwise when I directly participated in some of the events I describe.

Also, I believe nonfiction authors have a responsibility to reveal to the book buyer what their politics are. We may want to buy a pro-welfare book written by a liberal, or a welfare-bashing book by a conservative, but wouldn't it be nice to know the mind-set of the author in advance?

I will volunteer that I'm a lifelong moderately liberal Democrat, the very kind of person who has been Amtrak's staunchest defender. I and others like me now recognize Amtrak as a failed program that should be jettisoned. Consequently, this book's message will alarm liberals, but they shouldn't rush to call me a turncoat. I believe a true liberal is one who has faith that government can contribute to the public well-being, but only if it provides programs that *work*. So, call me a "sensible liberal" who refuses to be wedded to a failed policy. Or call me a practical fellow whose message is neither partisan nor ideological.

If liberals and conservatives admitted that developments have invalidated their earlier advocacy for this or that government effort, then useless federal programs could die. Special interests would be short-term losers, but the country would be a long-term winner. This has happened elsewhere; in New Zealand, for example, it was none other than the Labour government that was the primary force in privatizing its national airline and railway.

Does Amtrak have the influence to save itself? Quite possibly, because it showed staying power under assaults from the Carter, Reagan, and Bush Administrations. All bureaucracies in our nation's capital take on a life of their own and develop a cadre of influential special-interest friends.

Regardless of the future shape of federal transportation policies, my view is that there is no useful role for Amtrak. Amtrak has failed in what it was set up to accomplish. A fitting action to take on Amtrak's thirtieth anniversary—which will occur on May 1, 2001—would be to put Amtrak to rest, passing the baton to private-sector and state-agency successors.

This book addresses practical questions: Without Amtrak, what kind of passenger trains will Americans ride? Where should they run?

What mix of public and private financing will be necessary? Certainly, as our airports and highways become more crowded, we should develop the kinds of trains that we will need in the next century.

I am, at heart, an optimist. There is a future for passenger trains, especially as many Americans remain fascinated with them. Maybe it's because each of us can own an automobile or boat, or even an airplane, but we can't own a train. Perhaps that's why we acknowledge that trains are, well, *different.*

Dissolve Amtrak? Yes, but we need to do so carefully to keep useful trains running in the twenty-first century.

ONE

Riding Amtrak:
An Adventure

*"Twenty-five years after I set out to save the American
passenger train, I feel personally embarrassed
over what I helped to create."*

—Anthony Haswell, founder,
National Association of Railroad Passengers

T rain travel can be an enjoyable experience. On some days riding
Amtrak can be great; on other days, a disaster. One constant
through Amtrak's history is its widely uneven level of service. The result
is that people who like trains either love Amtrak or hate it. Why is
this?

Before looking forward, let's look back.

Anyone who has wondered what inspired Washington to create
Amtrak, or who wants to hear well-considered views of what we should
do about Amtrak today, should meet Anthony Haswell. In his sixties,
he is as lean as a track star, courteous in demeanor, and shy about his
genius. When he speaks, his sincerity shines in such a way that even

those who disagree with him respect him. Logic is his strong suit, perhaps because of his legal training, and his knowledge about railroads is encyclopedic.

In the days before Amtrak, he was known as the railroad industry's Ralph Nader—an allusion he probably liked—because he argued eloquently for better passenger train service to serve a neglected public. He knew his way around railroad offices in Chicago, having worked for the Illinois Central and the now-defunct Chicago, Rock Island & Pacific Railroad and learned the ins and outs of Washington, D.C.

He earned the moniker Father of Amtrak, which he is uneasy about today, as the founder of the National Association of Railroad Passengers. There, working out of a Capitol Hill office in 1970, he was the key proponent in persuading Congress to pass the Railpax ("railroad passenger") law that created Amtrak. Now he has the mettle to declare that his work was wasted. "Back then, if I could have seen what Amtrak would become, I would have sought some other way to save and improve our passenger trains."

Haswell would like to undo what he created. His is one of a growing number of voices who would replace Amtrak with new organizations in all parts of the United States. Meanwhile, others who've never met Haswell believe that some Amtrak trains could be operated profitably by new enterprises—provided the government makes policy changes. This claim of profitability is made because of a basic fact: the market for rail passenger service is much wider than Amtrak has ever been able to tap into.

Simply put, there are many reasons why customers are motivated to travel by train. A psychological factor is that trains are part of our human fabric. Children still ask for trains for Christmas (when has a child ever asked for a model bus?), and many of us are just older children. People of all ages anticipate with pleasure a long-distance train trip. In a few of our largest cities, some business travelers arrange meetings around train schedules whenever possible.

The lure of train travel can be understood by leafing through Amtrak's multicolor tour brochure, in which flowery prose can whet a traveler's appetite:

It rolls through majestic farmlands. Cuts through mountains so high they take your breath away. Just around the bend is something new—a mist-shrouded forest, an endless beach. And just out the window, America and her people thrive, raising a hand in greeting as the train hurtles by. It's the sound of the distant whistle. The rush of the wheels and the rhythmic sway. It's relaxing. Stimulating. . . . So close your eyes and clear your mind. Or spend hours looking at the scenery outside. Pick up a book. Or pick up a conversation with that fellow across the aisle. Watch your children watch for bears, deer and eagles. Lean back. Way back. And enjoy the entertainment of our great land.

That makes telephones rings down at the local travel agent's office, but so do other marketing efforts. Amtrak has earned some good marks by implementing a Smart Pass for frequent riders, upgrading equipment, developing new train-bus routes in conjunction with Greyhound Lines, and urging its employees to be friendlier. Its marketing efforts include an Internet site that describes routes and promotional packages.

Once aboard a train, travelers find an atmosphere unlike the strapped-in confines of an airplane cabin. Trains—particularly long-distance ones—offer room to stretch and places where it's easy to meet people. Sometimes, an employee with a sunny disposition creates a fun, relaxed atmosphere, which helps break the ice among passengers. Although unprovable, I suspect more friendships have started aboard passenger trains than on any other form of transportation except cruise ships.

Amtrak sometimes offers wine tastings on Sightseer lounge cars in America's West, where views of snowcapped mountains, sparkling rivers, and endless prairies captivate travelers. Dining cars offer sit-down dinners with fresh food prepared by chefs trained at the Culinary Institute. By boosting the quality of its meals, Amtrak is trying to please the aging part of the travel market who are fussy about lunch and dinner.

First class still exists on Amtrak. The opulence of Pullman service may be gone, but Amtrak's sleeping cars—with snug beds, individual temperature controls, linens, and private bathrooms—still provide the single most comfortable way to travel overnight.

An example of Amtrak's effort to target specific markets is found in several states where cycling enthusiasts can bring fully assembled bicycles aboard the train. This is an improvement over a time-consuming requirement that bicycles had to be disassembled and boxed for shipment as baggage.

There's some style left to train travel, a hint of which shows in train names. The *Capitol Limited* connects Washington, D.C., with the Midwest, terminating in Chicago. The *California Zephyr* starts in Chicago and links many communities with San Francisco. The *Coast Starlight* trundles along on a busy Seattle–Los Angeles route and has become Amtrak's "most respected train," according to Sylvia and Ted Blishak, who own a travel agency in Klamath Falls, Oregon, and are rail travel specialists.

For those who travel along the Eastern seaboard, Amtrak's *Auto Train* can transport them and their automobiles overnight between Lorton, Virginia (near Washington, D.C.), and Sanford, Florida, convenient to a host of tourist destinations. The train's biggest virtue is that passengers avoid driving a grueling nine hundred miles, parts of which offer highway congestion and speed traps. Also, passengers may pack as much baggage as their cars can hold, a benefit for those planning an extended stay.

In many cases, Amtrak passengers are riding in fairly new equipment, paid for by taxpayers, including double-decker Superliner cars (on long-distance trains) and single-level Viewliner cars (on Eastern routes). A significant number of Amfleet cars have been extensively rebuilt.

Train trips start at terminals, and Amtrak has done a decent job upgrading many of them. A stench-filled, decrepit station in Rochester, New York, has long been replaced by an attractive facility. Through painstaking restoration, Washington Union Station, once a boarded-up embarrassment, again reflects its classic splendor. Oakland, California, has a new station, required after the 1989 Loma Prieta earthquake nearly destroyed the old one. And in a unique arrangement,

Bellingham, Washington, converted an old salmon cannery into an intermodal facility that serves Amtrak, intercity buses, airport shuttles, and taxicabs.

Disappointing Rides

U nfortunately, Amtrak can be schizophrenic. While passengers may have delightful experiences, they also run the risk of enduring miserable rides. As Kevin P. Keefe, editor of *Trains* magazine, cogently put it: "You can still ride the Northeast Corridor at 125 mph, then endure 40-mph average speeds on the Chicago–St. Louis run. You can still board various short-haul trains that feature food service, and others that don't. These simple but maddening lapses of consistency prevent Amtrak from attaining anything close to world-class status."

Sad but true, many Amtrak passengers experience terrible trips. Amtrak's efforts are overshadowed by its unpredictability. Its on-time performance is uneven—a few trains generally run on time, such as the *Metroliner* between New York and Washington, while others are late, dirty, and worse. On some trains passenger cars run without heat in the winter or air-conditioning in the summer, windows are filthy, and garbage piles up in coaches. Even Amtrak president Tom Downs admits that many first-time Amtrak customers say, "Never again!"

In 1994 Amtrak received more complaint letters than ever before. After a subsequent decline, however, the letters are coming in again. Consider what happened during Thanksgiving week in 1996, when the Associated Press ran a story about Amtrak's "train from hell." The report chronicled numerous problems aboard Amtrak's *Empire Builder* and noted that the train arrived in Seattle twelve hours late. It quoted Tim O'Donoghue, a passenger from Reston, Virginia, as saying, "I was wondering if the stagecoach would be faster." Moreover, the food ran out, "forcing a stop to take on some Kentucky Fried Chicken in Spokane, Washington."

Even Amtrak's special trains filled with VIPs run poorly.

In 1996 the first run of Amtrak's *Gulf Coast Limited* between New Orleans and Mobile, Alabama, ran so slowly that it was called the "slow boat to China." It didn't help that it also ran late, keeping crowds at train stations sweltering in the summer heat.

Amtrak had not learned from a terrible inauguration several years earlier, when its *Sunset Limited* from Miami arrived in Los Angeles four hours behind schedule. According to Craig Wilson, a reporter for *USA Today*, "The toilets didn't always work. The shower was sometimes cold. The dishwasher broke down before New Orleans and the toasters were left behind in Miami. To make matters worse, the bar car ran out of vodka outside of Sanderson, Texas—just when you need a drink most."

Again and again, this is Amtrak's experience.

One episode in particular sticks in my mind as a way of illustrating Amtrak's problems. I was a public relations representative for Amtrak and at one point was in charge of promoting sparkling new equipment that was being put in service on a long-distance train. Our publicity about the new train offered hope to travelers: "Passengers riding the new Amfleet cars can expect to find the ride smooth because of an advanced suspension system and quiet due to extensive soundproofing. The cars are equipped with all the luxuries of modern travel—pastel colors, indirect lighting, roomy seats, automatic sliding doors, pull-down seat trays, and air-conditioning."

In addition to carrying paying customers, the train was filled with journalists, elected officials, and travel agents. Under the circumstances, it was reasonable to expect that the train would run on time. After all, the equipment was fresh from the factory; most of the guests were VIPs; the weather was perfect. The day was important enough for Amtrak to serve champagne. But all was not well. One media story after another reported that the westbound inaugural train pulled in to Kansas City nearly four hours late, while its eastbound counterpart limped into New York five hours behind schedule. This attempt at positive publicity resulted in widespread negative coverage, which of course turned off an untold number of potential customers.

That late-running train was the *National Limited.* This particular story happened in 1978, but it cries out for repetition because *nothing has changed*—the disappointing service offered back then is similar to disappointments today. It's also an important story to consider because the train was discontinued, having failed to pick up a decent share of the market in its service area.

On-Time Performance

I f Amtrak can't run trains filled with governors and mayors and the news media on time, when can it? Certainly its record with regularly scheduled trains will win no awards. The "late train story" has repeated itself often throughout Amtrak's history, causing great customer dissatisfaction. One result is that trains almost seem to compete for negative attention. AMTRAK RUN HAS "WORST TIME" RECORD was the title of a Champaign *Courier* (Illinois) story back when its local train, the *Illini*, was meeting its scheduled time of arrival "only once in 20 trips." Or, *BROADWAY LIMITED*'s ON-TIME RECORDED: 1 IN 60 headlined the *Chicago Sun-Times*, which reported that Amtrak blamed Conrail for the poor performance.

A feisty publication, the *Rail Travel News*, reported in early 1972 that the *Coast Starlight* had an abysmal on-time record over the just-ended Christmas holiday period, having an on-time record at Los Angeles of only 29 percent. Again, some things don't change—even after nineteen years. As reported by Michael Wright in *Condé Nast Traveler*, the on-time rate of Amtrak's *Coast Starlight* "dropped from a not-great 40 percent in September 1991 to an abysmal 8.3 percent one year later." This train was so tardy during 1995 that Amtrak employees began referring to is as the "Starlate." Riders aboard Amtrak's Chicago–New York *Lake Shore Limited* have been heard to call it the "Late Shore Limited." Newspaper headlines from the 1970s and 1990s about late trains are virtually interchangeable.

At times, Amtrak management has explained poor performance by pointing out that its routes are so long that many opportunities exist for things to go wrong. What, then, explains the problems on short-distance lines? The Train Riders Association of California reported that Amtrak service between Santa Barbara and Los Angeles was "extremely unreliable," as Amtrak trains were sidetracked for other trains. "In some instances passengers had to endure waits as long as an hour in the sidings," reported the group. It concluded, "This chaotic operation seems to be a standard feature of the route."

In its twenty-five-year history, four presidents preceded Tom Downs at Amtrak. The first was Roger Lewis, followed by Paul H. Reistrup, Alan S. Boyd, and W. Graham Claytor, Jr. All shared an inability to make the trains run on time.

Professors Tony M. Ridley and Francis R. Terry of the Centre for Transport Studies at the University of London report that European railways "exceed by a substantial margin the punctuality standards which Amtrak sees as the norm (70–80 percent on-time arrival)." The French railway system reported that after a decade of operating the TGV (*Train à Grande Vitesse*, or "train of great speed"), it has experienced a delay of ten minutes or longer *only once per year per trainset,* or every 248,500 miles. Further, a survey by *Railway Gazette International* revealed that nine European rail systems did better than Amtrak when tolerance differences were taken into account.

Amtrak's on-time performance has never been, nor will it ever be, at the point where passengers could expect European-like dependability. Amtrak owns tracks only in parts of the Northeast and a small stretch in Michigan, but virtually everywhere else its trains move over tracks owned and dispatched by America's freight railroads. The result is that Amtrak's on-time performance from 1983 to 1993 ranged from a low of 72 percent to a high of 82 percent. It has fallen again, with Amtrak's 1996 record of 70.9 percent lower than the previous year's 76.4 percent. For short-distance business passengers, that meant arriving late for meetings. For long-distance travelers, there were missed connections with other trains and countless personal inconveniences.

"I can personally testify that the *Southwest Chief* does not have a good reputation for on-time performance," said Haswell. "Twice in recent years I have inquired about renting a car at Flagstaff; both times the rental agency said they could not meet me at the train because it ran late so often. A cab driver in Albuquerque referred to the train's schedule as an 'estimated time of arrival.' On-time performance is particularly unimpressive when one keeps in mind that the *Southwest Chief* averages 55 mph."

John Reed, the president in the 1970s of the Santa Fe Railway, over whose tracks this train operates, was so disenchanted with Amtrak's stewardship that he ordered Amtrak to cease using the name *Super Chief,* which for years had been the name of Santa Fe's premier passenger train. Amtrak was forced for many years to rename the train, which it called the *Southwest Limited.*

Federal law gives Amtrak passenger trains priority over freight trains, but operating conditions often mean it's *impossible* for the freight railroads over which Amtrak operates to comply. For example, when a long freight train and a short Amtrak train run on a single-track line, and the passing siding is short, the Amtrak train often must take the sidetrack and wait for the freight train to pass. This is an operational fact that Washington policy makers who demand that "passengers come before freight" prefer to ignore.

An Amtrak analysis showed that 36 percent of the delays suffered by Amtrak were attributable to factors that are wholly controlled by the freight carriers. But Amtrak itself is responsible for many delays due to improper servicing of equipment, malfunctions at stations that it owns, trains being held for late-running connections, and other causes.

Amtrak in Chicago

What is surprising about Amtrak's having so much trouble arriving at the appointed hour is it liberally pads its schedules with extra time. This is most noticeable in the stretches at the end of a train's run. Henry Kisor explains this well in his book *Zephyr: Tracking a Dream Across America,* in which he urges readers to check the elapsed time between a train's point of origin and its first stop. Now do the reverse—compare the time between the same stations for a train going in the opposite direction. He gives as an example the 28 miles from

TABLE 1.1. Comparison of Amtrak's Chicago Operations and Third World Train Schedules

Route Portion	Miles	Amtrak Train	Average (mph) Speed	Country, Train Route	Average (mph) Speed
Glenview to Chicago	17	*Empire Builder*	25.5	Sri Lanka, Colombo–Batticaloa	25.5
Homewood to Chicago	24	*Illini*	22.9	Chile, Valparaiso–Los Andes	23.7
Hammond to Chicago	16	*Lake Cities*	22.3	Nigeria, Lagos-Kano	23
Naperville to Chicago	28	*Southwest Chief*	21.8	Zambia, Kitwe-Livingstone	22.3
Naperville to Chicago	28	*California Zephyr*	20	Algeria, Constantine-Jijel	20
Hammond to Chicago	16	*Lake Shore Limited*	17.1	Ghana, Accra-Kumasi	19.3
Hammond to Chicago	16	*Capitol Limited*	15.5	Angola, Luanda-Malange	18.5
Summit to Chicago	12	*Ann Rutledge*	15.3	Namibia, Windhoek–Gobabis	17.9
Dyer to Chicago	28	*Cardinal*	14.7	Ethiopia, Addis Ababa–Dire Dawa	15.4
Hammond to Chicago	16	*Three Rivers*	12.8	Peru, Cuzco–Quillabamba	13.1

Sources: Amtrak schedules effective through April 1997 and *Thomas Cook Overseas Timetable*, September–October 1995.

Chicago to Naperville, which takes "thirty-five honest minutes," but Naperville to Chicago takes more than twice as long.

This bizarre scheduling results in Amtrak trains' entering Chicago at speeds equal to some of the worst found on creaky railroads in Third World countries. Table 1.1 shows that Amtrak's New York–Chicago *Three Rivers* plods into Chicago from Hammond, Indiana, at an average speed of 12.8 mph, slower than trains in Peru. Other Amtrak schedules are also tedious: the *California Zephyr* at 20 mph mimics a timetable found in Algeria; the *Lake Cities* on Amtrak's "emerging high-speed corridor" from Detroit, creeping along at 22.3 mph, would lose a race to a train in Nigeria. Other trains in Chile, Angola, and Ethiopia are equal to or faster than Amtrak trains running toward Chicago Union Station.

A study of schedules shows that at least thirty less-than-advanced nations run trains twice as fast as Amtrak does in Chicago.* Amtrak

*Angola, Argentina, Bangladesh, Benin, Botswana, Brazil, Bulgaria, Cameroon, Chile, Egypt, Ethiopia, Gabon, Ghana, Indonesia, Ivory Coast, Malaysia, Mali, Mexico, Mo-

trains are painfully slow, which, combined with lengthy layovers between trains, means passengers passing *through* Chicago have to stay *in* Chicago much longer than if they had driven, taken the bus, or flown.

To add another disconcerting element, Amtrak's system of record-keeping tolerances makes Amtrak's on-time performance look better than it is. Trains traveling more than 550 miles are still considered to be on time even if they arrive thirty minutes late. Thus, on a day the eastbound *California Zephyr* is on time at Naperville, combining that allowance with the schedule of one hour and fifteen minutes means that the train can take one hour and forty-four minutes to travel 28 miles to Chicago and still be considered on time. That's an average speed of 16.2 mph, or slower than the Dar es Salaam–Mwanza train in Tanzania.

It was not always like this at Chicago. In 1952, for example, the Santa Fe's westbound *Grand Canyon* took fifty-four minutes between Chicago and Joliet, but eastbound took only four minutes longer. Today, in Europe and Japan, railroad managers schedule trains as expeditiously on final segments of routes as they do on originating legs.

Even more shocking, Amtrak's slowness isn't isolated to Chicago. Its trains are the slowest American trains in more than half a century. That finding came from research by Haswell, who went back to 1936, when Franklin D. Roosevelt was elected to his second term as President and Hitler's troops were occupying the Rhineland. It doesn't seem possible that trains running so long ago were faster than trains today, but they were. Haswell cites startling examples: Amtrak takes five hours and thirty minutes to connect Chicago with St. Louis, but that trip was forty-five minutes faster in the thirties. Amtrak's fastest train today between Chicago and Detroit covers the distance in five hours and twenty-four minutes, but that trip was thirty-nine minutes faster then. Similar comparisons could be made for other periods: a San Francisco–Los Angeles trip on Amtrak's *Coast Starlight* today takes eleven hours

---

rocco, Myanmar, Namibia, Senegal, South Africa, Sri Lanka, Tanzania, Thailand, Tunisia, Turkey, Venezuela, and Zimbabwe.

and twenty minutes, barely faster than the twelve-hour schedule launched in 1923 by the Southern Pacific Railroad.

It is logical to compare Amtrak today with schedules in 1952, when railroads had replaced steam engines with diesel locomotives similar to what Amtrak operates. Also that year the Interstate Commerce Commission implemented a rule that the top speed for passenger trains unequipped with special signal lights on engineers' control panels was to be 79 mph; other rules limited passenger train speeds to 60 mph. Amtrak has to observe the same regulations today.

The results shown in Table 1.2 are devastating to Amtrak. On many corridors—the routes most promising for passenger trains—Amtrak schedules are embarrassingly slow. For example, travel on Amtrak between Chicago and Cincinnati takes nearly eight and a half hours, almost three hours longer. Even very short routes aren't spared. The 86-mile Chicago–Milwaukee line sees a schedule more than a quarter hour slower than it was in 1952. Los Angeles–San Diego, where the state of California has spent millions of dollars to upgrade track, is ten minutes slower.

This is truly remarkable. In no other area of transportation can such a marked deterioration be found, as a comparison of 1952 and 1997 air and bus schedules or driving time charts would easily show.

It may be immaterial that schedules for long-distance trains have been lengthened because it is believed leisure travelers won't mind. That may be, but today's slower trains are failing to deliver their passengers to their destinations with the same degree of punctuality as their faster predecessors did.

A disturbing factor about lengthy schedules is their significance for the future. The New York Central Railroad offered a twenty-hour schedule between New York and Chicago in 1893 with the *Exposition Flyer*. If the best that Amtrak can offer on the same route more than a century later is a schedule only about an hour and a half faster, then Amtrak has reached its technological pinnacle *for long-distance trains*. Thus, fundamental changes must be made to the nature of the services offered aboard the trains and the markets to which they are targeted.

Some Amtrak trains are faster than their 1952 ancestors, as shown

TABLE 1.2. Schedule Deterioration over 45-Year Period

1997 Fastest Amtrak Schedules Compared with 1952 Railroad Schedules

Route	Amtrak Train	Time	1952 Train	Time	Amtrak Slower by
Chicago–Boise–Portland, Ore.	*Pioneer*	49:25	*City of Portland*	40:00	9:25
St. Louis–San Antonio	*Texas Eagle*	22:59	*Texas Eagle*	18:10	4:49
Portland–Oakland	*Coast Starlight*	18:40	*Shasta Daylight*	14:43	3:57
Chicago–Pgh.–New York	*Three Rivers*	19:55	*Broadway Limited*	16:00	3:55
Chicago–Cincinnati	*Cardinal*	8:25	*James Whitcomb Riley*	5:30	2:55
Chicago–Denver–Oakland	*California Zephyr*	52:35	*California Zephyr*	49:50	2:45
Chicago–New Orleans	*City of New Orleans*	19:00	*City of New Orleans*	16:25	2:35
Chicago–Denver	*California Zephyr*	18:40	*Denver Zephyr*	16:05	2:35
Boston–Chicagao	*Lake Shore Limited*	21:01	*New England States*	18:45	2:16
Chicago–Buffalo–New York	*Lake Shore Limited*	18:24	*20th Century Limited*	16:30	1:54
New York–Pittsburgh	*Pennsylvanian*	9:39	*Broadway Limited*	7:52	1:47
San Francisco–Los Angeles	*Coast Starlight*	11:20	*Morning Daylight*	9:45	1:35
New York–Charleston–Miami	*Silver Meteor*	26:25	*East Coast Champion*	24:55	1:30
Chicago–Pgh.–Washington	*Capitol Limited*	16:52	*Capitol Limited*	15:25	1:27
New York–Charlotte	*Carolinian*	13:56	*The Crescent*	12:30	1:26
Chicago–Indianapolis	*Cardinal*	4:45	*James Whitcomb Riley*	3:30	1:15
Chicago–Milw.–Twin Cities	*Empire Builder*	7:55	*Afternoon Hiawatha*	6:45	1:10
Chicago–Carbondale	*Illini*	5:30	*Panama Limited*	4:32	58
Chicago–Albuq.–Los Angeles	*Southwest Chief*	40:40	*Super Chief*	39:45	55
New York–Tampa	*Silver Palm*	23:37	*Silver Meteor*	22:44	53
New York–New Orleans	*Crescent*	29:05	*Southerner*	28:20	45
New York–Harrisburg	*Keystone Service*	3:45	*General*	3:02	43
St. Louis–Fort Worth	*Texas Eagle*	15:38	*Texas Eagle*	14:55	43
Chicago–Detroit	*Twilight Limited*	5:35	*Twilight Limited*	5:00	35
Chicago–Champaign/Urbana	*Illini*	2:25	*Panama Limited*	1:50	35
Oakland–Bakersfield	*San Joaquins*	6:15	*Golden Gate*	5:40	35
Sacramento–Oakland	*Capitols*	2:24	*No. 247*	1:53	31
St. Louis–Kansas City	*Kansas City Mule*	5:30	*Colorado Eagle*	5:00	30
Chicago–St. Louis	*State House*	5:30	*The Abraham Lincoln*	5:10	20
Chicago–Milwaukee	*Hiawatha Service*	1:32	*Afternoon Hiawatha*	1:15	17
Boston–New York	*Old Dominion*	4:15	(8 trains)	4:00	15
New York–Montreal	*Adirondack*	9:25	*Montreal Limited*	9:10	15
Los Angeles–Las Vegas	*Desert Wind*	6:50	*City of Los Angeles*	6:35	15
Los Angeles–Santa Barbara	*San Diegans*	2:35	*Morning Daylight*	2:20	15

Route	Amtrak Train	Time	1952 Train	Time	Amtrak Slower by
Los Angeles–San Diego	*San Diegans*	2:25	*No. 81*	2:15	10
Philadelphia–Harrisburg	*Pennsylvanian*	1:53	*No. 600*	1:45	8
New Orleans–Mobile	*Gulf Coast Limited*	3:10	*No. 6–65*	3:03	7
Washington–Springfield	*Nutmeg State*	7:05	*The Patriot*	7:00	5
Chicago–Quincy	*Illinois Zephyr*	4:23	*Kansas City Zephyr**	4:20	3
Washington–St. Albans, Vt.	*Vermonter*	13:35	*Washingtonian*	13:34	1
Seattle–Vancouver, B.C.	*Mount Baker***	3:55	*International*	3:55	0
Chicago–Fargo–Seattle	*Empire Builder*	45:00	*Empire Builder*	45:00	0

Sources: Amtrak schedules effective through April 1997, and *Official Guide of the Railways*, June 1952 edition.
*This schedule from April 1953.
**Identified by Amtrak as a high-speed train.
Trains running on Saturday- and Sunday-only schedules excluded from the study.

TABLE 1.3. Schedule Improvement over 45-Year Period
1997 Amtrak Schedules Faster than 1952 Railroad Schedules

Route	Amtrak Train	Time	1952 Train	Time	Amtrak Faster by
New Orleans–Los Angeles	*Sunset Limited*	40:50	*Sunset Limited*	42:00	1:10
New York–Washington	*Metroliner**	2:59	*Afternoon Congressional*	3:35	36
New York–Albany	*Hudson Valley Express*	2:10	*Knickerbocker*	2:40	30
New Orleans–Jacksonville	*Sunset Limited*	14:40	*Gulf Wind*	15	20
Washington–Cincinnati	*Cardinal*	13:55	*George Washington*	14:10	15
Boston–Washington	*New England Express*	8:01	*The Senator*	8:15	14
Chicago–Grand Rapids	*Pere Marquette*	3:55	*No. 8*	4:05	10
Seattle–Portland	*Mount Rainier**	3:50	*Daily Streamliner #457*	3:59	9
New York–Buffalo	*Empire State Express*	7:48	*Ohio State Limited*	7:53	5
Chicago–Port Huron	*International*	6:27	*The International Limited*	6:30	3

Sources: Amtrak schedules effective through April 1997, and *Official Guide of the Railways*, June 1952 edition.
*Identified by Amtrak as high-speed trains.
Trains running on Saturday- and Sunday-only schedules were excluded from the study.

in Table 1.3. There are a few reasons for this. First, on the New York–Washington, Boston–Washington, New York–Buffalo, and Seattle–Portland routes, federal and state funds have gone into upgrading the lines in order to shorten travel times. Second, the *Sunset Limited* is faster because a reroute means it no longer directly serves Phoenix, Arizona. Finally, some 1952 schedules required time to switch cars in and out of trains at junctions. When the westbound *George Washington,* for example, stopped in Charlottesville, Virginia, the Chesapeake & Ohio Railroad added sleeping cars that arrived in another train from Richmond and Tidewater-area points. Dining cars and coaches were also switched in and out of the train. Later, upon the train's arrival in Ashland, Kentucky, where routes diverged, time was needed to split the train into sections—one to Cincinnati, Ohio, and the other to Louisville, Kentucky. Amtrak avoids all that by running an intact train, but it is only fifteen minutes faster.

Meanwhile, travel has become faster on one system that competes with Amtrak—highways. In 1995 Washington repealed the nation's 55-mph speed limit that had been imposed to save energy during the mid-1970s Arab oil embargo. Most states have since increased their speed limits to between 65 and 75 mph, with highway patrols often ignoring drivers going faster than posted speeds.

Flying will become faster in upcoming years. The Federal Aviation Administration (FAA) will phase in new rules and technology to permit "free flight," meaning that pilots will be allowed to pick their routes, altitudes, and speeds, with controllers intervening only if flight plans conflict. This will eliminate many zigzag flight patterns and, in addition to saving money for airlines by easing delays, will save time for passengers.

Don't expect faster Amtrak trains in most of the country.

In the vast majority of the United States, Amtrak has no effective program to address causes of slow and undependable trains, including but not limited to poor track, inadequate signaling and grade-crossing protection, arbitrarily low municipal speed limits, freight congestion in yard and terminal areas, delays for passing freight and commuter trains, and insufficient operating supervision.

Late and slow trains aren't Amtrak's only problem.

The FDA's Permanent Injunction

Amtrak's service problems are numerous, but it's useful to examine a notorious case in which the U.S. Food and Drug Administration (FDA) cited Amtrak for unsanitary conditions. It's a little-known fact that the FDA regularly inspects food service of commercial airlines. During a typical year, the agency issues about nine warning letters to airlines. Southwest Airlines was cited for a lack of hand-washing sinks at a California facility, Aloha Airlines for mold in an ice machine, and Continental Airlines for storing meat and eggs at improper temperatures aboard a New York–Houston flight. In Washington, FDA spokeswoman Judith Foulke said, "There's a possibility of public health problems, or we wouldn't have issued warnings. But the airlines are very good about correcting problems immediately."

As FDA records show, Amtrak had problems that were far more severe—problems that festered for years.

In the 1970s and again in the 1980s, the FDA had issued warnings to Amtrak regarding unsanitary conditions and rodent problems in its commissaries. The warnings were issued locally, and no national coordination or investigation was evident. Amtrak responded by taking sporadic corrective action, which was only temporarily effective. Often, food-service personnel were confused by conflicting directives. For example, Amtrak—which has long been unable to keep refrigeration equipment in working order—encouraged its employees to use dry ice to keep food cold. The FDA opposes such a practice because dry ice has an uneven effect on food, which produces health hazards. Receiving conflicting directives from supposedly knowledgeable officials led Amtrak workers to be contemptuous of both the edicts and the officials.

In 1992 the FDA initiated a sweeping investigation of Amtrak because of reports about unclean conditions, mice-infested dining cars and commissaries, inoperative public toilets, and related conditions. The complaints were coming not only from passengers but from another public agency—the U.S. Customs Service reported that rodents were in evidence on the *Montrealer*. The FDA took action that was more severe than anything ever taken against an airline. The agency filed a complaint in federal court, which issued a permanent injunction against Amtrak that required a long-term "sanitation and food service program" to be implemented with the FDA's and the court's approval. Amtrak, which signed a consent decree, must for all time take the agreement seriously because the FDA has the authority to take strong measures when Amtrak falters.

For the first time, Amtrak began giving employees serious sanitation training: part of the effort included the banishment of dry ice. The organization also began a long-delayed cleanup campaign.

The immediate impact was to create havoc on Amtrak's operations. Within a month Amtrak fumigated more than six hundred cars outside the normal maintenance schedule, temporarily sidetracked a large segment of its food-service cars, rushed sixty-four cars with inoperative public toilets or sinks into the repair shops, and delayed sixty-eight trains for rodent problems. Another result was noticeable to passengers as infested equipment was shunted around—more and more trains were late. Very late.

Some railroad enthusiasts were unhappy that the FDA had opened fire on Amtrak with such force. But speaking a year later, Dennis F. Sullivan, then Amtrak's executive vice president and chief operating officer, conceded that "the FDA didn't do that to Amtrak; Amtrak did that to Amtrak. . . . It was a tough thing to go through, but I'm glad it's behind us."

It wasn't.

Two years later Amtrak had to close part of train number 477 in Springfield, Massachusetts, because of mice. After the mice were discovered, Amtrak planned to remove the coach at New Haven. However, no advance notice was given to employees there, and considerable discussion ensured about what to do. One worker speaking over a radio suggested allowing the car to continue to Philadelphia, where the mice might be happier. Another employee said that wasn't permissible because the mice didn't have tickets. When the joking ended, the train was evacuated and all passengers transferred to a later train.

Accidents and Their Aftermath

More serious than the mice are the mishaps and derailments. Amtrak trains derail too often, even while loping along at slow speeds. Meanwhile, high-speed trains overseas operate with astonishingly superb safety records. France's TGV, Germany's ICE Train (InterCity Express), and Japan's famed Bullet Trains have carried more than 3.5 billion passengers without a single passenger fatality. In rare instances when foreign high-speed trains are in an accident, the injuries have never been as extensive as on Amtrak.

A stunning high-speed accident was described by Mike Knutton, editor of the *International Railway Journal:* "What images spring to mind if you consider the possibility of a TGV train leaving the tracks at 183 mph? Mass destruction of life and equipment? Fortunately the reality is different, as was demonstrated when a derailment actually happened in northern France on December 21, 1993, when four cars of the early morning train from Valenciennes to Paris left the track. . . . The cars remained upright and attached to each other and the rest of the train, and only one of the 170 passengers on board was slightly injured—a remarkable testimony to the TGV's articulated design." The cause of the derailment was a collapse of underground trenches made during World War I, which had not been identified from official records during construction planning.

"One wouldn't wish it on anyone," wrote Knutton, "but this accident provided some sound evidence of the extremely high safety levels of the TGV and, perhaps perversely, it could actually enhance the safety image of the TGV system—the French press treated the incident as a triumph for the train."

An Amtrak train could never survive a similar right-of-way defect at even half the speed, because the design of its infrastructure and trains are inferior when compared with the TGV.

Admittedly, some Amtrak accidents are minor and cause no injuries. In one instance, Amtrak's *Coast Starlight* moving at 50 mph sideswiped a derailed Burlington Northern freight train in Winlock, Washington. Passengers were unharmed, although their fear turned to anger as delays set them nine hours behind schedule. In Memphis, the *City of New Orleans* derailed on the Illinois Central Railroad. The Federal Railroad Administration found that poor crossties had caused the rails to spread, but riders—who experienced the derailment while moving at only 18 mph—had to wonder about the quality of the tracks over the entire route.

To be fair, many accidents are not Amtrak's fault—particularly those at railroad-highway grade crossings. Nevertheless, there's much to be said for completely separating railroad tracks from streets and highways, especially when planning for high-speed trains.

Some Amtrak accidents are quite serious.

Amtrak's worst tragedy came at 2:50 A.M. on September 22, 1993, when the *Sunset Limited*'s locomotives and four cars plunged into the swamps and bayous near Mobile, Alabama. Forty-seven passengers and crew members lost their lives, most by drowning, and more people would have died except that passengers formed human chains to rescue nonswimmers. Another 103 were injured. Thick fog, smoke from a fire, and the murky waters of the Big Bayou Canot added to the chaos of the scene. Rescue workers had difficulty finding the remote site, an area with no lights and no nearby highways.

Some passengers were rescued by a towboat, *M/V Mauvilla*. It wasn't long, however, before National Transportation Safety Board (NTSB) investigators found that a barge had broken loose from that towboat and struck the bridge, knocking it out of alignment and causing the train to wreck. The NTSB did not fault Amtrak in the accident, although it recommended that Amtrak provide safety briefings to its passengers, much like airlines do, as well as install portable onboard lighting.

Some accidents bring with them lasting legal and contractual entanglements. On the first Sunday of 1987, a clear and dry day with heavy holiday traffic, Amtrak's *Colonial* was traveling at 120 mph when it slammed into three Conrail freight locomotives occupying the wrong track in Chase, Maryland. The impact caused one of the Conrail locomotives to explode, the passenger cars to derail in a zigzag pattern, and one car to screech along the ground on its side. Fifteen passengers and the Amtrak engineer died, and 175 passengers were injured.

A court found the Conrail engineer responsible for the accident because, by failing to comply with a stop signal, he had blocked the rightful path of the Amtrak train. It also was determined that he and the brakeman had been smoking marijuana on the trip. Investigators uncovered contributing factors: safety features on Conrail's locomotives were absent, malfunctioning, or purposely disabled. This accident, because of its lawsuits and financial losses by Conrail, caused long-lasting friction between Amtrak and Conrail. Further, it sparked demands throughout the freight railroad industry that passenger train operators carry more liability insurance.

Over the years, Amtrak has been at fault for accidents attributed to human error, poor maintenance, or acceptance of new equipment that had design flaws, but it was not responsible for the accidents discussed above. Amtrak has, however, gone too far to plead its innocence. After a rash of accidents, Amtrak issued a statement in September 1995 claiming that most of its reports to the Federal Railroad Administration (FRA) "concern minor accidents causing no injury and involving only slight inconvenience to passengers. On average, only .00007 percent of the annual FRA-reportable accidents result in injury to passengers."

The problem is, for a long time Amtrak has issued figures that cannot be trusted. *Washingtonian* magazine writer Steven D. Kaye reported in 1987 that the number of injuries found in FRA reports, which were compiled from Amtrak data, was lower than information compiled in NTSB reports. "We discovered a pattern of sharply lower FRA injury figures going back at least to 1975, when a collision in Illinois injured 41 people—according to the NTSB—but only 4 people according to the FRA," wrote Kaye. "A derailment in Montana injured 115 people or 31; a sleeping-car fire in California injured 61 people or 6; a New York City collision in 1984 injured 140 people or 23, depending on whose report we read."

Kaye's remarkable findings show that in twenty-five accidents, the FRA reported forty-four injuries while the NTSB found 1,388 injured. Amtrak later admitted that it counts as injured only those passengers admitted to a hospital, not those who are treated and released. The FRA acknowledged that its Amtrak-originated statistics were misleading, but it's unclear whether corrective action was taken; contradictory statistics again appeared after a 1995 derailment in Arizona.

Amtrak issued "safety comparisons" in its 1994 annual report that were misleading. It stated that the average annual fatalities in the 1978–92 time period mean that automobiles were the most dangerous way to travel, followed by commercial air, bus, then Amtrak trains. In other words, Amtrak is safer than everybody else.

That is misleading. The Amtrak comparison was for a contrived fourteen-year period, which included years when Amtrak's fatalities were lower. A better standard to use comes from the National Safety Council, which annually issues statistics for the preceding decade. More important, any useful comparison should be based on passenger-miles—the total of all miles traveled by all passengers. After all, the probability of being involved in an accident is based not on the number of people using a particular mode of transportation but on the exposure level as determined by miles of travel. When figures from the National Safety Council for 1983–93 are examined, and when weighted per 100 million passenger-miles, all passenger trains were the safest form of transportation in only one year (1985). Amtrak usually ranked second or third, switching places with buses, while automobile travel was always the least safe and commercial aviation usually the safest.

Even within the railroad community, Amtrak does not always stack up well. The National Safety Council reported that "in 1993, Amtrak accounted for about 46 percent of the railroad passenger miles and 42 of the 58 railroad passenger fatalities." While that was an unusual year, the bottom line is that Amtrak is not the most dangerous way to travel, but it isn't the safest, either, despite Amtrak's claims.

Amtrak statements about the safety of its future high-speed trains are deceptive. Amtrak said its new fleet of high-speed trainsets are "designed to be among the safest trains in the world." Significant differences exist, however, between the Amtrak design and those of the Japanese Bullet Trains and French TGVs. Also, Amtrak's signaling systems are less sophisticated and its track structure less advanced. Further, there is no evidence that Amtrak's tracks will receive the superior maintenance that is standard practice overseas. Thus, if a new Amtrak train were in a derailment such as the one the TGV experienced, it is likely that the human cost would far exceed the one injury suffered by the French.

Train-wreck pictures in newspapers cause a sensation. Cable News

Network's video footage of an Amtrak accident, sometimes aired for days, can rivet the public's attention with highly negative consequences. Amtrak spent $109 million for advertising and sales in 1996, which was offset by the media's focus on Amtrak accidents. Tom Downs said Amtrak was perceived as trying to sell a product that it couldn't deliver.

Late-night television hosts in their opening monologues have targeted Amtrak. On *The Tonight Show,* Jay Leno said, "They don't post arrivals anymore. They post the odds." Another Leno line was that Amtrak planned to get rid of about six hundred workers—by putting them on one of its trains. On CBS, David Letterman joined in: "Earlier today Amtrak announced its new name—Am-Not-On-Track." Another night, listed among Letterman's "Top Ten Signs You're Not Getting a Year-End Bonus" was the item "You're the Director of Safety for Amtrak."

Amtrak officials became so furious with Leno that they pulled advertising worth about $2 million a year from NBC. After forcing a promise from Leno that he would go easier, Amtrak told the network to begin airing its commercials again. In reality, this was a form of censorship, pure and simple. Why Leno and NBC caved in, and why those who strive to guarantee constitutional freedom of expression failed to censure Amtrak, was puzzling.

Amtrak safety became an issue again when a train derailed in November 1996 after crossing a bridge in Newark, New Jersey, forcing part of the train down an embankment. Investigators learned that Amtrak employees had been aware of track defects on the bridge for eleven months but had failed to take appropriate action.

Amtrak Train Discontinuances

A mtrak has problems that have nothing to do with accidents. The public has often been irritated with Amtrak service, and the result has been insufficient traffic. One example is telling.

On a Sunday evening several years ago, I was waiting in Chicago Union Station for an Amtrak train. Over a two-hour period the only arrivals and departures were the local trains operated by the regional

Metra commuter system. It struck me that Chicago's O'Hare Airport was operating at full capacity, as it does on many Sunday evenings, and Midway Airport was busy, too. Yet, the train station was oddly quiet—sad testimony to Amtrak's dismal reach into the marketplace.

It could be argued that Chicago Union Station should be full—especially at that hour—because Amtrak has launched many new marketing efforts. Amtrak became the first nonairline member of the Airline Reporting Corporation, increasing the number of approved Amtrak travel agents from four thousand to more than forty thousand; when the airlines reduced the commissions paid to travel agents, Amtrak decided to pay travel agents more; and as Amtrak gained more experience with airline-style yield management, it tweaked its computers to sell a greater number of seats aboard trains.

Amtrak also started a promotion aimed at college students by offering the Student Advantage Card, which for a low price gives users discounts on various products. Amtrak airs glitzy television commercials, which could win awards in the advertising community. Planners helped specific routes, such as by offering miles in Midwest Express Airlines' frequent-traveler program to Chicago–Milwaukee train riders.

Unfortunately, such efforts are offset by Amtrak's shortcomings. Even when serious problems have afflicted Amtrak's air and highway competition, travelers fail to shift to trains in big numbers. Amtrak suffers from an inability to effectively penetrate the travel market on most routes.

When ridership dries up, trains are discontinued. The late-running *National Limited* made its last run in the late 1970s, as did the Chicago–Houston *Lone Star,* the Chicago–Miami *Floridian,* and the *North Coast Limited,* a Chicago–Seattle train that ran on the historic Northern Pacific Railroad route through Billings, Montana.

As airlines added flight schedules to meet the mid-1990s travel demand—the strongest in America's history—Amtrak, to stop its financial hemorrhaging, cut back. In 1995 the mice-infested train number 477 disappeared from the timetable. The Chicago–Indianapolis *Hoosier State,* the Montreal–Washington, D.C., *Montrealer,* and the Houston section of the *Texas Eagle*—all slow trains—were discontinued. Also deleted from the schedules were Amtrak's Philadelphia–Atlantic City trains and the New York–Jacksonville *Palmetto*.

One train's demise was to eclipse all others: the last run of the famed New York–Chicago *Broadway Limited* was particularly painful for railroad buffs. Here was a train that began running in 1902 under the name *Pennsylvania Special;* it was renamed a decade later not for the theater district of Manhattan but for Pennsylvania Railroad's four-track main line promoted as the Broad Way of Commerce. "The train had operated day in and day out, year in and year out," said railroad historian Mike Bezilla in an interview with Associated Press reporter Ted Duncombe. "It's been there through the world wars, through the Depression, the Sputnik, the atom bomb, you name it—there's been a *Broadway*." Dan Cupper, an author and correspondent for *Trains* magazine, pointed out that the train, long the flagship of the Pennsylvania Railroad, "really was the Concorde of its day." Its passengers included Pearl Bailey, Jack Benny, Charlie Chaplin, President Eisenhower, and others foremost in American arts, politics, and business.

Where trains weren't discontinued, the level of service dropped from daily to three or four times a week. Amtrak reduced frequency on the Atlanta–New Orleans segment of the *Crescent,* the Ogden, Utah–Seattle *Pioneer,* the Salt Lake City–Los Angeles *Desert Wind,* and the *Empire Builder* between Minneapolis–St. Paul and Seattle. It also ran less frequently the *City of New Orleans* that links Chicago with its namesake, and the *California Zephyr* west of Salt Lake City. The logic Amtrak offered for keeping routes open but reducing the number of trains was that more passenger revenue would be retained by cutting the frequency of trains rather than eliminating routes entirely.

Amtrak can change its logic fast. A mere twenty months later, Amtrak announced a restructuring that would do the opposite. Randolph E. Schmid of the Associated Press reported: "Concluding that less than daily service doesn't work, Amtrak plans to close down four routes and return to daily service on several others in an effort to save money and increase income." The new plan, in response to another cash shortage, would restore daily service to the *Empire Builder, California Zephyr, Crescent,* and *City of New Orleans.* Amtrak would also add a Pittsburgh–Chicago train and another New York–Miami train, the *Silver Palm.* These enhanced services came at a cost, however, as forty-two stations would lose all service as trains like the *Pioneer, Desert Wind,* and *Texas Eagle* were to be discontinued. Dallas would become the largest city in the country to lose all intercity rail passenger service, although in fact its Amtrak service is a joke because the train runs only three times a week in each direction.

But that plan also was not to be. Congress, alarmed that trains would be discontinued near election time, voted $22.5 million to freeze the existing pattern for six months.

Despite what the latest schedules may be, the root causes for passenger displeasure remain. Too many Amtrak passengers have been angered for too many reasons on too many trains. An occasional cold car here or bad breakfast there could be understood. But the service deficiencies that existed in 1971 have been repeated with eerie similarity through Amtrak's history. In some cases, service is worse: in 1997 Amtrak was running an unprecedented number of trains without food and beverage service on its New York–Philadelphia–Washington route, the busiest in the nation. On twenty-five trains, customers couldn't purchase even a cup of coffee.

The organization simply cannot achieve a level of service that draws a significant amount of repeat business. This has disheartened Amtrak's biggest supporters—railroad buffs. In what appears to be greater numbers than ever, they are giving up on Amtrak.

This is the case even though some have been supporters throughout Amtrak's lifetime. For example, William S. Lind, an experienced Capitol Hill staffer, was influential in arranging the start-up of Amtrak's New York–Chicago *Lake Shore Limited* and is associate publisher of the *New Electric Railway Journal.* Several years ago he blasted Amtrak in a *Wall Street Journal* column for treating passengers on a stalled train "like convicts in a Soviet labor camp, bullying them, insulting them and ultimately enraging them." A letter about the incident from Amtrak's Graham Claytor was so nonresponsive that Lind denounced it, saying, "It suggests the fatigued helplessness of some Third World subminister explaining again why nothing in the country works."

Disappointment with Amtrak also runs strong outside Washington's famed Beltway. John Wegner of Roeland Park, Kansas, wrote in *Passenger Train Journal:* "Ask yourself this question: Can I recommend a long-distance Amtrak trip to my friends who are not familiar with Amtrak travel? For me, the answer is no. . . . I wonder what it will take to get Amtrak to shape up; a *60 Minutes* or *20/20* exposé perhaps?"

"We're tired of excuses," said Ken Bird, the president of Illinois Rail, an organization that promotes passenger train service. "Amtrak's history is one of missed marketing opportunities, lackluster operational performance, and poor equipment utilization. When you operate chronically late trains with dirty windows, revenue shortfalls are bound to be the result."

From Grand Rapids, Michigan, James C. Miller wrote to *Trains* magazine that "Amtrak is probably the worst passenger-train operator this side of eastern Europe," a view echoed by a professional railroader, Eberhard Jaensch of the German Federal Railway's high-speed train division. He told *Business Week* that Amtrak is "almost as bad" as the system in the former East Germany.

Anecdotal evidence suggests that when traveling on vacation, most Amtrak employees and their families avoid their employer's trains except on a few routes—the Northeast Corridor, New York–Albany, and Los Angeles–San Diego. This is startling because employees can travel on Amtrak for free. In fact, most employees fly or drive at their own expense because of Amtrak's poor scheduling, slow travel times, awkward routings, or unattractive service. My experience has been that spouses of Amtrak employees often gripe about how slow Amtrak trains are. Bottom line: Amtrak has difficulty giving its service away *for free* to its employees.

Amtrak's efforts to save itself have failed, and its time is running out. Anthony Haswell, along with others, applauds the congressional move to end Amtrak funding by 2002. They know that Amtrak, with few exceptions, simply can't deliver useful passenger trains in the next century. But before we can plan a system to replace Amtrak, we must move beyond an examination of Amtrak's symptoms and take an unprecedented look at Amtrak's underlying structural problems.

Amtrak's Structural Problems

*"These funding levels turn the glide path
to success into a slippery slope to extinction."*
—Thomas M. Downs, Amtrak chairman and president,
June 6, 1996

A mtrak continually complains that it is underfunded, and the quote above by its president is rather typical of comments made by Amtrak officials for more than a quarter century. While it is true that Amtrak has suffered from undercapitalization, Amtrak has itself to blame for lobbying excessively for operating subsidies (which only encourage inefficiencies) instead of putting more emphasis on capital funding (which would boost efficiencies).

Amtrak's problems are that it is a subsidized monopoly and that it has a vague public service identity crafted by Congress. The result is that Amtrak suffers from a form of schizophrenia, and its best performance is rarely better than lackluster.

Meanwhile, the United States needs several types of train service.

It needs *commuter rail* to carry tens of thousands of people into and out of large cities on a daily basis and needs clusters of *regional rail lines* for specialized markets. America also needs *long-distance trains* to carry tourists on seasonal travels to highly popular destinations and needs *high-speed trains* on selected well-traveled corridors. Some of these trains can't operate at a profit; some can.

Amtrak has become irrelevant to the future of all of them.

Amtrak's difficulties started at its very beginning. When the Nixon Administration agreed to Amtrak's creation in 1970, then–Southern Pacific Railroad president Benjamin F. Biaggini said, "I think Amtrak's function should be to preside over the orderly shrinkage of rail passenger service." Since then, Amtrak's route system has grown, but much has gone wrong. The repercussions to its bad start are many: a poor corporate culture, lack of vision, faulty standards of measuring performance, and credibility problems. Periodic amendments to the law that created Amtrak haven't helped much.

Public Monopoly

Amtrak's biggest problem is that it is a monopoly in the classic economic sense. It is a government-created, government-protected, and government-guided legal monopoly. Any individual who creates a company and attempts to provide rail service in competition with Amtrak, without first obtaining Amtrak's approval, is subject to prosecution under civil law because of the following clause in Amtrak's enabling legislation: "No railroad or any other person may, without the consent of Amtrak, conduct intercity rail passenger service over any route over which Amtrak is performing scheduled intercity rail passenger service pursuant to a contract under this section." At the time this provision was passed, nobody thought about the effects that requiring Amtrak consent would have on private rail initiatives; there were no such initiatives.

At first blush it appears there could be exceptions to Amtrak's monopoly. Independent operators might run passenger trains on routes that are outside Amtrak's "basic system" that it started in 1971; on routes that involve railroads with which Amtrak has no operating contract; or on routes where all-new infrastructure is built by state agencies or private interests. Not so, however, as Amtrak will torture logic to maintain its monopoly even on routes where it has never operated and has no plans to operate.

Amtrak's ploys were explained a decade ago by Mari Gursky, a Philadelphia attorney, but her views are germane today. "Amtrak asserts that 'route' means market area. Thus, Amtrak asserts a right to license and exact fees from a parallel line, even one operating between cities not served by Amtrak, if those cities are within what Amtrak sees as its 'market,'" said Gursky. "Further, Amtrak insists that it is not limited to fees which reflect damage done to Amtrak through the loss of ridership due to competition. Rather, Amtrak argues that [the law] permits it to charge a license fee that reflects the value of the license to the licensee. The fee, according to Amtrak, should be calculated according to the profits of the competing line."

Amtrak flexed its monopolistic muscle in the 1970s when it sought to prevent the private Auto-Train company from establishing service between Louisville, Kentucky, and Sanford, Florida. Amtrak took this action even though it was trying to discontinue the *Floridian*, which served essentially the same line. Auto-Train successfully argued that its contract with the freight railroad, which had antedated Amtrak's contract with the same railroad, included that route. Auto-Train's service on the route never did as well as its East Coast train, primarily because it ran as part of Amtrak's *Floridian,* a painfully slow train with an atrocious on-time performance record.

Amtrak exercised monopoly rights in the mid-1980s, again with poor results. Then, Amtrak insisted that the Colorado Midland Railway pay an initial fee and 5 percent of its earnings for the right to run passenger trains in Wyoming—a state in which Amtrak service has been on-again, off-again. Eventually, the proposal died, although Amtrak's demands were changed to a one-dollar-per-year fee after Senator Malcolm Wallop intervened.

It is important to consider this monopolistic behavior because it leads to questions about Amtrak's motivation in Florida in 1996. A few months after that state granted a franchise to the Florida Overland Express to build a high-speed Miami–Tampa line—rejecting the application from a team that included Amtrak—Amtrak voluntarily began operating a train between Miami and Tampa named the *Silver Palm*. The train follows an oddball routing, leaving Miami on the Atlantic Coast, proceeding to Tampa Bay on the Gulf of Mexico, and returning to the Atlantic at Jacksonville before heading to New York. The train, with its route and slowness, could not realistically be promoted for local Florida travel. Yet Amtrak's Mark S. Cane, president of the Amtrak Intercity Business Unit, said the *Silver Palm* would help in "developing a new intrastate route in Florida." This appears to be an Amtrak maneuver to establish "rights" to the Miami–Tampa route, thereby enabling it to elbow its way into the affairs of the Florida Overland Express high-speed train plan.

A public monopoly is likely to be as anticompetitive as any private monopoly. That's Amtrak—an unprogressive agency whose behavior has a chilling effect on independent proposals that are imaginative and visionary. Amtrak acts in ways that are typical to monopolies: it has interfered with potential competitors, issued wretched cost estimates to those wanting new services, turned in disappointing performance, demonstrated inadequacies in dealing with new technologies, and is downright arrogant and inflexible.

Amtrak's monopoly is harmful because it serves to dampen marketplace interest in rail service. As long as Amtrak exists and claims privileged status, entrepreneurs and investors will almost universally shy away from new rail passenger enterprises. As long as Amtrak prevails in imposing itself as a middleman between private operators and the freight railroad industry, operators' profits will be minimized as Amtrak takes part of the pie. As one example, the American Orient Express (AOE), an enterprise that runs long-distance trains offering a land-cruise experience, has to pay Amtrak per-mile charges to operate over freight railroads. It is perceived that Amtrak has a statutory right to its go-between role, even though Amtrak would never run the train that the AOE does. Without Amtrak, the AOE could negotiate arrangements directly with freight railroads, could reduce costs somewhat by eliminating Amtrak's markup, and as a result earn more of a profit or lower its ticket charges as it wishes.

Would America stand for the U.S. Postal Service demanding payments from Federal Express or United Parcel Service for every mile their trucks operated? Absolutely not, and any postal executive proposing such an arrangement would be met with shock and outrage. Yet that's what Amtrak has done and will do in the future—impose costs on private train operators that they wouldn't have if Amtrak didn't exist.

Mysteriously, Amtrak's boosters tolerate behavior by Amtrak that they would condemn if emanating from a private cartel.

Many in transportation recognize the dangers of letting Amtrak's monopoly stand and have acted to protect non-Amtrak proposals. In commenting on the Swift Rail Development Act supported by the Clinton Administration, the former chairman of the Pennsylvania high-speed rail commission, Richard A. Geist, objected to its potential strengthening of Amtrak's monopoly, saying, "We cannot allow Amtrak's track record to adversely affect our proposed Supertrains." Echoing his view was every developer of independent high-speed rail proposals from Florida to California.

Amtrak's status must change, as explained by William Lindley of the Arizona Association of Railroad Passengers, who wrote in a letter posted on the Internet: "The first item of business should be to strike from the 'Amtrak Law' the clause giving Amtrak exclusive right to operate intercity passenger rail services. This would allow private companies and regional systems to bid on operation of existing routes, or to run routes of their own choosing."

Like all monopolies, Amtrak is unable to adapt well to change and has ossified. One Amtrak board member, Robert Kiley, sees the need to transform Amtrak into something else, telling *Traffic World* that Amtrak "may soon be national in name only" and that perhaps Amtrak should delay purchasing more equipment until it redefines its mission.

Public Agency Status

At times, an organization can be such a hybrid that it takes on multiple personalities. That, unfortunately, is Amtrak—uncertain of itself.

At first, Amtrak was routinely referred to by the term in its 1970 enabling legislation, a "quasi-public" organization. For some time, no one was quite sure what *quasi-public* meant. In the 1950s an examiner with the Interstate Commerce Commission, John Messer, concluded that the Southern Pacific, "as all other railroads, is a quasi-public corporation in nature, having been chartered to serve the public convenience and necessity." Yet today the U.S. Postal Service, whose assets are publicly owned, also is a quasi-public entity. Multiple understandings seem to exist for the term.

Perhaps that's why in 1981 Congress discarded part of Amtrak's "private" status by issuing preferred stock to the U.S. Department of Transportation and eliminating common stockholder seats on Amtrak's board of directors.

Amtrak, officially known as the National Railroad Passenger Corporation, would define itself something like this: "Amtrak is incorporated under the laws of the District of Columbia as a private corporation, with a board of directors, a president, and an executive staff. Although it was created by an act of Congress, Amtrak is not an agency of the federal government, and its employees are not part of the federal civil service system." Amtrak's business plan states that "Amtrak is a private company wholly responsible for its own cash management and liquidity."

On the surface, that makes Amtrak appear to be a private corporation.

But appearances can be deceiving. Unlike most corporations, Amtrak receives *direct* financial support from federal, state, and local governments. More important, Amtrak must receive such funding in order to maintain operations and stay alive.

Thus, on reflection, Amtrak looks like a public agency.

Consider more. Eight Amtrak board members are political appointees, and together they elect the ninth. The board includes the Secretary of Transportation, a state governor, and two members who must be affiliated with public commuter agencies. What private company names sitting public officials as directors? What private company has the composition of its board dictated by Congress?

A board like that reinforces Amtrak's public agency status.

The preferred stock, which is voting stock, is held by the federal government, giving the public preferential rights in any liquidation of Amtrak. The common stockholders place little value in their holdings—three railroads purchased common stock when Amtrak was created, and they each later wrote down the value to one dollar and took tax deductions. These shareholders have no voting rights, quite unlike an independent, investor-owned corporation.

Amtrak has been subject to the Freedom of Information Act, another indicator of Amtrak's public status.

The courts have had their turn at defining Amtrak. Consider Michael Lebron, an artist, who at one point sued Washington's Metro subway for its refusal to rent him space to display work that contained a political theme. He won his case in a U.S. court of appeals, with a strong majority opinion emphasizing the constitutional protection citizens have against government censorship of speech. In effect, the court decided that the subway was a public agency.

Several years later, a similar dispute erupted when Amtrak denied renting to Lebron billboard space in New York's Penn Station for a potentially controversial parody of a Coors advertisement. Again Lebron sued, and a lower court ruled that Amtrak is a private corporation. The Supreme Court agreed to review the case. The *Washington Post* editorially observed that "the court had to resolve a preliminary question first: Is Amtrak a government entity that may not restrict speech, or is it a private corporation without the same constitutional obligations?" The Court ruled that Amtrak is in fact a government entity that can be sued for a violation of constitutional rights.

It was a victory for those who want to end the pretense that Amtrak is a private corporation.

British professors Tony Ridley and Francis Terry at the University of London's Centre for Transport Studies have no doubt what Amtrak is: "Amtrak is in effect a nationalized industry." That is a common-sense conclusion, considering that Amtrak is backed by the full faith and trust of the U.S. government; without government backing, Amtrak would disappear. The federal government holds title to most Amtrak assets not already pledged to creditors.

I consider Amtrak a *nationalized* entity, notwithstanding its employees being outside of the civil service system. Congress and special interests in Washington avoid that term because they do not want to highlight an unpleasant fact about a program they created.

U.S. General Accounting Office Evaluations

However defined over the years, Amtrak lacks direction and performs poorly. The U.S. General Accounting Office (GAO) has repeatedly confirmed that Amtrak has deteriorated and cannot maintain a national system without increases in federal and state funding. In a comprehensive review requested by five congressional committees, Kenneth M. Mead, when serving as the GAO director of transportation issues, testified several times that "Amtrak is at a crossroads, and we believe that important decisions need to be made that will affect Amtrak in both the short and the long run."

Part of Amtrak's ineptitude is an inability to make realistic ridership projections. One 1979 GAO study looked at earlier Amtrak reports, to learn what its ridership estimates would be for that year. It found that in 1974 Amtrak filed with Congress a projection that ridership in 1979 would be a stunning 37 million; in 1975 Amtrak revised the figure downward to 29.2 million. In fact, both estimates were way off—Amtrak carried 21.4 million passengers in 1979—illustrating the extent to which Amtrak filed distorted figures with Congress. (Amtrak's 1996 ridership was only 19.7 million.)

Poor estimates go back further than that. Amtrak's first president, Roger Lewis, told *U.S. News & World Report* in 1972 that two to three times as many people would be riding Amtrak within five years. It never happened. Five years later, his successor, Paul Reistrup, approved a report that estimated a rise in Amtrak's patronage to 26 million in 1982, a figure Amtrak has never achieved.

When ridership estimates are off, so are revenue estimates, and this inaccuracy is a continuing problem. In 1995 testimony to Congress, the GAO's Mead said that Amtrak's problems have accelerated, and one reason is that "Amtrak overestimated passenger revenues by $600 million from 1991 through 1994."

Other figures can't be fully trusted. In 1995 Amtrak ran an advertisement in the *Wall Street Journal* boasting that "last year, 55 million passengers rode Amtrak-operated trains." The phrase *Amtrak-operated* is clever but ambiguous. In reality, about 33 million were commuters on trains financed by agencies that contract with Amtrak for services. Not even a footnote appeared in the advertisement to clarify that only about 22 million rode on Amtrak trains. Amtrak's Tom Downs stated in an annual report that these 55 million customers "are the soul of Amtrak." That is misleading. If Amtrak disappeared, the 33 million would still have commuter trains to ride; it's just that other entities would contract to run them.

None of this is a surprise to George W. Hilton, an economic historian who has long been skeptical of Amtrak. In a study for the American Enterprise Institute for Public Policy Research, Hilton declared, "The Amtrak experiment has been unsuccessful by any standards." He wrote that "Amtrak's failure stems directly from the logic whereby the corporation was established," discussing such fairly complex issues as elasticities of demand and measures of consumer responsiveness. When all is said and done, what Hilton said was that Amtrak proponents just don't understand how much travelers value their time or how they view the cost of train tickets relative to rival modes of transportation.

Hilton's study was published in 1980, and it is notable for concluding that in the remainder of the century, Amtrak's system will probably atrophy to the Northeast Corridor.

Anthony Haswell provides additional perspective, believing Hilton is right if Amtrak is viewed purely as a private corporation and tied to the usual profit/loss measure of corporate success or failure. "However," said Haswell, "in my view, the correct measure is whether Amtrak has or has not returned public benefits relative to its public costs. My answer is no. So while Hilton and I reach the same conclusion, we do so by applying fundamentally different criteria."

Amtrak Financial Allocations and Deficits

Much has been written about how much money Amtrak loses, and the annual figures are always in the hundreds of millions of dollars; in some years it was more than a billion. Amtrak's federal subsidies will soon exceed $21 billion, as shown in Table 2.1, but Amtrak also enjoys additional subsidies. For example, eleven states provide operating subsidies—sometimes combined with capital for track improvements, cars, and locomotives—for regional trains to be run at the states' discretion.* In 1996 alone, state contributions totaled $64.2 million, up significantly from the year-earlier total of $35.7 million. In the last six years California alone has spent about $1 billion to cover various Amtrak costs.

TABLE 2.1. **History of Federal Subsidies/Loans to Amtrak (in millions)**

Fiscal Year	Operating Funds	Excess R.R. Retirement	General Capital	Bos–Wash Capital	Totals
71/72	$40.0				$40.0
73	$170.0				$170.0
74	$146.6		$2.5		$149.1
75	$276.5				$276.5
76	$357.0		$114.2		$471.2
TQ	$105.0		$25.0	$50.0	$180.0
77	$482.6		$93.1	$225.0	$800.7
78	$561.0A		$130.0	$425.0	$1,116.0

*California, Illinois, Michigan, Missouri, New York, North Carolina, Oregon, Pennsylvania, Vermont, Washington, and Wisconsin.

Fiscal Year	Operating Funds	Excess R.R. Retirement	General Capital	Bos–Wash Capital	Totals
79	$625.0A		$130.0	$479.0	$1,234.0
80	$670.4		$191.0	$362.0	$1,223.4
81	$709.2		$187.1	$350.0	$1,246.3
82	$522.4	$36.0	$176.6	$170.0	$905.0
83	$561.5	$44.0	$94.5	$115.0	$815.0
85	$562.1	$56.0	$98.3	$100.0	$816.4
85	$551.7	$76.0	$52.3	$27.6	$707.6
86	$500.7	$88.0	$2.0	$12.0	$602.7
87	$468.5	$112.0	$26.5	$11.5	$618.5
88	$413.6	$121.0	$46.2	$27.5	$608.3
89	$410.6	$144.0	$29.4	$19.6	$603.6
90	$388.1	$133.0	$83.6	$24.4	$629.1
91	$343.1	$144.8	$132.0	$179.0	$798.9
92	$331.0	$150.2	$175.0	$205.0	$861.2
93	$351.0	$146.0	$190.0	$204.1	$891.1
94	$351.7	$150.5	$195.0	$225.0	$922.2
95	$392.0	$150.0	$230.0	$200.0	$972.0
96	$285.0	$120.0	$230.0	$115.0	$750.0
97	$222.5	$142.0	$303.0B	$175.0	$842.5
98C	$245.0	$142.0	$751.0	D	$1,138.0
Loans			$1,110.6E		$1,110.6
Totals	$11,043.8	$1,955.5	$4,798.9	$3,701.7F	$21,499.9

Sources: *Background on Amtrak*, Amtrak Annual Reports, Amtrak Finance Dept., GAO.
TQ—Transition Quarter as Federal fiscal year changed from July 1 to Oct. 1.
A—Includes appropriations of $25 million in 1978 and 1979 for loan payments.
B—Includes $80 million for "high-speed rail" in 1997.
C—Amtrak's request of Congress for fiscal year 1998.
D—Amtrak placed Boston-Washington capital request in General Capital.
E—Amtrak failed to repay $880 million in government-guaranteed loans for 1971–75 capital. Loan obligations plus $239.6 million in interest was paid by the FRA in fiscal 1984. Amtrak then executed a new $1,119,635,000 note with the U.S. Government that matures Nov. 1, 2082. It will be renewed for successive 99-year terms with interest payable only in the event of prepayment or acceleration of principal.
F—Capital funds for upgrading; includes $86 million in 1977–80 to purchase the line.
Note—With inflation, the GAO reports Amtrak has received more than $29 billion in real 1995 dollars. This is understated because of uncalculated state subsidies, later federal subsidies, and failure to include principal and interest for loans as identified in Footnote E.

There's more: several states have purchased cars that Amtrak uses for free on service within their borders; Pennsylvania recently funded $1 million in Amtrak costs to locate a regional headquarters in Philadelphia, and Illinois issued low-interest loans to persuade Amtrak to keep a reservations office in Chicago. At the municipal level, communities have purchased stations and improved them for Amtrak's use.

Amtrak's losses will continue, a hard fact acknowledged in Amtrak's 1995 strategic plan: "Without changes in how we do business, where we do business, and how costs are shared we will post $7.3 billion in operating losses from 1995–2000." That sum doesn't count capital funds needed for new locomotives and cars, track repairs, and other items in what is a capital-intensive industry.

On an operating-cost basis, Amtrak is losing disproportionate amounts on trains outside the Northeast. For fiscal year 1996, Amtrak's total losses by business units amounted to $763.6 million, of which $151 million was attributable to its Northeast Corridor Business Unit and $342.6 to its Chicago-based and Oakland, California–based Business Units. The "Corporate" unit accounted for $270 million. The net losses were reduced somewhat by state subsidies, but this essential truth remains: the faster trains in the Northeast enjoy better revenue-to-cost ratios than long-distance trains and slow short-distance trains on virtually every other line in the nation. This is why, by Amtrak's own admission, the Boston–Washington line can eventually operate at a profit while the others cannot.

It's difficult to persuade some rail passenger advocates that Amtrak's deficits are what Amtrak says they are. This is because Amtrak suffers from an unfair criticism from advocates—generally located in the West and South—who claim that Amtrak cooks its books to worsen the financial results of long-distance trains and to help the balance sheets of trains in the Northeast.

Such criticism doesn't stand up to scrutiny. Amtrak's route-by-route financial performance reports appear accurate for three reasons. First, if Amtrak had any motivation to tweak figures, it would do the *reverse*—it would make its short-distance trains appear to be the poorest performers because it's in Amtrak's interest to improve the financial picture of its politically vital long-distance trains. Second, for Amtrak to purposefully file false cost data would violate federal statues regarding its duty to provide accurate information to the Office of Management and Budget, the U.S. Department of Transportation, several congressional committees, and the General Accounting Office. Last, although railroad buffs and some Amtrak employees decry Amtrak's cost allocations, no one has alleged to the Federal Bureau of Investigation or the Justice Department that Amtrak is issuing misleading financial information.

In all likelihood, such a complaint wouldn't go far. Over the years, auditing firms such as Price Waterhouse and Arthur Andersen & Company have reviewed and approved Amtrak's cost-accounting system. These companies audit Amtrak in accordance with private sector and government auditing standards and have found Amtrak to be in compliance with laws and regulations. While, as I noted previously, Amtrak has provided inflated ridership and revenue estimates to Congress, filing *estimates* that turn out to be incorrect is hardly a violation of the law.

The GAO has reviewed Amtrak's costing practices for particular trains. In one case, the GAO selected a Detroit-to-Chicago train for intensive study and concluded that Amtrak's accounting process provided a generally correct report. In fact, the GAO in 1994 specifically reviewed whether Amtrak properly accounts for the funding it receives and has a "reasonable system" for allocating costs. The agency found that "Amtrak accounts for its federal subsidies in accordance with federal requirements and agreements and with generally accepted accounting principles."

The GAO explained that Amtrak's cost-accounting systems are capable of various calculations. One system assigns expenses to individual routes in two categories, avoidable and fixed. Avoidable costs, such as for fuel and labor, vary with the operation of a route and would cease if the route were eliminated. Fixed costs found in maintenance and administrative facilities would remain relatively constant if a single route were discontinued. The system is capable of calculating fully allocated costs—non-route-specific costs such as salaries, advertising campaigns, equipment depreciation, and so forth—and allocating them to all trains. Another accounting practice produces avoidable-costs reports on routes. These reports approximate the incremental costs gained or lost from adding or eliminating service.

Of course, costs to operate trains can vary considerably. One Amtrak train a day contributes little to the expense of maintaining a track used primarily by heavy coal trains. On the other hand, Amtrak's four-track railroad between New York and Philadelphia, used more or less half by Amtrak and half by commuter and freight trains, presents a different cost picture. There, it could logically be argued that a discontinuance of all Amtrak trains would reduce the number of tracks to two. Thus, about half the fixed expense of operations there should be attributable to Amtrak trains.

Even though Amtrak's expenses in the Northeast are higher than elsewhere in the nation, its revenue base is sufficiently healthy to result in a lower subsidy per passenger than that of long-distance trains.

Despite this defense of Amtrak, there is one way that Amtrak's financial analysis becomes very questionable: the way Amtrak calculates its overall "revenue-to-expense" ratio, a standard performance measure, to lead observers to conclude that Amtrak performs better than European and Japanese railroads. In fact, its ratio has improved only because of artificial changes in cost allocations.

According to the GAO's Ken Mead, again in congressional testimony, "Amtrak's revenue-to-expense ratio for fiscal year 1993 indicated that revenues were covering about 80 percent of operating expenses. However, the calculation of this ratio excluded certain expenses, including (1) depreciation; (2) the Federal Railroad Administration (FRA) mandatory retirement payment; (3) various taxes paid to federal or state governments; (4) user fees assessed by the FRA; (5) other miscellaneous expenses relating to accident claims; and (5) losses incurred in providing [state-subsidized] service and disbursements for labor protection, which according to Amtrak, are excluded at the direction of the Congress."

Thus, Amtrak reduces its ratio by removing from the calculation tens of millions of dollars in costs, allowing Amtrak to show progress that in fact it is not making. If such additional expenses for fiscal year 1993, which totaled about $370 million, had been included in the calculation, the ratio would have been only 66 percent, or 14 percentage points lower than reported by Amtrak. It would have plunged further had Amtrak included interest on government-guaranteed loans.

These practices are unacceptable to Mead, who said, "We believe all relevant costs, both capital and operating, should be included in any performance measurement." Such criticism does not prevent Amtrak from boasting that its ratio is better than rail systems overseas. The truth is that foreign systems haven't played such hocus-pocus with their obligations; most perform better than Amtrak would have Americans believe.

An additional point, an aberration according to the GAO, is that Amtrak's emphasis on improving its revenue-to-expense ratio could actually cause it to take actions that have adverse effects. When an organization is operating at a financial loss, an improving ratio does not necessarily indicate that the need for subsidies is decreasing.

"The true test of whether a new business benefits Amtrak is whether the new business contributes more to revenue than expenses in the short and long term," said Mead. He explained to Congress how Amtrak could actually improve its ratio with new business that brought in $100 million in revenues but cost $125 million to provide. In such a case, if everything else were equal, Amtrak's ratio would improve by nearly one point. This has happened—Amtrak's ratio increased from 65 percent to 66 percent between fiscal years 1992 and 1993, but Amtrak's net loss actually climbed from $712 million to $731 million, and the federal operating grant rose from $331 million to $351 million. As distressing as this is, Congress gave Amtrak its approval for creative bookkeeping, thereby enabling Amtrak to make efficiency claims based on calculations that would be ridiculed in the business community.

Comparative Subsidies

Some defend Amtrak's subsidies because they are lower than those benefiting aviation and highway systems.

In one way, that claim is true. A 1993 GAO analysis shows that federal operating and capital subsidies to Amtrak amounted to about $35 per passenger; the Essential Air Services Program provided a subsidy of $50 per passenger; and private airplane users enjoyed a $65 per-trip subsidy. (The Amtrak figure must be viewed with caution, because passengers on some trains are highly subsidized, while those on other routes receive little.) Nevertheless, what gets lost in the argument is that none of these subsidies is defensible. All three should be ended.

Some subsidies are acceptable because of the true mobility and social benefits they bring to millions of daily users. For example, subsidies to commuters aboard public bus and rail transit systems average $1.61 per passenger. That's a more reasonable amount, especially considering that the loss of these subsidies would induce millions of Americans to shift to automobiles; congestion-related delays and smog costs alone would exceed any savings.

Another agency, the Congressional Budget Office, tried to put a value on aid to Amtrak in a 1982 study entitled *Federal Subsidies for Rail Passenger Service*. The comparison showed that on a passenger-mile basis, Amtrak passengers were subsidized at a level more than one hundred times the next closest alternative means of passenger travel. Each Amtrak passenger was subsidized at the rate of 23.6 cents per passenger-mile, while commercial airline passengers received two-tenths of one cent, and private auto passengers about one-tenth of one cent.

Subsidies become confusing for commercial aviation and highways, where on an *absolute* basis the subsidies are greater than Amtrak's. Yet so many people use those systems that on a *relative* basis the subsidies are lower per passenger-mile. Hundreds of millions of users regularly rely on the aviation and highway systems; about 9.5 million passengers fly on commercial airlines *daily*, and a greater (incalculable) number rely on streets and highways. To put it another way, subsidies for air and auto travelers at least go to systems enjoying an astonishing level of use. America just can't survive without its aviation and highway systems, while Amtrak's disappearance would be insignificant because of its infinitesimal market share outside of a few routes. Thus, on a quantitative basis, Amtrak's subsidies are excessive and indefensible.

Anthony Haswell justifies ending Amtrak subsidies based on a qualitative view. In *Passenger Train Journal* he wrote, "Amtrak presides over the worst intercity rail passenger service of any technologically advanced nation. . . . The benefits of such services are not worth the public funds which support them."

Reorganization at Amtrak

Amtrak has been unable to make itself relevant, unlike other old-line industries that have changed with the times. For example, the American steel industry has outlived the obituary written for it in the early 1980s by building mini-mills that use labor more efficiently. There is one watchword that applies to the steel industry's resurgence—flexibility. Production methods have changed so much that factories are able to turn out high-quality products in different shapes and sizes. This turnaround, based on increased efficiencies, has been aided by skilled workers using computerized equipment. Managers, meanwhile, are paying constant attention to marketplace messages about what their companies are producing.

Amtrak is the reverse; it fails to pay close attention to the marketplace. That failure is why it has a fairly rigid route structure that languishes outside the public's consciousness. Amtrak's inability to make fundamental product changes means it suffers from an inflexibility typical of monopolies.

Downs has tried to change Amtrak by modifying the organizational structure, putting energy into establishing "business units" in regional offices. But Amtrak also created regional staffs in the 1970s, a fiasco as on-time performance suffered and deficits increased. Amtrak later abandoned regionalization and returned to centralized management. It's doubtful that Amtrak's continual shuffling of staff will do much other than enrich moving van companies that scurry about with employees' household goods. The much-touted Amtrak reorganizations amount to repainting a house while its foundation crumbles.

Success and Failure

Amtrak's messages to employees and supporters also are unrealistic. Annual reports, for example, amount to fiction. Such reports are filled with language about Amtrak's providing "superior" service, becoming "customer-driven," enjoying high "revenue-to-cost ratios," employing new long-distance cars that symbolize "the challenges of the next century," anticipating a "shining future"—all while "in the midst of a historic transformation."

It's rhetorical nonsense. Amtrak does not evaluate itself properly, confuses action with results, claims any change as progress, and does so while its ridership is falling.

Here's where it pays to turn to the late John W. Barriger III, a forward-thinking president of several smaller railroads and author of *Super-Railroads for a Dynamic American Economy.* This monograph, published in 1956, is a classic in business literature for offering sensible concepts on how to evaluate success or failure of a railroad.

Barriger wrote about *technical efficiency,* in which results are expressed in ton-miles or passenger-miles per train-hour. By this standard, the freight railroads today are very successful while Amtrak is a failure—on some lines its productivity has deteriorated, and on others it's only minimally improved. This is a shocking failure, considering the federal capital infusions that have exceeded $8.5 billion in Amtrak.

Another index by Barriger was *economic efficiency,* by which he means converting capacity into "revenue units of salable service." Again, the freight railroads have made great strides by improving facilities and earning higher revenues on what had been excess capacity. Amtrak has not done so anywhere outside the Northeast Corridor and routes in New York, Wisconsin, Washington, and California—and the latter improvements are thanks to state initiatives.

The last item Barriger considered, *commercial efficiency,* refers to "characteristics of price and service" that attract customers. He specifically mentions punctuality, convenience, accessibility, schedule frequency, transmission of information, price, condition of equipment, politeness of employees, and station locations. Amtrak's performance on each of these factors varies widely.

Some believe Amtrak might score better on standards more in line with contemporary responsibilities of a public or nationalized agency. Consider then the standards in *Reinventing Government,* by David Osborne and Ted Gaebler. This 1993 book alerts readers to note that "there is a vast difference between measuring process and measuring results." Amtrak will measure a process, such as the number of new cars put in service in a given year, but is remarkably mum about the failure of that act to draw more customers. Its 1996 annual report boasts of conducting "public forums around the country to invite comments about how we can better serve our passengers," and Amtrak's *Fiscal 1996 Business and Financial Performance Report* cites an increase in the number of days that employees are in training classes. Are these achievements? How about trains as fast as they were in the thirties, forties, and fifties? Now that would be an achievement.

Last, Osborne and Gaebler advise of the "important difference between 'program outcomes' and broader 'policy outcomes.' " To put this in context, a program to carry more mail would boost Amtrak's revenues. Passenger trains, however, are limited to a certain number of cars; and when mail cars displace coaches, fewer people are able to ride the trains. Amtrak's New York–Chicago *Three Rivers* typically is limited to eighteen cars. It has operated with as many as a dozen "head-end" cars and one RoadRailer (all used to carry mail, express and baggage), three coaches, and one dining car. Is this "program success" really a "policy success," when passengers are denied space by limiting the number of available seats? Does this much "head-end" traffic have an adverse impact on schedule convenience to passengers? Also, it is a national "policy success" to shift to Amtrak mail that might otherwise move in fast trains at a profit to the freight railroads—companies that pay dividends and taxes?

The somewhat dated business book *In Search of Excellence* offers food for thought. The authors, Thomas Peters and Robert Waterman, Jr., studied management techniques to better understand the secrets of successful businesses. They found eight basic practices that generally characterize winning companies: having bias for action; staying close to the customer; permitting autonomy and entrepreneurship; relying on rank-and-file employees for quality and productivity gains; being run by hands-on management in which executives inspect facilities that customers use; sticking to business that it knows how to run; keeping a simple structure and lean staff; and maintaining a tight control over core values even with a decentralized structure.

Amtrak has displayed some of these practices a few times, but far too erratically to ever have the "shining future" it claims in a recent annual report. I believe an honest Amtrak annual report would say: "We at Amtrak are mediocre, although on some days we're worse."

A Note About Maglev

Any look ahead requires consideration of another type of train that will come into its own in the twenty-first century, with a design based on principles of magnetic levitation. These trains, commonly called maglev, will not run on tracks but on "guideways" and will float on waves of magnetic fields. German and Japanese maglev technologies are capable of carrying passengers at 300 mph, permitting a New York–Washington trip to take only an hour.

If Amtrak is unable to make decent progress with today's rail technologies, it certainly lacks the distinctive competencies and high-tech proficiencies required for maglev. In fact, maglev is closer to aerospace and airline technologies and practices, and there are those who want maglev not as a *part* of Amtrak but *in place* of Amtrak.

In a February 1995 congressional hearing on Amtrak, Congressman Jay Kim of California asked, "Instead of upgrading this obsolete system . . . why don't we focus, refocus all this money, shift the money into a more futuristic system such as Japan and Germany [have], a maglev high-speed train? I know we have a sentimental value on this Amtrak, but I think it is time now to bite the bullet, go in and proceed for the future . . . rather than just keep repairing this thing and pouring money down into a bottomless pit."

Responded Kenneth M. Mead of the General Accounting Office: "I can tell you that is certainly an option."

Like any monopoly wishing to shove its way into another territory, Amtrak has exploited interest in maglev by printing brochures associating itself with the new technology. That's arrogant, considering that Amtrak lobbied on Capitol Hill to shift National Maglev Initiative (NMI) funding to its own budget; the NMI was a joint government-industry program to develop an American maglev prototype to compete with foreign models. Every maglev designer, planner, and advocate in the United States eager to see progress should strive to keep maglev independent of Amtrak.

Maglev may be the future, but something must be done today about America's underperforming national rail passenger service provider.

Amtrak has an identity crisis, is unable to chart a productive direction for itself, is reluctant to admit to its nationalized nature, works to preserve its monopoly status, and is unable to evaluate itself in a credible manner. Amtrak violates the most important advice that Peters and Waterman preach: "Decide what your company *stands for.*" It is no wonder that Tom Downs once told *Journal of Commerce* reporters Stephanie Nall and William L. Roberts, "We are Chapter Eleven–able by our creditors. We can be put in bankruptcy with relative ease."

This discussion began by mentioning four types of trains running today: commuter, regional, long-distance, and high-speed. Amtrak is becoming irrelevant to the future of each.

THREE

New Long-Distance
and Regional Trains

"You should see the giant canyons, towering peaks,
noble cataracts, bubbling hot springs, spouting geysers
and weird formations of rock and lava."

—Northern Pacific Railroad advertisement promoting
travel to Yellowstone National Park, 1910

S till today, captains of American industry demonstrate their faith
in the appeal, romance, and luxury found in long-distance passenger trains.

The Union Pacific Railroad meticulously maintains locomotives
and passenger cars so its sales executives can give shippers a luxurious
firsthand look at the railroad. That's cultivating customers in a grand
style. The trains sometimes are pressed into service for general corpo-
rate-image purposes, too. In 1996 it was the Union Pacific's executive
train that carried the Olympic flame through hundreds of communities
to the Atlanta Games. It generated an incalculable amount of goodwill.

The Burlington Northern Santa Fe uses its private passenger train during Christmas to carry children on trips in Southern California aboard its annual *Santa Claus Express*. Other railroads maintain a fleet of passenger train equipment to run Christmas specials and pamper their friends year-round.

Perhaps that's to be expected of railroads, which, after all, already own the equipment. What do we make, then, of the efforts by Playboy, Neiman Marcus, the Walt Disney Company, and others over the years to run special trains? The answer is that long-distance trains, like cruise ships, can be magical.

But there is a difference between special trains and Amtrak. Even Amtrak's best long-distance trains, says Amtrak itself, will forever be unprofitable. If true, shouldn't the government discontinue them?

Yes and no. We should discontinue the operations *as they are today* and put the trains under the direction of market-sensitive organizations. We must change the nature of the long-distance trains so that they link places Amtrak doesn't serve, operate on schedules Amtrak has never tried, and serve a travel sector Amtrak has virtually ignored.

Common-Carrier Service and Market Share

Amtrak is misdirected by running long-distance trains the way railroads did when they provided "common-carrier passenger service" as defined by the now-defunct Interstate Commerce Commission. In short, a railroad was a "service for hire," required to transport anyone with a ticket getting on at a scheduled stop. The problem is, a common-carrier long-distance train is no longer vital to mobility. In fact, the market penetration of such trains is so infinitesimal as to be meaningless to virtually every community in America.

Amtrak, in a 1997 statement filed with a Senate committee, claimed that Amtrak "serves more than 93 percent of the continental United States." That's fiction, as a glance at Amtrak's map shows. Amtrak fails to provide any service whatsoever on literally thousands of city-pair combinations because at least one of the communities has no Amtrak service. Examples: New York–Scranton, Detroit–Louisville, Tucson–Amarillo, Kansas City–Tulsa—the list is endless.

Examples of Amtrak's uselessness where it does stop are numerous. The *Lake Shore Limited* can hardly be vital to Dunkirk, New York, when this Chicago–New York train appears in the wee hours—it's nearly 4 A.M. when both the eastbound and westbound trains stop there. Does the *Cardinal* serve a public need as it departs Cincinnati at 1:10 A.M. on a painfully slow trek to Chicago? The situation is little better for stations where trains stop at more marketable hours. At Charleston, South Carolina, the number of passengers waiting for the "All aboard!" call made at 9:06 A.M. for the long-distance *Silver Palm* is far less than the number boarding a Boeing 737 at the city's airport at that hour. Trains are volume carriers, yet Amtrak is not carrying volumes on most routes.

Amtrak poorly serves many passengers when connections are required. Consider this Dallas-to-Atlanta trip comparison: Amtrak requires nighttime layovers in San Antonio and New Orleans, resulting in a trip taking fifty-one hours. Want daytime layovers? Amtrak's computer offers a ludicrous routing via Chicago and Washington, D.C., taking sixty-three hours. Travel by automobile over 782 miles of highway can be completed in about fourteen hours. Delta Air Lines offers one-hour flights.

Amtrak's common-carrier charade has been costly because it has been unable to expand its market penetration despite the 1990s travel boom. The reverse is happening—Amtrak is losing market share. According to Timothy R. Jorgenson, a Milwaukee-based transportation consultant writing in *Trains*, "Passenger rail miles have dwindled from somewhat under 1 percent to about two-thirds of 1 percent of national passenger miles. . . . Whatever Amtrak may have accomplished, the national significance of intercity passenger rail service has diminished during Amtrak's existence."

He's right. As each year passes, a greater number of Americans are nonusers of Amtrak than are users.

It isn't getting any better. As 1997 opened, numerous stories appeared about America's growth in travel: for the preceding year, the Travel Industry Association of America (TIAA) said winter travel had increased 5 percent over the year before. Highway travel set records generally, and the Pennsylvania Turnpike concluded the year racking up more than 4 billion vehicle-miles of use, an all-time record. The airlines did so well that the industry chalked up record earnings, and the FAA predicted airline traffic climbing to a new record of 667 million travelers. Motor-coach and tour operators say the group travel market will increase, according to the American Bus Association.

Amtrak was odd man out.

Key Amtrak indicators for 1996 are shocking. Amtrak carried 19.7 million passengers, down 1 million from the previous year and fewer than in fifteen of Amtrak's twenty-five-year history. Compared to the prior year, passenger-miles declined nearly half a billion to about 5 billion, equal to Amtrak's 1987 traffic. Passenger-miles-per-train-mile dropped to 168, Amtrak's lowest in a decade. Average trip length dropped for the fifth consecutive year, down to 257 miles per passenger (a distance equal to that between suburban Washington, D.C., and suburban New York City).

One problem for Amtrak is that long-distance trains will never again effectively tap into the business-travel market, which is changing as more high-income executives hit the road. According to the TIAA, in 1995, for the first time ever, the majority of domestic business travel was done by people who earned more than $50,000 a year. The number of travelers with incomes above $100,000 has doubled, meaning that they account for almost 20 percent of the business-travel market segment. Amtrak attracts virtually none of these travelers except for short distances on four routes: Boston–New York–Washington, New York–Albany, Chicago–Milwaukee, and Los Angeles–San Diego.

It's difficult to stereotype who drives automobiles on business and personal trips, but experts generally agree that middle-class travelers opt for the highways, not trains, when air travel doesn't meet their needs.

At lower socioeconomic levels, travel also looks good—so good that Greyhound has turned around its ridership decline; its traffic rose 6 percent through most of 1995. For the nation's nine largest regional bus lines, the traffic increase was more than double Greyhound's.

Thus, high-, middle-, and low-income people are traveling more than ever, but not on Amtrak. What this translates to, according to economist Robert Samuelson, is that "Amtrak provides only 0.7 percent of intercity transportation. Its annual ridership of 22 million has barely increased since 1979. By contrast, the number of airline passengers rose by 149 million (to 441 million) over the same period."

Past is prologue for Amtrak—even in the leisure market. For example, it would appear that Amtrak's long-distance *Sunset Limited* would do a respectable level of business in California, Arizona, and Florida because of the population growth in these states. Also, that type of train should appeal to Sunbelt retirees. Yet, traffic is so slim that Amtrak has never made a serious move to increase the frequency of the train from three times a week to daily.

With America's population aging, the ridership on such trains should be increasing. The number of Americans fifty-five and older will reach 75 million by 2010, up from about 55 million in 1995, according to the U.S. Census Bureau. Amtrak shows little evidence that it will be able to reach more of these passengers, a bad omen. Considering that Amtrak has had many years to perfect its craft, it nevertheless is unable to lure the unhurried travelers with what certainly is a leisure-travel vehicle.

To a degree, Amtrak has tried. Many vacationers book trips through travel agents, and Amtrak increased its commissions to agents at the same time the airlines reduced such payments. Over time, Amtrak also increased the number of approved travel agents from four thousand to more than forty thousand. Still, travelers more often ignore Amtrak than ride it.

Even when many travelers become concerned about safety on competing modes of transportation, Amtrak's blip in traffic has little staying power. A significant example can be found in the peak of the 1995 summer travel season, when New York's three airports were placed under tightened security because of threats of terrorists attack. Airline passengers were delayed as security checks intensified. United States Transportation Secretary Federico Peña announced new precautions nationwide to "deter possible criminal or terrorist acts." For several weeks hundreds of flights were delayed in response to additional bomb threats at New York's airports.

Airline-safety fears intensified the following year when, within weeks of each other, a ValuJet aircraft disappeared into the Florida Everglades and a TWA jumbo jet plunged into the Atlantic Ocean off the Long Island coast. All lives were lost in both accidents. Shortly thereafter, the Commission on Airline Safety and Security recommended installing sophisticated bomb-detection equipment at airports, another grim reminder that all was not well with the aviation system. Stories into 1997 focused on major aircraft accidents in the Dominican Republic, Peru, India, and Nigeria. The scare factor can't get much worse over a three-year period.

A few additional passengers temporarily took to the trains in the Northeast when the airports were snarled. Overall, however, travelers were undaunted and continued to fly. Many passengers believe that Amtrak's service leaves much to be desired and won't climb aboard, and those who do often fail to become repeat customers.

Political Trains

S hocking but true—if Amtrak continued to run only the short-distance trains in the Northeast and Southern California, about half of Amtrak's total ridership would be retained. Many other trains are running for political reasons, not marketing potential, pure and simple.

This has been true since Amtrak's beginning in 1971 when Senate Majority Leader Mike Mansfield, a Democrat, tried to block Amtrak's start-up because train service through his home state of Montana would be reduced. His delaying tactic was defeated by Senator Winston L. Prouty, a Vermont Republican.

If politics could not stop Amtrak from discontinuing trains, it could be used to force Amtrak to start running them again—even though every index showed these trains would fail. Within four months of Amtrak's start-up, House Commerce Committee Chairman Harley

O. Staggers forced Amtrak to begin running a train between Washington, D.C., and Parkersburg, in his native West Virginia. One "marketing opportunity" seized by Amtrak was to locate a stop in a small town, Keyser, Staggers's hometown. As if running this worthless train was not absurd enough, Amtrak assigned one of its fairly new Turbo Trains to the route. The analogy may be imperfect, but it an airline had assigned a Boeing 747 to Washington–Parkersburg service, it would have felt the outrage of stockholders and the snickers of aviation experts throughout the world. What taxpayer outrage or disparagement came Amtrak's way was irrelevant because Amtrak was establishing a pattern of doing what it could, when it could, to please members of Congress.

Eventually, other political routes were added. Restoring the *North Coast Limited* between Chicago and Seattle via Billings pleased Senator Mansfield. Amtrak trains ran in Indiana, to the delight of Senators Birch Bayh and Vance Hartke, even though poor tracks meant meandering routes and unmarketable schedules. Even rural Idaho saw the *Pioneer* added between Salt Lake City and Seattle. Political considerations have influenced Amtrak service in every region of the nation.

Running trains for a tiny market means they eventually are discontinued because of poor ridership. Despite this reality, some rail enthusiasts and public officials have advocated other sure-to-fail routes in the 1990s, including the revival of a Chicago–Florida train (with start-up capital estimated at a quarter billion dollars); Denver–Spokane via southern Montana; and Chicago to anywhere in Oklahoma ("because Oklahoma doesn't have Amtrak"). If those aren't bad enough, Amtrak has also considered starting a New York–Atlanta route via a time-consuming line through rural Tennessee.

It's been said that "all politics is local," which is true when it comes to pork barrel spending for Amtrak. The major argument used to gain or retain Amtrak service is that it will "help the local economy." Mayors and civic boosters want trains to their towns, even if few people ride them.

In some instances, intercity train service helps a city's mobility and economic health. New York is a prime example. It's reasonable to believe that business and tourism would suffer in Manhattan if intercity trains quit serving the city. It's logical to hypothesize that its status as a commercial center would suffer without trains, especially considering the city's problems with its crowded airports and highways. It is even sensible to argue that Amtrak trains somewhat affect the economies of Boston, Philadelphia, and Washington, D.C.

But in hundreds of other communities, Amtrak trains could be discontinued tomorrow without hurting local economies one iota. First, Amtrak serves but a tiny portion of the travel market in most urban areas. Houston and Atlanta are enormous cities, but it is a rare taxi driver who waits at the station in either city for fares, knowing that only a trickle of people arrive by train. Las Vegas, San Antonio, and Tucson are fast-growth cities, but there's nothing fast-growing about Amtrak's microscopic ridership. Even where railroads historically were indispensable—San Francisco, Cincinnati, Minneapolis, and Pittsburgh come to mind—Amtrak's disappearance would leave local economies unharmed. Pittsburgh in 1921 was served by 266 daily intercity trains; Amtrak runs six. In such cities, the number of people using Amtrak is so small that they could easily be accommodated on other means of transportation.

This is hardly a new view. A study group led by John P. Doyle conducted an extensive transportation review for the U.S. Senate during the Kennedy Administration, and the widely heralded Doyle Report concluded that "railroad intercity passenger service meets no important needs that cannot be provided by other carriers. . . . It serves no locations which cannot be adequately served by air and highway." Doyle did concede the possibility of renewed demand in later years, which is evident today, particularly on Northeastern and California short-distance routes.

Another way of looking at the myth that Amtrak helps local economies is to examine growth rates of cities with and without Amtrak. This effort exposes how Amtrak service is inconsequential. For example, cities with many years of Amtrak service have lost population. A review of U.S. Census Bureau data of the thirty cities with the largest percentage population loss between 1980 and 1990 reveals that the majority of them (twenty-two to be exact) have been served by Amtrak for many years. Some population losses, such as Detroit's, have been devastating.

Communities that have never had Amtrak service—or have gone for long periods without it—have some of the highest growth rates in the nation. The census shows big population gains in Naples and Daytona Beach, Florida. Many people have moved to or vacationed in Aspen, Colorado. These and other places have never had Amtrak service and have done just fine.

Of course, Amtrak advocates can selectively point to Amtrak-served cities that have grown. That's true of Las Vegas, Atlanta, and Tucson. What those advocates fail to volunteer, however, is that the fastest-growing transport mode in these cities is aviation. If anything, business leaders often make decisions on where to place facilities based on the quality of air service. Only a dreamer would argue that two Amtrak trains a day (or six per week, in Tucson and Las Vegas) assist development. In virtually all of America's fastest-growing cities, Amtrak is irrelevant. Yet it is difficult to dispel the myth that small and medium-sized towns need Amtrak long-distance train service.

Service to Smaller Communities

" A mtrak advocates often assert that Amtrak is vital to small towns and rural areas," said Anthony Haswell. "I invite you to compare the number of communities under 50,000 [that have] Amtrak service to the total number of such places located along rail lines. The ratio is probably less than one to ten. It is difficult to believe that Amtrak is so important to these places when so many of them do not have it . . . Amtrak is a very inadequate device for meeting the transportation needs of smaller communities around the nation."

Amtrak advocates argue that many types of people—the elderly, disabled, students, those with medical conditions who cannot fly—need trains as a travel option. In fact, these assertions are hollow when one looks at Amtrak's map. Indisputably, vast areas of America have no Amtrak service whatsoever and never will. Are we justified in subsidizing hopelessly unmarketable Amtrak service for the elderly, disabled, and student populations of, say, Stanley, North Dakota, and Alpine, Texas, when the equally worthy elderly, disabled, and student inhabitants in thousands of other American communities (far too encyclopedic a listing to put here) will never see Amtrak service?

Furthermore, less-than-daily frequency in many communities flies in the face of assertions that Amtrak is an essential transportation service.

Haswell believes that smaller communities do have a claim to adequate intercity public transportation, but Amtrak long-distance trains are not the answer. He would change government policies to permit the optimum mode of transport to be used—whether a bus, commuter airline, or regional train—depending upon demand.

When Amtrak uses the argument of maintaining rural service as a justification for long-distance trains, its real motivation is to please rural members of Congress, who will continue to vote for Amtrak subsidies. Amtrak's Tom Downs told *Railway Gazette International* that "Amtrak gets support in Congress from a wide range of places; if we don't provide national coverage, we cannot expect national support."

Another claim is that Amtrak's long-distance trains are important to low-income groups. That was called into question by Wisconsin Department of Transportation findings in a planning effort called Translinks 21. The agency surveyed passengers aboard Amtrak's *Empire Builder,* which operates through the state on its Chicago–Seattle route. Although the report was limited in its scope, the responses are interesting. The report found that "about 32 percent of all passengers—and 40 percent of 'regional' travelers—had household incomes of $40,000 or more." Had the survey been conducted in the middle of summer, when more affluent passengers take vacations, the income levels would have been even higher.

The survey also determined that minuscule number of people reported having "no other mode" of transportation available to them. Fully 90 percent of the Wisconsin travelers would have taken their trips even if Amtrak's *Empire Builder* were not operating.

Rerouted Trains

Many of Amtrak's problems today are the same ones Amtrak experienced in its early days. For example, poor tracks have forced reroutes away from potential markets. Amtrak in the 1970s could not serve Indianapolis and abandoned service to Columbus and Dayton, Ohio, because of poorly maintained track or abandoned track. For years track problems caused Amtrak to link Washington, D.C., and Pittsburgh on a preposterously circuitous route through Philadelphia.

History is repeating itself as railroads abandon routes that see little or no freight traffic. When routes aren't abandoned, tracks are downgraded and speed limits lowered to reduce maintenance expenses. Small towns in Mississippi lost Amtrak service recently when the Illinois Central Railroad wanted to downgrade tracks. Amtrak, unable to fund track maintenance appropriate for passenger trains, agreed to reroute its *City of New Orleans* away from Batesville, Grenada, Winona, Durant, and Canton.

The most conspicuous case is the *Sunset Limited*, which operates between Southern California and Florida. In 1996 this train was routed away from Phoenix, Tempe, and Coolidge, Arizona. Phoenix is one of America's largest and fastest-growing areas, and its population of discretionary travelers represents ideal demographics for Amtrak. Yet, service was shifted to another line when the Southern Pacific Railroad wanted to abandon track near Phoenix.

Passengers willing to journey on a bus at less than ideal hours could still connect with the *Sunset Limited*, but the schedule was beyond belief as the connection was established in Tucson. A Phoenix–to–Los Angeles passenger would first have to travel in the wrong direction to Tucson, only to ride west on a line that passed south of Phoenix. This resulted in a Phoenix–Los Angeles trip time of eleven hours, forty minutes, meaning that while one traveler was on Amtrak, another could drive from Phoenix to Los Angeles, have a cup of coffee, drive back toward Phoenix, and be in Arizona before the Amtrak passenger arrived in Los Angeles.

Saying it another way, calculating Amtrak's schedule on direct mileage, Amtrak offers an average Phoenix–Los Angeles speed of 36.5 miles per hour—slower than average speeds for trains in Indonesia, Malaysia, Egypt, South Africa, Morocco, Algeria, and other underdeveloped countries.

With Amtrak giving little attention to the *Sunset Limited*'s intermediate markets, and with weak ridership, no policy maker can justify giving Amtrak the $27.5 million in capital funding that would be needed to retain Southern Pacific's entry from the west into Phoenix. The result is that the Amtrak train operates on segments that hold little promise while missing lucrative Phoenix–Los Angeles traffic. According to the Air Transport Association, the number of passengers flying between those cities totals more than 1.3 million annually, making it the seventeenth-busiest domestic air route. Before the train's rerouting, according to Haswell, Amtrak daily counts were less than 0.1 percent of air traffic at Phoenix and only 0.7 percent at Tucson. The contrast in Phoenix traffic has gotten worse for the train.

Long-Distance Trains Overseas

Amtrak's long-distance trains are a type of service that failed in America in the past and—perhaps even more important—is diminishing today in other parts of the world. A little-known fact, and one that Amtrak officials keep mum about, is that conventional train traffic is falling in other industrialized nations. In Europe the high-speed trains in busy corridors are very popular, commuter train traffic into and out of cities is growing, regional trains are seeing rather static traffic levels, but Amtrak-style long-distance trains are in big trouble. They are losing customers and market share even in historically train-dependent counties. Moreover, when South American countries privatize their railways, usually one of the first actions taken is to discontinue money-losing long-distance passenger trains.

If long-distance passenger trains are in trouble across the world, it's no wonder they are suffering the threat of discontinuance here, too.

A report in *Railway Gazette International* about European railways' joint decision to end some first-class sleeping-car services reveals that high-speed trains and airlines have eroded Europe's traditional sleeper traffic. "*Trans Euro Nuit* sleeping car traffic fell by an average of 17 percent between 1991 and 1993. The France-to-Italy services, subject to particularly strong air competition, lost 18 percent." Although many sleeping cars remain, particularly where air service is poor, the railways are increasingly nervous about their long-term outlook. Admittedly, the sleeping-car decline is slightly offset by new overnight trains, such as a Glasgow–Brussels service, which would not be possible except for the existence of the Channel Tunnel, which was built primarily to serve rail freight and high-speed passenger markets.

"On the face of it, this could be a recipe for a slow decline in overnight sleeping car and couchette services, ensuring that they will progressively disappear as rolling stock reaches the end of its useful life," concluded the magazine.

Rail market share continues to erode in Europe. According to the Institute for Transport Studies in Leeds, England, data for fourteen European railroads (when averaged) show that in 1990 rail lines had a modest share of the passenger market at about 7 percent, down from 12 percent in a similar 1977 survey. The findings would have been worse had it not been for dramatic growth in high-speed train traffic, particularly in France and Germany. That means a big shift away from Amtrak-type conventional trains in Europe. Later data show that one route alone, Paris–Netherlands, has lost half of its million annual passengers, making the Brussels–Amsterdam high-speed line vital for that railway.

Social factors are playing a big part in that change, with a major influence being a growing reliance on automobiles. Between 1980 and 1992, according to Geneva's International Road Federation, European private car transportation increased a remarkable 46.5 percent, and for coaches and buses, 17.5 percent. Every European nation is improving its road network. A report issued by the Office of Technology Assessment (a component of the U.S. Congress that has been dismantled as part of Washington cutbacks) found that "European travel is nearly as automobile-dominated as U.S. travel," and air travel gained so much over an eleven-year period that rail and air went from having equal shares of the intercity market to a rail share now about half of the air share.

As would be expected, much of the increase in automobile travel was in Western Europe, but what's happening in former Eastern bloc countries is telling. A reporter for the *Wall Street Journal,* Barry Newman, in a story about the Czech Republic, wrote that new highways are fanning out in all directions. "Four countries in the fast lane— Poland, Hungary, Slovakia and the Czech Republic—intend to spend $20 billion over the next decade or so building their freeways to freedom." In the Czech Republic alone, five hundred thousand automobiles were added to the 2 million private cars in only six years. It's a microcosm of Europe.

Improved airspace and airports are also having an impact. European airline traffic demand is expected by 2010 to more than double, to 774 million passengers. The most heavily traveled routes, according to the Geneva-based Air Transport Action Group, will be centered in Western Europe. As congested airports become busier, policies will be geared to shift passengers to high-speed trains for trips of three hours or shorter. Europeans are not planning to increase overnight long-distance train service as an option to airport congestion for one simple reason: the long-distance strategy won't work.

Amtrak has asserted that all its trains can help reduce airport and highway congestion. The argument is absurd because of the small contribution long-distance trains make to mobility—and that won't change, because it is nearly impossible to convince travelers to shift to slow trains for long-distance trips.

A Cato Institute study in late 1996 found that "closing down Amtrak would increase auto traffic imperceptibly." Discontinuing the *Sunset Limited,* for example, would put less than one additional motor vehicle per "lane hour" along the California–Florida route, or one vehicle every 86.2 minutes. If Amtrak's *Coast Starlight* between Seattle and Los Angeles were discontinued (a train Amtrak touts as having high load factors), a vehicle would be added to nearby highway lanes only every 18.8 minutes. (See Table 3.1.)

TABLE 3.1. **Maximum Diversion to Highways Through Closure of Amtrak Long-Distance Train Services**

Long-Distance Route	Minutes Between New Vehicles	New Vehicles Per Lane Hour
Los Angeles–Houston–New Orleans–Florida	86.2	0.7
Chicago–Albuquerque–Los Angeles	65.3	0.9
Chicago–Minneapolis–Fargo–Seattle/Portland	50.6	1.2
Chicago–Cleveland–Pittsburgh–Washington	40.1	1.5
Chicago–Denver–Oakland	34.0	1.8
Chicago–Memphis–New Orleans	33.7	1.8
New York–Atlanta–Birmingham–New Orleans	28.4	2.1
Washington–Cincinnati–Chicago	27.5	2.2
Chicago–Cleveland–New York/Boston	19.9	3.0
Los Angeles–Oakland–Portland–Seattle	18.8	3.2
Washington–Richmond–Raleigh–Charlotte	10.7	5.6
New York–Jacksonville–Miami/Tampa	9.0	6.6

Based on 1996 Cato Institute study by Jean Love, Wendell Cox, and Stephen Moore entitled *Amtrak at Twenty-Five: End of the Line for Taxpayer Subsidies.*

Amtrak management has failed to adapt the product to the market and, as a result, has frittered away tax dollars. Amtrak has spent about $2 billion for sleeping cars, dining cars, coaches—and the locomotives to pull them—for long-distance trains. Part of that investment went to stations used exclusively by such trains and for maintenance shops and yards. Thus, Amtrak has sunk scarce resources into equipment for common-carrier services that can never thrive. That money would have been better spent on short-distance corridor services, on regional trains, or on local commuter trains, or even to operate a government-guaranteed loan program to help private operators willing to innovate.

Some rail enthusiasts would rather remain unaware that Amtrak's long-distance trains are doomed. Instead, they would argue to preserve Amtrak's network because traveling by train from coast to coast is a part of America's heritage. That argument is weak. After all, aviation enthusiasts have strong attachments to vintage aircraft, but they don't expect the government to run them. Others remember U.S. Route 66 with great fondness, but since its replacement by interstate highways, no one seriously suggests reopening more than a few historic portions of the route.

Long-Distance Tour Trains

A market does exist for a certain type of long-distance train. Again, Haswell: "While ideally we would all like to see more funding made available for all kinds of train services, that is very unlikely to happen. We must make a choice, and for me the choice is clear. Long-distance services should be confined to a seasonal operation aimed at tourists and vacationers who are willing to pay the price for a unique travel experience."

A niche market exists for long-distance trains that take travelers to the nation's most popular tourist spots. For example, the economics of long-distance trains would improve if the trains were run between big cities and the national parks. Such trains would run seasonally, with fares geared to target audiences.

An eloquent case for such *National Park Specials* was made by historian Alfred Runte in his instructive and wonderfully illustrated book *Trains of Discovery*. Few realize it today, but the national parks came about not only because of a desire to preserve scenic wonders but also because of an alliance forged by preservation groups and the western railroads. Establishing parks was an idea that coincided perfectly with railroad marketing strategies at the turn of the century. The railroads became so involved that several built tracks and stations immediately adjacent to or in the parks. For example, in 1905 the Santa Fe Railway completed construction of the El Tovar Hotel on the South Rim of the Grand Canyon; it continues to enjoy a thriving business today.

"On the Santa Fe Railway, the streamliner *Grand Canyon* provided daily service between Chicago and Los Angeles, with through-cars to the canyon by way of the spur track from Williams, Arizona," wrote Runte. "Similarly, the Union Pacific added the *National Parks Special* for seasonal traffic to Zion, Bryce, and the Grand Canyon; it also expanded service to include the *Yellowstone Special,* whose summer runs ferried patrons between West Yellowstone and connecting main line trains at Salt Lake City." Also running such trains were the Northern Pacific, Great Northern, and Southern Pacific. Amtrak's *Empire Builder* still stops at Glacier National Park.

The parks are groaning under the burden of millions of visitors each year, with studies by the Wilderness Society and others projecting further growth. The majority of visitors arrive in automobiles, which is jeopardizing the environment within the parks.

Runte's book makes a common-sense call to revive the use of trains to bring visitors to parks, and recent developments are on his side. "On September 17, 1989, for example, the first passenger train in 21 years left Williams, Arizona, for Grand Canyon National Park over the fully restored Grand Canyon Railway. Similarly, since the mid-1980s, upward of 300,000 people annually have been recapturing a sense of the past at Denali National Park (Mount McKinley) in Alaska. The Alaska Railroad, Holland America Westours, and Princess Tours have combined to provide the latest in rail travel amenities, including full-length vista domes and modern sightseeing coaches." Alaska is where to find the most alluring train name around today— the *Midnight Sun Express.*

Railroad tracks remain in place to permit passenger trains to serve some of America's national parks. An inspired management could sell the combination of breathtaking scenery, the monumentalism of the national parks, and the "land cruise" concept of long-distance trains.

A few trains operate to the national parks, and do so to great acclaim. One private operator is TCS Expeditions of Seattle, a specialist in marketing unique travel experiences. It runs the *American Orient Express,* a train owned by the Swiss company Reisebüro Mittelhurgau, which also owns the *Nostalgic Istanbul Orient Express.* The *American Orient Express* is a deluxe train in the tradition of the legendary trains of Europe. "In the two dining carriages, tables are set with china, silver, crystal and linen, and menus offer a delicious taste of regional cuisines. In the two club cars you can relax around a baby grand piano. At the end of the train there is a historic observation car, the ideal place to watch the rails and passing scenery," wrote company president T. C. Swartz in a sales pitch to potential customers. The train has sleeping cars, which come equipped with showers.

This is indeed a private luxury train: "The vintage carriages are appointed with rich mahogany and polished brass, exquisite fabrics and custom carpets. Sleeping compartments have large picture windows and private bathrooms. . . . Attendants are on duty 24 hours a day." The train, rebuilt from the streamliner era of the 1940s and 1950s, was restored at an investment of $14 million.

The tours on this train—billed as a "cruise ship on rails"—cost several thousand dollars per person for a nine-day experience (shorter trips are also offered), but included are train and hotel accommodations; gourmet meals; group activities, including local tours; transfers and baggage handling; and pampering by tour directors and train staff. Aboard to give lectures are various experts, including one who speaks about the century-old relationship between the national parks and the railroads—Al Runte.

During 1996, the first year of operating the *American Orient Express*, the company broke even on a 165-day operation. The trains continue to sell out despite premium fares, and a profitable operation is expected in coming years.

Companies elsewhere offer unique train travel experiences. The *Northern Parks Limited* carries tour groups between Yellowstone and Glacier National Parks. The *Mountain Rockies Daylight*, offering "Big Sky" dome car service, runs between Laurel, Montana (near Billings), and Sandpoint, Idaho, and rides over rails not used by passenger trains in more than fifteen years.

North of the border, Rocky Mountaineer Railtours, owned by the Great Canadian Railtour Company, offers the *Rocky Mountaineer* between Vancouver in British Columbia and Banff, Calgary, and Jasper in Alberta. The company was founded by Peter Armstrong, a former Gray Line Tours executive who has tapped the luxury rail travel market at a profit. The operation is different from the *American Orient Express* in that the fares on the Canadian trains are lower and thereby appeal to a broader range of travelers. This train can carry more than seven hundred passengers. Another Canadian company, BC Rail, is planning a new operation to begin in 1998, *Westcoast Explorer,* a summertime "touring train" to operate on a twice-weekly schedule.

The financial results for the independent operations described above, and others like them, range from worrisome to thriving, depending upon circumstances. The unifying feature, however, is that lessons are being learned in how to privatize cruise-type passenger trains. Amtrak's common-carrier long-distance passenger trains may operate at a loss; yet, innovative "travel experience trains" are earning varying degrees of profit.

Organizations devoted to serving seasonal travel markets can be designed at the outset to be flexible in how they will use capital assets. A train operating to national parks in the summer could easily be devoted, say, to winter-season luxury runs between New York and Florida.

Some rail advocates would like to strengthen rail service to the parks by restoring rail links, bringing trains closer to lodging and dining facilities. Al Runte, for one, would like to see eighteen miles of track put back so that special trains to Yellowstone could once again terminate at the historic Gardiner Gateway. Meanwhile, Christopher C. Swan, of Suntrain Transportation Development Corporation in San Francisco, proposes an ambitious plan to rebuild the now-abandoned Yosemite Valley Railroad.

The market is growing for these trains, especially as baby boomers age and become more interested in unhurried cruise-style travel. It is unlikely that Amtrak will shift from its common-carrier role to a land-cruise one, nor would doing so be appropriate. If Amtrak abandoned stops and bypassed others in a shift to seasonal tourist trains, elected officials would howl protests in the name of bruised civic pride. If Amtrak upgraded passenger car appointments to the more luxurious standards required for the land-cruise market, egalitarians would decry the special treatment accorded to "wealthy travelers." The fact that reconfigured services could operate at a profit would simply be lost in the emotional fray. Amtrak should not try to do this job; private-sector newcomers should.

To illustrate how removed Amtrak is from this thinking, consider a unique proposal it received only six months after Amtrak's birth. The U.S. Department of Interior in October 1971 urged Amtrak to designate ten of its routes spanning 3,000 miles as parts of a National Scenic Railway System similar to the National Wild and Scenic Rivers System and the National Trails System. The Amtrak routes would help promote "both domestic and international travel to the network of national parks." Amtrak never took action.

Specialized land-cruise trains run overseas. The *Thomas Cook European Timetable* warns that "normal rail tickets are not valid" on the privately operated *Venice–Simplon Orient Express*, on Waterman Railway's Premier Land Cruise in Great Britain, and on the *Al Andalus Express* and the *Transcantabrico* in Spain. Meanwhile, in India, where the luxurious *Palace on Wheels* has operated for years, new arrangements call for the private sector to operate five land-cruise rail routes.

Amtrak operates one passenger train that makes no intermediate stops and appeals almost exclusively to leisure travelers—the *Auto Train* on a 900-mile route between Lorton, Virginia, in suburban Washington, D.C., and Sanford, Florida, near Disney World. It carries passengers in coaches and sleeping cars while their automobiles, vans, and motorcycles ride in special cars.

Should Amtrak be dismantled, it seems logical that private companies would vie to operate not only the East Coast *Auto Train* but others as well. The potential for new routes was acknowledged by Amtrak's vice president of marketing and revenue development, Steve Scott, who said that *Auto Train*, now a $50 million revenue opportunity, with two additional routes could grow to a $175 million operation. Candidate routes for *Auto Train* service include the Midwest–Florida, Seattle–California, Chicago–Denver, and Denver–California.

Short-Distance Train Options

Americans today can ride trains from earlier eras, usually for short distances, in all regions of the nation. Vacationers can visit about 150 railways and museums in the United States devoted to railroading as recreation. The Tourist Railway Association, based in Aurora, Colorado, indicates that many of these organizations do a splendid job running steam locomotives and quaint passenger cars. Operating museums like the Steamtown National Historic Site in Scranton, Pennsylvania (financed by $80 million in federal funds, so this one is subsidized), offer trips through scenic countryside. Others specialize in white-linen dining experiences, with California's *Napa Valley Wine Train* but one example. Excursion companies elsewhere capitalize on their locales—such as the *Ozark Zephyr* and *White River Eagle,* which are part of the growing tourist industry in Branson, Missouri, or the ski trains that link Denver with the slopes at Winter Park. In some cases, these are the places to find historic railroad stations that have been painstakingly restored.

A market also exists for specialized short-distance leisure-style trains.

An example can be found in Florida, where First American Railways Inc., of Miami, has plans to operate the *Florida Fun Train* between Fort Lauderdale, near where twenty-five cruise ships dock, and Orlando International Airport. Entertainment cars will feature movies, music, dancing, video games, and, of course, a gift shop. If the first train succeeds, the company will start another to Kennedy Space Center, to be called the *Space Coast Fun Train.* In both cases, a significant portion of revenue would come from wholesale tour operators. First American Railways describes itself as a "publicly held, entertainment-based passenger rail company."

Cynics have hinted that individuals who propose to run passenger trains outside the Amtrak system might somehow be naive characters—either uninformed about railroad operating costs or perhaps dreamers or even speculators. The *Florida Fun Train* dispels that notion. The company's registration statement with the Securities and Exchange Commission lists its management, all of whom are professionals ranging in age from thirty-eight to seventy-four; they have faced harsh business realities and are serious about making their train a going concern. These entrepreneurs know that trains—if operated as an experience rather than as mere transportation between origin and destination—could be profitable. The participants in the *American Orient Express* are also professionals who recognize the business risks they face.

Then there is the potential for running trains to special events.

For many years, Amtrak has run special trains between Oakland, California, and Reno, Nevada; trains to Army-Navy football games played in Philadelphia; and an occasional "party train" to the Mardi Gras in New Orleans. These are traditional rail operations that required no innovations on Amtrak's part. Amtrak has broken with custom to run the *Seahawk Special* from Portland to Seattle (which is easy to market since the Kingdome is adjacent to the Seattle train station) and a few other trains.

New local or regional organizations, closer to their customers, with operations designed from the beginning to run highly marketable special and seasonal trains, could reap the rewards of serving this enormous market. Think a *Watermelon Special* from Little Rock to Hope, Arkansas, for the annual Watermelon Festival is a silly idea? Well, special Garlic Festival trains to Gilroy, California, do a brisk business, according to CalTrain, a commuter agency for the San Francisco Peninsula, as does its *Sun Tan Special* to Santa Cruz. The Los Angeles Metrolink commuter rail agency in 1996 reported that its first efforts at running San Clemente beach excursion trains quickly sold out, making a modest profit in the process.

Amtrak has missed the market for special events that attract tens of thousands of people from, literally, around the world. The 1996 Summer Olympic Games in Atlanta is an example. Three years earlier, the Council of Cooperating Governments in Birmingham, Alabama, headed by John Katopodis, launched the Olympic Train Demonstration Project. The council was helped by Richard Arrington, Jr., and Bill Campbell, the mayors of Birmingham and Atlanta, respectively, who appealed to Congress, saying that the trains could help move thousands of Olympic guests through the region during what would certainly be crowded conditions. Former Atlanta Mayor Andrew Young praised the idea as the type of forward thinking representative of the New South.

By January 1995 the council's project manager for rail, Milton Bagby, testified before Congress that the Olympics would bring about a voracious need for train service. "Transportation needs around the region during the Olympics will stretch capabilities to the limit," said Bagby. "There is already a plan to bring hundreds of city buses into Atlanta for urban transport. Many regional intercity bus companies have already chartered their entire fleets. The always-crowded Atlanta airport will become jammed." His predictions were more or less accurate. The number of obstacles to running special Amtrak trains for the Olympics proved too much, however, and Amtrak abandoned the attempt.

State-Developed Regional Trains

As Amtrak was planning to curtail service in the mid-1990s, Congress voted to save only long-distance routes. It fell upon states to save short-distance or regional routes, which they did by providing additional subsidies to Amtrak. The state actions spoke volumes about what types of trains are important.

Not that these "Save Amtrak" relationships got off to a great start. John F. Hynes, railroad administrator for the Missouri Highway and Transportation Department, said in congressional testimony that Amtrak's retrenching came without warning: "We received a telephone call from Amtrak informing us that a press release was to be distributed that morning announcing a number of route reductions and eliminations. . . . We were completely taken by surprise. There was no discussion, no opportunity to meet with Amtrak in advance of the announcement to review the considerations that went into their decision-making process. We felt that Amtrak had breached a fourteen-year partnership." Nonetheless, Missouri moved ahead with a program to save trains between St. Louis and Kansas City.

Amtrak fared well in Wisconsin as Governor Tommy Thompson negotiated retention of Chicago–Milwaukee *Hiawatha* service. Illinois assumed a greater share of funding for trains that radiate out of Chicago: the *Illini* to Carbondale and the *Illinois Zephyr* to Quincy—both used by college students—and the Chicago–Springfield runs, which see legislators and state employees as passengers.

Some went further than saving trains. Despite the odds, several states revived regional trains by providing not only operating subsidies but capital funding. Officials in Olympia, Washington, found $24 million to fund Amtrak's *Mount Baker International* between Seattle and Vancouver, British Columbia. North Carolina launched the *Piedmont* between Charlotte and Raleigh. Vermont helped to bring about the *Ethan Allen Express* between Rutland and New York, with the state managing to tap into federal transit funds to help finance the Amtrak train. Maine, using state as well as non-Amtrak federal funding, is working for the return of Portland–Boston service.

The results? Examine the *Vermonter*, which Amtrak describes as "a state-supported train that has significantly exceeded ridership projections and planned revenue targets. The strength of this train is attributable to grassroots marketing, supported by the state tourism office and local bureaus," and, of course, a strong regional market. Remember—Amtrak would have abandoned such promising markets, the places where America needs trains, but for state government action.

The question is, how much will Amtrak bleed the states? The GAO reported that Amtrak plans to increase the costs borne by states for the Amtrak service they receive. Amtrak in 1996 increased its take in state subsidies 79.8 percent (from $35.7 million a year earlier to $64.2 million.)* Amtrak plans to boost subsidies from states to $132 million in 2001.

Amtrak's management has squandered resources trying to preserve long-distance trains while failing to develop regional and seasonal services with higher potential. Amtrak's long-distance trains running as common-carrier vehicles will never become popular enough year-round to warrant their continuance.

---

*Subsidies were higher from California, Illinois, Michigan, Missouri, North Carolina, Oregon, Pennsylvania, Vermont, Washington, and Wisconsin.

Murky Answers for Some Routes

Will states work to preserve long-distance trains? Not likely.

For some Amtrak routes, there are no solutions other than outright discontinuance or breaking them into segments that might become regional trains. It is highly doubtful that any new operator could save an excessively long Amtrak route struggling to survive. For example, the eight states served by Amtrak's *Sunset Limited*—California, Arizona, New Mexico, Texas, Louisiana, Mississippi, Alabama, and Florida—would gain little by preserving the common-carrier nature of this train. With jetliners and interstate highways, the *Sunset Limited* has become irrelevant.

Only once was an effort made to preserve a long-distance train with subsidies by a multitude of states. It occurred at Amtrak's start-up, when the New York–Chicago *Lake Shore* was to operate on a six-month experimental basis. Ridership was low, the states reneged on their funding promises, and the train was discontinued. A modified version of the route was revived later as the *Lake Shore Limited*, with all operating subsidies coming from the federal government.

Some insist that long-distance trains that operate with high passenger loads—such as the Seattle–Los Angeles *Coast Starlight*—can thrive in their common-carrier role if only an imaginative organization replaced Amtrak.

While I'm skeptical, I'll concede that American ingenuity is up to the task on *some* routes. Selected cross-country passenger trains can survive, but only if the train's makeup is changed to include high-priority express or high-value perishable items. Such freight could be carried in cars adapted for passenger trains—a revival of the Railway Express Agency operation that antedated Federal Express and similar companies. (Amtrak, in a drive to survive, hopes to establish express service.) Also, long-distance trains can continue to roll if service is expanded to include auto-ferry capability so that travelers can travel with their motor vehicles.

New managers luring high-revenue traffic to the trains, managers freed of Amtrak's shortcomings, might be able to operate a successful long-distance passenger service on a few routes. Its success in a common-carrier role, however, will most likely result from cross-subsidies made possible by express, freight, or auto-ferry revenues.

A bright future lies ahead for land-cruise trains as envisioned by Haswell, Runte, and the entrepreneurs who have started them, as well as for sensible regional trains and local fun trains. Americans will ride trains that offer style and romance, trains that serve the national parks, trains that meet changing travel needs by altering their routes according to the seasons, and trains that offer auto-ferry services. It is time to turn to imaginative and energetic organizations that know how to enhance revenues while making passengers happy.

FOUR

Sidetracking
High-Speed Trains

"The great irony is that Graham Claytor,
the man who saved Amtrak, may go down in history
as the man who destroyed Amtrak."
—Paul Weyrich, former Amtrak board member

When it comes to Americans involved with high-speed trains, it appears that two basic types exist: visionaries and incrementalists.

A visionary wants to build high-speed trains as good as or better than the French TGV or Japanese Bullet Trains. The challenge for visionaries is to find ways to boost confidence in such projects so that adequate financing can be arranged. Lines built by visionaries, if they ever are, will be wildly popular.

An incrementalist wants to improve rail lines a bit here and a bit there to bring about higher speeds and generally is satisfied with using public dollars to do so. This group often is willing to accept abysmal objectives, including those set by Amtrak, because incremental projects are "easy" and "affordable" compared with visionary ones. Unfortunately, performance on incrementally improved lines can be poor, as Amtrak experienced on the Philadelphia–Atlantic City line. After spending millions to upgrade the route, Amtrak stopped service because of low patronage. On a broader basis, the danger of expecting too much on an incrementally improved line is that it will be seen as a dud, potentially dooming public support for further improvements.

Japan learned this lesson. When Bullet Train proposals were being evaluated in the late 1950s, incrementalists proposed building new narrow-gauge lines so that the trains would be compatible with the rest of Japan's railway system. The problem is, such trains would have been limited to 125 mph. The visionaries argued that partial improvements would not solve transport problems. They argued to build a standard-gauge system in which trains would run at higher speeds and allow quicker schedules, permit use of larger trains with a greater carrying capacity, and bring about modernized facilities in one comprehensive project. Had the visionaries lost that battle, Japan would be ill-served today with lines built to incrementalists' standards.

This doesn't mean every incremental rail project is bad. The shortest train routes, those generally about 150 miles long, are where such improvements—if done properly—can be justified. Outside of the Boston–Washington line, six currently operated routes qualify for incremental investment when ridership level, travel distance, and condition of the track and infrastructure are considered.* Although even after ridership increases, the number of passengers on the Amtrak routes is small compared with lines overseas, such improvements are nonetheless useful efforts.

The primary funding for such projects comes from state treasuries,

*New York–Albany, Philadelphia–Harrisburg, Chicago–Milwaukee, Los Angeles–San Diego, Oakland–Sacramento, and Seattle–Portland.

which means only incremental projects, not the more costly high-speed ones, can be funded. Further, the state transportation departments involved are staffed with incrementalists (although there are exceptions); thus, incremental projects become institutionalized.

Well and good for those routes, but the key to incremental projects is not expecting too much of them in situations that call for true high-speed trains. State high-speed rail commissions in Florida, Texas, Pennsylvania, Nevada, and California have studied and rejected the incremental approach for longer routes (generally longer than 250 miles, end to end). These commissioners and staff members, most often visionaries, have called for construction of new high-speed rail lines and air-competitive train service.*

That incrementalist versus visionary analysis may be simplified, but it is useful to remember as we examine how Amtrak has set low goals for its Northeast Corridor rail project and has damaged prospects for high-speed service elsewhere in America.

Northeast Corridor Programs

Amtrak has botched its mission. When Congress passed the Rail Passenger Service Act of 1970, it clearly identified Amtrak's purposes and objectives: to provide modern, efficient intercity rail passenger service and to employ innovative operating and marketing concepts to develop fully the potential of rail service.

Billions of dollars later, Amtrak is only partially modernized, is far from efficient, and has failed to employ innovative concepts. Amtrak has carried off a major hoax in making itself appear to be launching the new millennium in train service. The organization is so inept that it cannot even bring about high-speed train service on the Boston–Washington route equal to the train service overseas. Those who doubt it should consider this: when the high-speed rail project is completed

---

*High-speed lines are suggested for Tampa–Orlando–Miami, Dallas–Houston, Las Vegas–Los Angeles, San Francisco–Los Angeles–San Diego, and Philadelphia–Harrisburg–Pittsburgh.

in 1999 after more than two decades, Amtrak's top speeds will be slower than the Spanish trains were in 1995 or French or Japanese trains were in the early 1980s. Yet this is a line into which Amtrak has sunk billions of dollars of public funds.

The Northeast Corridor is a tale of low goals.

Before there was an Amtrak, Conrail, or Penn Central, there was the mighty Pennsylvania Railroad (PRR), whose web of routes linked the Atlantic seaboard with much of the Midwest. It held the majority of traffic on the New York–Washington route in the heyday of rail travel. The PRR invested heavily in the line, and in 1935 trains dashed between New York and Washington in three hours and forty-five minutes. Ridership peaked during World War II, then started a decline that continued through the 1960s.

Some astute observers, however, started to notice troublesome delays in the air and on the roads. In 1963—perhaps with Japanese Bullet Trains serving as an inspiration—a professor at Princeton University, Richard Rice, urged that a new high-speed train line be built in the Northeast. We still haven't built that new line; Amtrak doesn't even talk about building it.

Senator Claiborne Pell of Rhode Island persisted in a campaign on behalf of high-speed trains in the Northeast, and his work paid off when President Lyndon B. Johnson, in his 1965 State of the Union address, sought funding for high-speed train tests. The senator gave another boost to the program when his book *Megalopolis Unbound* appeared the following year.

What resulted was the *Metroliner*, which in 1969 went into New York–Washington service at a top speed of 110 mph, offering a two-hour-and-fifty-five-minute trip (four minutes faster than Amtrak's early 1997 schedule). It was no surprise that passengers flocked to the *Metroliner*. According to Joseph R. Daughen and Peter Binzen, authors of *The Wreck of the Penn Central*, "For sixteen years, ridership in the New York to Washington corridor had been decreasing. The *Metroliner* reversed that trend. It carried more than two million passengers in its first two years of operation. In the first year, ridership on this route increased by 8 percent."

Promise after promise to bring the *Metroliner* to higher standards have been broken.

In 1971 Transportation Secretary John Volpe issued a report recommending a New York–Washington travel time of two hours. The same year, the Geo-Transport Foundation proposed that a new railroad be built between Providence and New Haven to allow Boston–New York schedules of two hours. This would have been a "super-railroad" to eliminate many curves on the shore line route. Also that year—a big one for high-speed rail promises—Amtrak incorporators, according to Don Itzkoff's book *Off the Track*, said that "the Northeast Corridor would be the corporation's focal point" and that the Boston–New York–Washington service could largely supplant air shuttles before the end of the decade. The following year Amtrak president Roger Lewis said that maybe by the 1980s the New York–Washington run might take only an hour and a half. Despite all this talk, Amtrak did not assign even one staff member to plan a higher-speed system, and nothing happened.

In 1973 Senator Lowell Weicker, Jr., of Connecticut, introduced legislation that would give the Army Corps of Engineers a supervisory role in creating a "super-speed" system to allow trains to connect New York–Boston and New York–Washington in two hours. Amtrak didn't lift a finger to boost Weicker's idea, and the measure died.

In 1976, for the first time in history, Amtrak owned a rail line. The Railroad Revitalization and Regulatory Reform Act permitted Amtrak to acquire from the bankrupt Penn Central most of the Boston–Washington line. The law authorized the $2.5 billion Northeast Corridor Improvement Project (NECIP) to upgrade track and facilities, an amount that was later increased. But little would improve right away. In fact, *Metroliner* schedules were lengthened as tracks deteriorated. It would be six years before the trains would run on faster schedules, a time span when Japan, France, and Spain could and did build all-new lines from scratch.

In fact, by 1980 Japan's first Bullet Trains were heading to museums while Amtrak dithered.

By 1981 Albro Martin, then a Harvard Business School professor, testified before Congress that America wasn't getting true high-speed trains because we lacked the vision. His statement remains pertinent today: "The truth is that what we assume about the future almost always is the most important factor in making that future come true. If we do not a assume a high-speed corridor system, we almost certainly can assume that we will not attain that level of development that requires one. More simply put, we will not much miss the high-speed system if we do not build it. What we *will* miss will be the busy, prosperous, balanced American society that we could have built with its indispensable help."

By the mid-1980s the Coalition of Northeast Governors formed a high-speed rail task force because of "the failure of the NECIP to accomplish fully its goals of rapid, reliable, and economically sound intercity rail passenger service." It said, "Some of the projects identified by NECIP remain incomplete, including ones that would lead to trip-time reductions and improved reliability." Amtrak had abandoned certain projects on the New Haven–Boston end, like extending electrification and straightening out the curviest rail line in Amtrak's system. (With so many curves, a train makes the equivalent of twelve full circles on a New York–Boston trip.) The line fell victim to Amtrak's poor planning, optimistic cost estimates, and work delays.

The saga of inaction and poor work continued.

By 1990 Amtrak was carrying about 2 million *Metroliner* passengers, below the peak of 2.5 million in 1972 and no better than the Penn Central carried in its first full year of *Metroliner* operations.

Amtrak stepped forward with a new plan for New York–Boston dubbed the Northeast High-Speed Rail Improvement Project (NHRIP), which called for electrifying the line and improving tracks but not for eliminating many curves. Amtrak's pace was slow. According to writer David C. Warner in *Passenger Train Journal,* "Unfortunately, problems with the track-laying system equipment and other unforeseen difficulties combined to limit the amount of track actually replaced during the 1993 work season to about half the initial plan. Thirty-six miles of new rail and 80,000 new ties were installed between Old Saybrook and Kingston." Wait—36 miles of new rail in one track-laying season? Clearly, this is no Japanese Bullet Train or French TGV system.

Meanwhile, in July 1993 a study was issued for the Massachusetts Aeronautics Commission by Arthur D. Little, Inc., stating that additional capacity will be required by 2010 to meet travel demand and that building a high-speed train system should be an option. The report stated that 200-mph trains would relieve congestion at Boston's Logan International Airport and that 230-mph trains on new alignments would do more to relieve crowding than building another airport. The conclusions were remarkable because they came not from any dogmatic high-speed rail group but from aviation experts. And the 230-mph speed is not much faster than France has planned for the next generation of TGVs. The report was in contrast to Amtrak's plans for a 150-mph top speed in the Northeast.

The Amtrak project underway today is substandard when compared with lines elsewhere in the world. Despite promises, Amtrak will be unable to make a real dent in Boston's airport congestion even after its program is completed. Amtrak ignored the pro-train report by the aviation panel and sought every opportunity to reiterate the logic of its incremental approach for the Northeast. Clearly, Amtrak was exploiting for its own means what the editor at *Railway Gazette International,* Murray Hughes, identified as a North American "failure to understand the fundamentals of high-speed trains."

Meanwhile, the Federal Railroad Administration estimated that $1.255 billion (in constant 1993 dollars) would be needed to reduce the Boston–New York trip time to three hours, but only after an additional $606 million was committed to build extra capacity for commuter and freight train operations. Costs were climbing for Amtrak's incremental rail program.

Also by 1994 some opposition was building to the Boston–New York project, and residents began to file objections with environmental authorities. In Connecticut inhabitants resisted closing grade crossings. Area boaters and marina owners initiated court action, fearful that when Amtrak added trains, drawbridges would close too often, denying access to open water. Numerous businesses and the Providence & Worcester Railroad objected to the increase in Amtrak service because it would delay freight deliveries. That issue was settled when the federal government financed new tracks to keep the freight moving. So much for the "ease" of incremental high-speed rail.

By 1995 David Carol, Amtrak's vice president for high-speed rail, said that the Northeast Corridor Improvement Project has been underway for over twenty years. Recent estimates indicate that through 2010, a total investment of as much as $6.7 billion will be required for the entire Boston–Washington program.

These figures do not represent the full picture.

Many other costs apply to Amtrak's Northeast Corridor work, but they are carried on books of other agencies. The Long Island Rail Road paid $100 million of the $110 million cost for a new computerized control system for tracks leading into Amtrak's Penn Station in New York. New Jersey Transit will contribute $125 million out of its capital budget to improve track and rehabilitate related infrastructure on the Newark–Trenton portion of Amtrak's Northeast Corridor. Delaware recently spent $1 million to upgrade two Amtrak rail yards. States have funded new roads and bridges when Amtrak closed grade crossings. Millions of dollars in private funds have gone into restoring Washington Union Station, and grants from the Federal Transit Administration (FTA) and local tax dollars have paid to renew stations in Baltimore, Newark, New Haven, and elsewhere.

Further, commuter coaches purchased by Massachusetts, Pennsylvania, and Maryland are leased by Amtrak during busy periods, giving Amtrak greater capacity without its paying ownership costs. Some expenditures are a give-away. In Some expenditures are a give-away. In 1997 Pennsylvania committed $4.67 million and the FTA $18.7 million to finance $23.4 million in new self-propelled diesel-powered cars for Amtrak. These capital disbursements will not appear on Amtrak's books.

Amtrak fails to volunteer that such expenditures are *in addition to* the $3.7 billion cost (to date) of Northeast Corridor work. Amtrak prefers that those amounts be left undiscussed, because Amtrak doesn't really want the public to understand how much its "bargain" incremental project really costs.

In 1996 Amtrak finally began working on the electrification project between New Haven and Boston that was promised in the 1970s, a slow pace considering that Amtrak by law is *supposed* to bring about modern, efficient intercity rail passenger service.

It its defense, Amtrak would say that it has been undercapitalized since its formation. But to a large extent, that is because Amtrak has failed to make a convincing case that it can spend capital funds in sensible ways. Also, it takes Amtrak an inordinate amount of time to achieve incremental goals. To spend the period from Amtrak's birth to 1999—a total of twenty-eight years—to bring about a three-hour New York–Boston schedule, only forty-five minutes faster than in the late 1960s, is pitiful.

Amtrak High-Speed Trains

Amtrak has selected new trains to run in the Northeast, although again not in a timely fashion. According to a 1995 dispatch by Gene Kramer of the Associated Press, "The race to build America a new generation of fast passenger trains is running late. . . . Two years ago, Amtrak said it hoped to award the contracts in early 1994 among six groups then competing." Delays were due to Amtrak's drawing up custom-made specifications, but two years is unjustifiable. Amtrak was not designing an all-new train—it was merely "Americanizing" proven technologies from overseas.

Beginning in 1992, several foreign-designed high-speed trains were turned over to Amtrak for demonstration in the United States. The first test was of the Swedish X2000 over the Northeast Corridor. The train allows faster schedules by using tilt technology, which permits up to 40 percent faster speeds on curves.

Amtrak created much hoopla over the X2000, but it was exaggerated because it really wasn't that new. A train built by United Aircraft in the 1960s, the TurboTrain, with a passive tilting system, was put in Boston–New York service and its fast schedules were popular. Also, record books show that a TurboTrain set a Northeast Corridor speed record of 170.8 mph on December 20, 1967. That record still stands, despite the speed trials of the X2000, which hit 155 mph a quarter century later.

Going back further, tilt-trains were developed by a Spanish engineer, Alejandro Goicoechea, and in 1942 prototypes ran between Guadalajara and Madrid. Continual refinements over the years have been incorporated into the Talgo 200, a popular train in Spain, which Amtrak operates on routes serving Seattle.

Over the years, tilt-trains have found a niche in operations in Spain, Switzerland, Germany, Poland, Finland, Sweden, Italy, and Japan, and several manufacturers build them. The trains will prove useful for additional applications in Great Britain, France, and—in limited cases—the United States.

Amtrak also tested the nontilting German InterCity Express (ICE Train) train, the most attractive of any ever run by Amtrak. The ICE Train and the X2000 rambled about on coast-to-coast tours, and people waited in long lines to walk through them.

By March 1996 Amtrak ordered new trains for the Northeast— the *American Flyer*—from Bombardier Incorporated of Quebec and GEC Alsthom, a British-French venture. In announcing the deal, Vice President Al Gore and Transportation Secretary Federico Peña showed off a model of the train, which will be slower than its French TGV forerunner.

The costs for eighteen *American Flyers* and portions of three new maintenance shops will total $611 million. Private funds are involved, according to Amtrak's Tom Downs, who said, "High-speed rail is moving forward because the private sector is convinced it will succeed. Lenders obviously feel confident about the prospects for high-speed rail service in America."

Matthew L. Wald, a reporter for *The New York Times,* explained it this way: "Just as General Motors finances car purchases, Bombardier and GEC Alsthom will provide financing for much of the deal, evidently sharing the railroad's belief that the trains will generate more than sufficient revenues to pay for themselves. Bombardier and GEC Alsthom plan to borrow the money from banks at preferential rates, because the loans will be guaranteed by the Export-Import Bank, according to Bombardier."

Amtrak also negotiated a requirement for the winning bidder to sign long-term maintenance and management contracts that include performance guarantees. Bombardier has agreed to pay Amtrak damages if specified travel times are short by even seconds or if trains are not available for service ninety minutes prior to departure.

Here's how the terms were viewed by Amtrak-watcher Don Phillips, writing in *Trains:* "The new equipment is actually projected to produce an additional $150 million a year in revenues after loan payments are subtracted. In other words, Amtrak pays almost nothing out of pocket, gets brand-new trainsets (plus fifteen new electric locomotives for conventional trains) and then waits for the money to flow in. On top of that, Bombardier agreed to some amazing penalty clauses. The Canadian company will pay $20,000 for every train that runs late for mechanical reasons after the first nine late trains in any year.... Unless Bombardier produces an unusually superior product, it will lose money on the deal."

There is an important lesson here that has gone unreported—Amtrak's operating goals for the Northeast are so low that modifying French TGVs to meet them should not be a real challenge. Perhaps that is why Bombardier agreed to Amtrak's terms.

A difference exists between tilting systems: the Talgo and Turbo-Trains were designed with passive systems relying on pneumatic cylinders, while the *American Flyer* relies on mechanisms guided by sensors, computers, and hydraulics. The latter's design is based on a system installed in Canada's Light Rapid Comfortable (LRC) trains, which is cause for concern. Dan Cupper wrote in *Trains:* "One nagging question that remains is whether history will repeat itself. The TGV is the finest high-speed passenger train in the world, but because of France's high-speed right-of-way, it requires no tilting mechanism. The LRC-style tilting-carbody mechanism proposed to be used in the *American Flyer* has not been proved at world-class high speeds, let alone while carrying carbodies with which it has never been mated, or in the brutal environment of daily revenue service. Can the combination of two technologies that have never been mated work?"

Southern California Fiasco

I f Amtrak's high-speed effort in the Northeast has been tarnished by Amtrak's low goals, delays, cost overruns, and broken promises, Amtrak has been an unmitigated failure everywhere else in the world of high speed.

Amtrak in the early 1980s created the American High Speed Rail Corporation (AHSRC) to plan a Los Angeles–San Diego line. According to Alan S. Boyd, the first U.S. transportation secretary and former Amtrak president, who also served as AHSRC chairman, the goal was to run trains between the cities in fifty-nine minutes. Amtrak loaned funds to the AHSRC at a commercial rate to finance studies. The company lost credibility, however, by issuing ridership estimates that were discredited and led to disbelief among the public, investment community, and government officials.

The effort turned into a fiasco as Amtrak's loaned executives made serious mistakes. For example, the AHSRC obtained a state exemption from all environmental requirements—a useless effort, as the state attorney general ruled that a full review was needed anyway. This was one of the worst moves the Amtrak team made because it turned potential allies into foes. Amtrak-AHSRC insensitivity meant that concerns about trains from trackside residents were ignored. As writer Tom Belden pointed out in *Passenger Train Journal,* "AHSRC from the outset essentially told Southern Californians what it was going to do for them, rather than asking what people wanted." Belden concluded that "AHSRC officials placed virtually all the blame for the collapse of their project on money troubles, despite the fact that other important issues, including political diplomacy, environmental impact, and the reliability of ridership figures were also at work, as they are in all proposed high-speed projects."

Amtrak's AHSRC unit folded up shop.

Redefined High-Speed Rail

Today, Amtrak is campaigning to redefine high-speed rail as any train traveling at a minimum of 100 mph; unfortunately, it has been successful at this semantics game. The problem is, these types of trains—sometimes derided as "high-speed lite"—are incapable of luring enough air travelers to rail so that the rail line can become profitable. Also, the important social and economic contributions that high-speed trains can make, such as relieving airport overcrowding, cannot be achieved by the kinds of trains that Amtrak is calling "high-speed trains."

Amtrak at one time admitted that it could not bring about air-competitive high-speed rail outside of the Northeast Corridor. In a 1983 letter to the Midwest High Speed Rail Compact, Amtrak's Graham Claytor was clear about not interfering with independent efforts. He said that "we believe that the kind of service, the technology, the financing mechanisms, the operating entity, the sponsoring agent, and so on may appropriately vary from corridor to corridor, according to each corridor's distinctive characteristics and commercial potential, and we accordingly welcome the diverse approaches that are being offered today. In that sense, there is indeed no conflict between the rail projects [the compact] and others are proposing on the one hand and Amtrak's own mission on the other."

That was at a time when Claytor was preoccupied in opposing the Reagan Administration's efforts to gut Amtrak's national route structure. Claytor won the battle to keep long-distance trains in operation, and railroad buffs have lionized Claytor as a result.

As high-speed rail planning increased around the nation, Claytor repeated his stance in a 1988 speech before high-speed rail advocates: "While we have a common objective, we are following different routes to achieve it. You with advanced technology high-speed rail projects and we at Amtrak with conventional passenger trains operating on existing railroad tracks. I think we can, however, work together to our mutual benefit in a lot of ways."

But things changed in an enormous way in 1993 when Amtrak started to issue misleading statements. Amtrak began telling the news media that the "only" way high-speed rail would come about was by upgrading existing rail lines. In one interview, an Amtrak public relations spokesman had sufficient nerve to criticize France's profitable and extremely safe TGV system. Also, Claytor dismissed new high-speed lines as "incredibly expensive" but failed to specify the numerous hidden costs for the Northeast's incremental high-speed project. Amtrak's public posture offended many high-speed rail advocates, who had worked for more than a decade—with zero help from Amtrak—to broaden support for new trains, new technologies, and new private and public funding sources.

This is when the rail community began to fall into two camps: the visionaries and the incrementalists. The visionaries understood that Amtrak was intentionally setting out to undermine independent high-speed rail projects, efforts that were superior to Amtrak's and, if successful, would embarrass Amtrak.

Claytor threw fuel on a growing fire. The most peculiar communication ever sent to the High Speed Rail Association (HSRA) was a January 20, 1993, letter from Claytor stating that "there is general public misunderstanding of the expression 'high-speed rail.' I believe that to avoid this, it is important to use two different expressions for two different types of operations. Here at Amtrak, we are making it very clear that we consider 'high-speed rail' to involve operations over existing railroad tracks at speeds from 100 mph up to 150 mph. . . . On the other hand, the Japanese Bullet Train, the French TGV and maglev operations are at far higher speeds than this, somewhere in the 160-mph and up to 300-mph range and require construction of a new dedicated railroad or guideway. We call this 'ultra high speed,' and we support these projects as well."

That reference to "support" was disingenuous, as we shall see.

The die had been cast. Amtrak and its friends would give all Amtrak rail projects, no matter how puny or absurd, the full push. The same people would fail to support, and would often ridicule, non-Amtrak high-speed rail projects in Texas, California, Nevada, Pennsylvania, and Florida. They would pooh-pooh the independent projects—no matter how socially useful, no matter how safe, no matter how technologically advanced, and no matter how potentially profitable.

Amtrak's coining the term *ultra high-speed rail* was a way of making the high-speed train systems of France, Japan, Germany, Italy, and Spain appear impossible to build in America. Contrary to Claytor's assertion, there was little "public misunderstanding" about the nature of high-speed rail, at least prior to his campaign to redefine it. What confusion existed could be found in Amtrak's muddleheaded management. Amtrak's solution was to mislead the news media, Capitol Hill, and the American public about high-speed rail.

Supporting Amtrak were wistful incrementalists who believe any schedule improvement, even just a few minutes, will draw hordes of new customers. They stubbornly cling to this belief despite harsh evidence that many Amtrak lines are hopelessly unmarketable. In this category are members of Congress who want "better trains" for their hometowns, Federal Railroad Administration staff who are more comfortable with Amtrak's old ways than with independent ventures and their new ways, some railway suppliers, and railroad buffs who will ride any train, no matter how slow. These interests demonstrate a fierce devotion to the status quo. Thus, we have Amtrak talking about high-speed trains between Chicago and Detroit (talked about since the 1970s) and between New York and Jacksonville (much too long to be a sensible high-speed route).

The visionaries want the United States to be careful about what kind of rail lines are built, because systems called "high-speed" must generate exceptionally high ridership to avoid financial losses and public ridicule. Unfortunately, Amtrak's incremental proposals show little promise of meeting future market requirements, and when they flop will jeopardize meritorious proposals by non-Amtrak interests.

Human behavior has for years demonstrated that speed sells. The system of transport offering the fastest trip always emerges with the most market share, provided the service is reasonably priced. That's why German high-speed trains offer service "half as fast as the plane, twice as fast as the car." Amtrak will not do that anywhere outside the Northeast Corridor.

Amtrak's goal of operating at 100 mph outside the Northeast Corridor was a throwback to past railroading practices. Steam engines pulling passenger trains on the Milwaukee Road and Chicago & North Western Railroads more than fifty years ago were hitting that speed, and trains elsewhere were close to it. If 100-mph trains were unable to keep their customers when airports and highways were underdeveloped, then they sure won't build traffic in today's competitive environment.

A reading of the law shows that Amtrak does not have legal grounding for its redefinition effort. Federal statutes have interpretations for what constitutes high-speed rail, and they are higher than Amtrak's. In the Railroad Revitalization and Regulatory Reform Act of 1976, the definition is service that is "reasonably expected to reach sustained speeds of more than 125 mph," a definition also used by the U.S. General Accounting Office. A higher threshold was established twice in the 1980s when the government amended the Internal Revenue Service code regarding private activity bonds. Both times Congress specified that tax-exempt bonds may be authorized for systems "using vehicles that are reasonably expected to operate at speeds in excess of 150 mph between scheduled stops."

An explanation for Amtrak's behavior might be found in the book *In Search of Excellence,* in which Peters and Waterman describe studies by Andrew Pettigrew, a British researcher, into strategic decision making and organizational behavior. They wrote that Pettigrew "showed that companies often hold on to flagrantly faulty assumptions about their world for as long as a decade, despite overwhelming evidence that the world has changed and they probably should too." That's Amtrak. Instead of changing, Amtrak would rather the rest of the world change. If Amtrak executives, in order to reach a narrow objective, had to "redefine" a McDonald's by calling it the Sistine Chapel, they would.

Thus, perhaps it should not have been a surprise that Amtrak would publicly redefine high-speed rail in a manner that conveys low goals, the only type Amtrak knows. Further, with high-speed rail increasingly positioned for federal assistance, Amtrak made it easier to lay claim to government funds that had been intended for non-Amtrak projects. This aim was clear in a letter from the National Association of Railroad Passengers to its boosterish membership, stating that "high-speed rail funding may function as supplemental Amtrak capital."

Death of the Texas TGV

I was president of the HSRA when the Claytor "redefinition" letter arrived, and its divisive nature meant something had to be done. I wrote to Claytor and appealed for his support in a March 1993 House Transportation Appropriations Committee hearing on high-speed rail. The committee chairman, Bob Carr of Michigan, wanted to kill high-speed rail because of fears that better trains would hurt automobile sales.

Carr had invited Herb Kelleher, chairman of Southwest Airlines, to appear, after Kelleher had widely publicized his position in favor of killing the ambitious Texas high-speed train project. I appealed to Claytor to support the Texas plan, urging a "united front, so that Mr. Kelleher will be unable to play us against one another. . . . The bottom line regarding the hearing is this: if you fail to give a ringing endorsement of the Texas TGV project, your comments will be used by Southwest Airlines to discredit the project."

Kelleher was indefatigable in vilifying high-speed rail and falsely claiming that aviation isn't subsidized. Meanwhile, Claytor created problems for the high-speed community by testifying incorrectly about how the French TGV lines were financed, by casting unjustified doubts on the profitability of TGV routes, by misleading the committee about electrical power issues, and by falsely claiming that "our tracks between New York and Washington are the best in the world."

It was a classic case of special interests speaking for their own concerns, no matter what the facts were.

Claytor launched into a poor-man's version of high-speed rail, asking for funds to develop diesel or turbine locomotives that would

TABLE 4.1. **Top Speeds of Fastest Trains Worldwide**

Country	Train	Top Speed/mph
France	*Eurostar*	186.4*
France	TGV Atlantic	186.4
Japan	Series 500 Bullet Train	186.4
Germany	InterCity Express (ICE Train)	173.6
Japan	Series E2 Bullet Train	170.5**
Japan	Nozomi Bullet Train	170.5
France	TVG Southeast	167.8
Spain	Alta Velocidad Español (AVE)	167.8
Italy	Pendolino	155.3
United States	*American Flyer*	150***
Great Britain	Various	125
Sweden	Various	125
United States	*Metroliner*	125

*Increase to 200 mph planned.
**In Fall 1997 will enter service to Nagano, site of 1998 Winter Olympics.
***Will not enter service until 1999 or 2000.

reach 125 mph, which wouldn't be as fast as the TurboTrains that had run in the Northeast nearly thirty years earlier. Also, Claytor failed to state that the French were phasing out turbine-powered trains, with the Lyon–Strasbourg service just about the only intercity turbine route left in that country.

Few in the hearing room realized it at the time, but in arguing for 125-mph trains, Claytor was calling for service slower than what already existed in France, Germany, Japan, Spain, and Italy and slower than systems planned for Russia, South Korea, and Taiwan. (See Table 4.1.) Further, Claytor was arguing for trains no better than what Turkey and Ireland are thinking of building.

Even the 150-mph *American Flyer* for the Northeast Corridor fails to rank high in an international comparison of top speeds, as Table 4.1 shows. Some will argue that comparing top speeds is unfair because it's average speed that counts in the marketplace. There is some truth to that criticism, but as shown in Table 4.2, on that basis Amtrak ranks even lower—at the bottom.

TABLE 4.2. Average Speeds of Fastest Trains Worldwide

Country	Train	Average mph	Over Track Between
France	*Eurostar*	165.7	Eurotunnel–Paris outskirts
Japan	Series 500 Bullet Train	162.3	Hiroshima–Kokura
France	TGV Atlantique	155.3	Roissy Charles de Gaulle–Lille
Japan	Nozomi Bullet Train	142.8	Kokura–Hiroshima
Spain	Alta Velocidad Español (AVE)	135.1	Madrid–Cuidad Real
Germany	InterCity Express (ICE Train)	125	Fulda–Kassel Wilhelmshöhe
France	TGV Southeast	123.9	Lyon–Paris
Great Britain	IC225	109.8	Stevenage–Doncaster
Sweden	X2000	108.6	Hallsberg–Skövde
Italy	*Christoforo Colombo*	100.4	Florence–Rome
United States	*Metroliner*	95.2	Baltimore–Wilmington

Sources: *Railway Gazette International* (October 1993, October 1995) and *International Railway Journal* (March 1997).

Carr asked Kelleher, "Do you have any serious reservations about Mr. Claytor's incremental approach, as he laid it out?" Kelleher responded, "No sir, Mr. Chairman, I really do not." Of course not. Claytor-type trains running on upgraded tracks in Texas, intermingled with slow freight trains, could never compete with Southwest Airlines' jetliners between Dallas and Houston. With Claytor in charge, Kelleher would never have to worry about losing market share to trains.

After Kelleher lambasted the proposed Texas TGV system, Congressman Frank Wolf, of Northern Virginia, suggested, "Mr. Claytor, it seems easy to reconcile your statement with that of Mr. Kelleher's." Claytor shocked the audience by responding, "That's right." Yet, *Aviation Daily* knew what Kelleher was up to and headlined its report SOUTHWEST TO CONTINUE ATTEMPTS TO DERAIL HIGH SPEED TRAIN.

A subhead could have read, AMTRAK'S CLAYTOR, TOO.

At that very time, Amtrak was running its Dallas–Houston *Texas Eagle* on a six-hour schedule—two hours longer than the schedule forty years ago of the *Sam Houston Zephyr*, and much longer than the ninety-minute schedule possible on a Texas TGV. Also, Amtrak had no plans to provide high-speed rail in Texas, incremental or visionary, publicly or privately financed, in this century or the next. Considering Amtrak's pathetically slow Texas operation and no strategy whatsoever to improve it, Claytor's performance was outrageous. Amtrak's Dallas–Houston train has since been discontinued because of poor patronage.

Amtrak's most important institutional imperative is to perpetuate itself, meaning it is no different from virtually every other organization in Washington. If Amtrak's self-interest required it to sabotage the Texas project, then by all means it would do so. This was devastating to high-speed advocates because Claytor, with his expert knowledge of railroading and masterful political skills, carried weight with Congress. It also was sad to see respect for an experienced leader start to evaporate in the visionary part of the rail community.

Claytor pretended to be for high-speed rail when in fact he damaged it. His performance was as phony as American professional wrestling. This was the day I began using the term "dinky-rail" to describe some of Amtrak's incremental programs.

The Texas team went into damage control. Its vice chairman at the time, Larry Salci, a veteran of the railway supply industry, sent a lengthy statement to Carr—thoroughly researched and footnoted, and understated in tone—to refute erroneous and misleading statements.

Salci wrote that the incremental alternative had been evaluated by the Texas Turnpike Authority and was found wanting. The study, with its cost and ridership estimates and transport time simulations, indicated that incremental rail would *not* be cost-effective in Texas, because of its low ratio of revenues to capital costs. In effect, Amtrak-style incremental rail in Texas would be a Texas-sized boondoggle. This isn't a surprise. Long ago the French had learned that all-new lines on deserving routes would amortize capital debt more quickly than with the incremental approach.

Salci clarified that the all-new Texas TGV would operate at a profit, while the alternative would not. An incremental failure "would assure Southwest of continued dominance in intercity travel in the Texas Triangle for another ten to twenty years, if not longer." Salci said the prime corridors for high-speed rail outside the Northeast are in Texas, California, Illinois, and Michigan—and all have become strong markets for Southwest Airlines. If only incremental upgrades are done in those states, the airline would have no serious competition.

Other airlines understand this. In late 1996 Robert Ayling, chief executive of British Airways, told *USA Today* reporter David Field that "I don't think you will see a Southwest-type airline within Europe. There is the tradition of long car trips, and when high-speed rail is in place, it will offer too much competition for a high-frequency, low-fare operation like Southwest's."

Contractors have estimated that under certain conditions, where work has to be scheduled around train operations, incremental costs can be higher than those for all-new systems. Wrote Salci: "Building rail to run at 125 mph, let alone 150 mph, involves much more than buying a few trainsets. Roadbed, tracks, curvature, signaling and communications, electrification, grade crossings, and safety barriers must all be modernized and upgraded, sometimes in the middle of active rail operations."

The Texas Turnpike Authority study indicates that incremental rail upgrades for the Dallas–Houston–San Antonio triangle would require 686 miles (compared with 618 miles for new high-speed rail) and would cost 78 percent of high-speed rail. It could even rise an additional 16 percent if railroads concerned with freight traffic required that passenger train tracks be built on dedicated rights-of-way.

Then there are operating costs. French railway data show that high-speed tracks used only by the TGV are less expensive to maintain than traditional mixed freight and passenger lines. Prohibiting freight train operations on such lines simplifies potential safety problems, too.

Profitable High-Speed Trains

An issue that embittered visionary high-speed rail advocates was Claytor's simplified claim that European systems require large subsidies, implying that high-speed trains lose money. Amtrak has had definitive evidence for years that *high-speed lines* within those systems earn a profit. In testimony before Congressman Dan Glickman in the early 1980s, Amtrak vice president Lawrence D. Gilson discussed the profitability of a high-speed service. He explained that "the 59 percent operating ratio in Japan for the Bullet Train is sufficient to throw off cash which is able to subsidize or offset losses in the conventional trains." In the railroad business, operating ratios are a standard measure of financial performance, and no service provided by Amtrak comes near the Japanese ratio.

In case the point was lost, Gilson explicitly stated that $4 billion a year in subsidies was given to the Japanese railways but that it was attributable to the losses accrued by the conventional trains "even after factoring in the surplus funds which are available to the conventional trains as a result of the profits of the Bullet Train." Remember, this came from an Amtrak vice president.

True high-speed trains operate at a profit, whereas Amtrak-like trains lose money; and Amtrak has known this data for years.

"High-speed rail has actually revitalized what had been an aging and inefficient conventional rail system," according to Salci. "High-speed rail has actually boosted the net revenues of the total system . . . [and] is carrying the burden of the rest of the French rail system." The Paris–Lyon TGV line was constructed with private funding, while the government issued grants totaling 30 percent of the construction costs to the TGV Atlantic line. The investments have been wise, as TGVs carry about half of main-line passenger traffic in France. Jacques Fornier, the former chairman of the French National Railways, stated that the railroad is making "substantial profits from TGV traffic."

These views were echoed by Mitchell P. Strohl in his book *Europe's High Speed Trains: A Study in Geo-Economics,* in which he reports that "for every 100 francs of income, operation costs take 38.8 francs, 23.10 go to paying infrastructure and rolling stock costs, and 39.10 francs go as a net profit to the [French National Railway]."

Because of technological advances, TGV operating costs per kilometer have dropped 37 percent from 1982 to 1990, and the Paris–Lyon route has generated something on the order of a 12–15 percent profit and paid for itself by 1993, several years ahead of schedule. Also on the record with Amtrak are statements furnished by German officials that several of their ICE Train routes operate profitably.

While a common ground exists among high-speed train experts overseas that speeds will rise to 215 mph after the turn of the century, Amtrak remains stuck in the past. Amtrak management looks at a situation, has little or no dialogue with others outside the organization and issues an edict—and that's that. The problem is, so many times they're wrong.

Oust Claytor Effort Debated

Claytor knew that by kicking the Texas TGV project, he would help perpetuate Amtrak. Believing something had to be done, I asked trusted HSRA board members to consider our options. It was clear from my conversations with Claytor that discussing the topic with him again would lead nowhere. Finally, I asked the sensitive question: Should we ask Claytor to resign? I was in favor of quietly asking for his departure, even volunteering for the task. If rebuffed by the autocratic Claytor—which was a certainty—I was prepared to make his resignation a public demand. We realized, however, that roughly one-third of our members (the visionaries) would cheer the effort, one-third (the incrementalists) would denounce the move, and the reactions of the rest were difficult to predict.

Claytor—supposedly Amtrak's best president—was failing miserably as a leader. But without a consensus, we did nothing. The failure of visionaries to stand up to Claytor was counterproductive because Amtrak's absurdities about high-speed rail intensified. I resigned from the association two years after the Carr hearing, weary of the charade that Amtrak's dinky-rail plans are worth much.

After Amtrak made nonsensical pronouncements about high-speed rail, others followed. The Georgia Department of Transportation, for example, urged high-speed rail on a Washington–Atlanta route. Yet the line is much too long to compete with air travel, and considering it was an absurd waste of tax dollars.

Elsewhere, with funding from Washington State, Amtrak began promoting another "high-speed" train—the Talgo 200—between Vancouver, B.C., and Seattle. It's a decent train, and its number signifies a 200-kilometers-per-mile capability, or 124.3 mph, which it reaches in Spain. On its Amtrak route, however, it is limited to 79 mph, and it travels even more slowly for part of the way. The Talgo has a three-hour-and-fifty-five-minute schedule—the identical running time as the schedule in effect when Harry Truman was President—and takes fifteen minutes longer than the bus or driving. The Spokane *Spokesman-Review* headlined its story on the train SLOWER THAN A SPEEDING BULLET, showing that some people can't be fooled by Amtrak's silly redefinition effort. The headline could have been harsher. Amtrak's Talgo to Vancouver, running at an average speed of 39.8 mph, can claim as its counterpart a Santiago–Concepción train in Chile that runs at the same average speed.

Most incremental improvements to Amtrak are a questionable use of capital. For example, the fastest train connected Seattle with Portland in three hours, thirty minutes when Amtrak was born. Under a state proposal to spend $266.2 million to improve this and another line, the best schedule in 1999 would be a mere four minutes faster than Amtrak's 1971 schedules. A long-range plan for Vancouver–Seattle–Portland also is inadequate because, even when nearly $1.3 billion is spent by 2020, the trains will not serve SeaTac Airport—the biggest single travel destination north of San Francisco and west of Chicago and a surefire traffic generator for the trains. Linked with the airport, the trains could be a success; without it, a failure.

It's true that the improvements carried out thus far have increased ridership on the Vancouver–Seattle–Portland line, but when the level of ridership was tiny to begin with, large percentage gains are possible.

Visionary Rail

A myth about high-speed rail needs to be exposed. Critics claim that true high-speed rail like the French TGV can't work in the United States because the nation does not have the population density of Europe or Japan to justify the cost of building it. What the critics miss, however, is that the United States is the most highly mobile society in the world, with destinations such as Las Vegas that are unlike anything that can be found overseas. Thus, few people live in the desert between Los Angeles and Las Vegas—a *low population density*—but the intense flight schedule between Southern California airports and Las Vegas and the level of highway traffic indicate a *high travel density* that can justify a high-speed train line. A study issued several years ago indicates that trains operating on a new line between Southern California and Las Vegas could operate at a profit.

For a look at a visionary rail project, consider Florida. As explained by Brendan Read in *International Railway Journal*, "Florida does not favor an incremental approach to high-speed rail using conventional trains except as a stopgap. The principal reason for this is that it would be quite costly to upgrade the CSX-owned line to high-speed rail standards. There are about 100 level crossings on the Tampa–Orlando section, plus signaling problems, and stretches of single track."

Early in 1996 Florida Transportation Secretary Ben Watts awarded a franchise to the Florida Overland Express (FOX) team, making it the state's partner in developing a high-speed program. The Orlando-based consortium (composed of Bombardier, GEC Alsthom, Fluor Daniel, and Ombrecht Contractors) won out over four competing groups. Interest in bidding stemmed from Florida's being the first state to commit significant public funds to a public-private partnership for high-speed rail, including public ownership of the tracks. The state offered about $70 million annually for thirty years for capital development. The FOX team proposal, estimated to cost $5.3 billion in 1995 dollars, includes a dedicated right-of-way for about 65 percent of the Miami–Orlando–Tampa line. The 200-mph all-electric TGV train system is to be financed with bonds to be repaid by ticket sales. All is not yet resolved: at the end of a three-year certification process, FOX must provide the state with a fixed price and start date for service. Also, a critical hurdle will be obtaining funding commitments from the federal government.

The first Miami–Orlando train to be run by FOX is planned for

2004, with operations to Tampa coming later. It is unclear whether FOX will give Amtrak a role, as "private business" is expected to operate the trains. Indeed, a team that lost to FOX was Rail Florida, a group that included Amtrak and proposed a $4 billion incremental program. It would have taken the Amtrak team *seventeen more years* to reach the speeds FOX hopes to reach in 2004.

The fate of the FOX proposal bears watching, but this much is certain—should the effort succeed, Florida will be a model for other states. Should it fail, Florida would be wise to steer clear of Amtrak and attempt to develop another financing package for a visionary project.

Examining California is useful because it has dealt with both incremental and visionary high-speed rail.

In 1990 the state began investing $2.99 billion in incremental rail improvements through general obligation bonds from passage of Propositions 108 and 116. The total available for Amtrak routes and services amounted to $658 million, not counting millions from other state funds (e.g., Petroleum Violation Escrow Account) and local agencies over the years. For Amtrak, California has financed track upgrades, including installation of new rail and additional passing sidings, bridge repairs, grade-crossing improvements, station and parking lot upgrades, new signals, and even the purchase of locomotives and cars.

Results? Of a $246 million capital program planned for Los Angeles–San Diego (not counting additional millions spent to purchase the route), the state has spent at least $46 million. After the upgrades thus far, Amtrak's 1997 schedules show six trains operating faster than the two-hour-and-forty-five-minute schedules in effect at Amtrak's 1971 start-up. Three trains offer the same travel times. Eight others are slower than their counterparts more than a quarter century ago.

It's true that more people ride the line today—about one million per year compared with the three hundred thousand in Amtrak's early years. However, that is more a function of increasing the frequency of train service at the same time that Southern California's population continues to grow and freeway traffic gets worse. If Amtrak's express *San Diegan*s ran faster than their 53.4-mph average speed—which makes them slower than trains in Morocco—many more would ride, and their financial performance would be better.

An even slower service exists between Sacramento and Oakland. The fastest *Capitol* train takes two hours and twenty-four minutes to travel its mere 89-mile route, for an average speed of 37.1 mph. Even though Amtrak's traffic has climbed impressively, it started from a tiny base. This train's schedule is so slow that it runs at about the same speed as the 36.8-mph average of Malaysia's Kuala Lumpur–Butterworth train and the 37.6-mph rate on Egypt's Cairo–Port Said train. Incremental improvements worth $67 million are under way, with the funds coming from California rail bonds, federal approtiations, a state grade-crossing program, and federal highway money that paid to straighten the rail alignment between Oakland and Emeryville. When the work is completed in early 1998, about twenty minutes will have been removed from the schedule. The average speed on this line will improve to 43.1-mph, slightly faster than the 42.3-mph average of a Dacca–Chittagong train in Bangladesh and the 42.2-mph rate of a New Delhi–Bombay train in India.

Meanwhile, rail visionaries have been active in the Golden State. The California Intercity High-Speed Rail Commission in late 1996 took the visionary route. It concluded that San Francisco–Los Angeles high-speed trains are necessary and that extensions to Sacramento and San Diego are desirable. "High-speed trains must be separated from other incompatible rail services, such as conventional freight operations," and "to attain the safety record of high-speed trains in other countries, California's system must be entirely fenced and grade-separated." The system that officials hope will be built through a public-private partnership is projected to generate annual surpluses over operating costs exceeding $376 million for steel-wheel trains and $600 million for maglev. Contributing to this effort was Ed Jordan, who built Conrail's freight traffic while serving as its chairman and, as a member of the commission, has become convinced of the importance of high-speed passenger rail.

Examine incremental work in other states.

Has New York's $120 million investment to upgrade Conrail

tracks to allow faster Amtrak trains been worthwhile? Maybe—for Albany–New York. Here, the trains are only thirty minutes faster than their counterparts in 1952, but highway entry into New York City is so difficult that this improvement deserves some applause. Even with the upgrades, however, Amtrak's fastest New York–Albany express train, at a 65.1 mph average speed, is only about one mile an hour faster than Portugal's Lisbon–Porto train. Part of those funds, however, went to improve Conrail's track to Buffalo, and New York–Buffalo trains are only five minutes faster than in 1952.

Has the $150 million in Detroit–Chicago work by Michigan and federal taxpayers been worthwhile, when Amtrak is thirty-five minutes slower today than a 1952 train? Well, "pointless" would be a good answer. On this line the fastest Amtrak train is only a hair quicker (0.1 mph) than the 49.9 mph average speed of the Yaoundé–Douala train in the West African nation of Cameroon.

Transportation Imperatives

Future concerns about airport congestion in many cities will intensify, and truly fast trains are the only kind that will relieve it. Airport traffic can be staggering, even in one city. In 1996 Los Angeles International Airport served nearly 58 million passengers, about a 20 percent increase over 1990, and predictions are that traffic will grow to 62.2 million passengers after the turn of the century. The airport's annual volume surpasses by almost three times the 19.7 million who rode Amtrak nationwide in 1996. When one airport's usage outdistances an entire national rail system, then something is very wrong with the rail system.

Airport problems are widespread. *Aviation Week* reporter Edward H. Phillips, interviewing David R. Hinson when he was FAA administrator, wrote that capacity constraints at major airports will become increasingly severe and threaten the viability of the airline industry. It's expected that U.S. air travel will increase 60 percent in the next decade, and within twenty years airports will be serving as many as a billion passengers annually—nearly twice today's number.

Amtrak won't ever be much of an option. Most freight railroad executives have become anti-incrementalist, alarmed by the prospect of squeezing higher-speed passenger trains onto lines crowded with heavy freight trains. Edwin L. Harper, when president of the Association of American Railroads, testified before Congress that "high-speed rail offers no quid pro quo for America's railroads. In essence, high-speed rail improvements do not benefit freight service. Our review shows virtually no values transferable to freight operations." It has since become clear that some railroads will refuse contracts for high-speed improvements to their lines, meaning that Amtrak's redefinition effort was for naught in many areas of the nation.

These freight railroad concerns are not new. In a speech given in 1982, Reginald E. Gilliam, Jr., then vice chairman of the Interstate Commerce Commission, had this advice for rail planners: "It would be counterproductive and politically unwise for high-speed passenger rail to inject itself into the freight modernization process. . . . It would be best to leave the old inherent conflicts of priorities, people versus freight, behind." The visionaries took his advice.

It has been acknowledged by rail advocates friendly to Amtrak that its future is in question. J. David Ingles, a longtime *Trains* editor, wrote on Amtrak's twentieth anniversary that "we won't be so bold as to predict Amtrak's future. Our system may even wind up with more than one 'Amtrak,' perhaps some sort of integrated urban rail transport entity and another for true intercity rail travel, be it a new high-speed rail network of some sort, or juiced-up versions of today's medium-haul corridors, or both."

Whatever happens, Amtrak should be written out of the equation. The major blame for high-speed rail inaction rests with Amtrak for its uninspiring leadership and spoiler tactics.

Listening to Amtrak testify before Congress today is unbearable to a visionary. If French rail officials gave the kind of testimony to their *Assemblée nationale* that Amtrak presents to Congress, the French would not be enjoying their marvelous TGV system. If German railway leaders gave an Amtrak-type performance to the Bundestag, the ICE Train would be only a sketch on an engineer's notepad. The same contrasts could be drawn between Amtrak and the Japanese, Spanish, and Italians. Amtrak's behavior on high-speed rail represents a shameful episode in American transportation history.

If airline presidents in the 1960s had adopted Amtrak's low-goal philosophy, they would have declined to purchase jetliners, saying, "propeller-driven aircraft are just fine." Or trucking executives in the 1950s would have told President Eisenhower, "No need to build interstate highways, these two-lane roads are splendid." A more absurd example would be if, when President Kennedy announced, "By the end of the decade, we will go to the moon and back," the aerospace community had replied, "No, let's only go *halfway* there."

Pioneers, regardless of whether they were developing steam-powered boats, interstate highways, or jetliners, knew that *faith*—an unwavering belief in the enterprise—is the crucial prerequisite for success. Amtrak, suffering from institutional inertia, lacks faith and remains unable to incorporate technology and infrastructure advances in use elsewhere in the world.

Not once in Amtrak's history—*not once*—has an Amtrak president or director laid out to the public an articulate, insightful, persuasive call for a future rail passenger system so dazzling that it would help Amtrak escape its mediocre condition. Worse, Graham Claytor blemished visionary high-speed rail in America to no good end. Considering that Amtrak's long-distance trains have a bleak future, while high-speed rail has a bright future, Amtrak's leadership has contributed de facto to Amtrak's eventual demise.

FIVE

Big Future for
Commuter Rail

*"Commuter rail on existing lines
makes a lot of sense."*
—Union Pacific Railroad brochure, 1995

C ommuter trains are vital to the United States, an increasingly urbanized nation. A commuter rail revival is underway in the largest metropolitan areas, the very places where highways are most congested. From rail-dependent New York to sprawling Los Angeles, such trains are enjoying their highest levels of ridership in years.

Commuter rail growth began nearly twenty years ago and shows every sign of continuing, as suburban areas mushroom and a sizable portion of their residents need to reach crowded commercial centers. Many rural counties are growing at their fastest rates in more than two decades, often attracting professionals who work in cities, thus causing existing trains to be upgraded and new rail projects to be launched.

The term *commuter* goes back to the 1850s. When railroads started running local trains between small towns and nearby cities, they "commuted" fares, or substituted lower fares in place of standard charges. Later, monthly commuter tickets were offered to those who bought a fixed number of trips during a limited period, usually over the same route. Up through the 1960s the term was applied to those who traveled short distances between work in the morning and home at night. Today, it has become acceptable for travelers to say they commute between New York and Los Angeles when they mean to say they are frequent flyers.

This chapter addresses traditional rail commuter service. Such trains usually operate no more than 50 miles from a city center (although there are exceptions), offer multiple-ride tickets, and generally run concentrated service into the city in the morning and back out at night. Although Amtrak contracts to operate commuter trains in several cities, agencies other than Amtrak hold the statutory and financial responsibility for such service. Federal law prohibits appropriations to Amtrak to be used to subsidize commuter trains.

Commuter trains operate over only 4,830 miles of track in this country, meaning that quite a few people ride in concentrated numbers on key routes. This is a job that trains, with their high capacities, are well suited to do.

While there is a hue and cry over Amtrak intercity service and subsidies, the public is fairly positive about the commuter systems. Even conservatives who generally oppose taxpayer-supported programs have blessed public investment in commuter rail. Paul Weyrich, president of the Free Congress Foundation, has pointed out that "the dominance of the automobile in the United States is not a free market outcome . . . it is a direct result of massive government intervention on behalf of automobiles." He says Chicago's commuter rail system, on which more than sixty thousand people with incomes greater than $35,000 ride, has customers who are members of the conservative constituency. It's no wonder that Chicago's suburban Republican officials have called for new commuter service.

New federal laws have helped. Since Congress passed the Intermodal Surface Transportation Efficiency Act of 1991, local and state decision makers have more freedom to fund programs that best suit their needs, including commuter trains. Another event motivating rail development has been the attempt to divert more auto commuters to rail as a way to comply with the Clean Air Act amendments regarding levels of ozone pollution.

While commuter rail enjoys relative stability at the policy level, it also offers a technologically sensible way to move people.

Commuter trains do not compete against airline travel; thus, high speeds are not as important. Moreover, the frequent stops made by commuter trains can negate the benefits of speed as trains lose time at each station. Therefore, traditional railroad operating practices—the very kind that stifle Amtrak's intercity traffic—are quite standard, logical, and acceptable on commuter trains. Also, where incremental improvements to Amtrak intercity service can amount to a waste of money, the reverse is true of busy commuter lines, where such improvements are more cost-effective.

Commuter trains provide vital mobility in urban areas, and they carry many more people than Amtrak ever will on any of its trains.

A surprisingly high number of passengers ride commuter trains in the United States. In 1995 about 348 million commuters rode the rails. Of that number, about 33 million were commuters on services for which Amtrak is the contract operator, and 315 million were on trains run independently of Amtrak.

Non-Amtrak Commuter Rail

Dramatic developments are evident on the commuter systems that serve those 315 million riders, the bulk of America's train-riding public, in New York, New Jersey, Philadelphia, Chicago, Miami, Dallas, and parts of Maryland. Amtrak does not operate these trains, although some facilities are shared with Amtrak.

These commuter authorities operate some of the busiest lines in the United States, purchase and maintain their locomotives and coaches, and hold title to most of the stations they use. They or their state governments own or lease the tracks over which they operate, except in parts of the Northeast where Amtrak is the owner and in Chicago and a few other places where some tracks are owned by freight railroads. These agencies conduct marketing and advertising programs, sell tickets, employ engineers and conductors, run the trains, undertake capital improvement programs, run purchasing departments that buy everything from diesel fuel to paper clips, purchase and lease real estate, and establish numerous agreements with contractors and public agencies. They do all these things without Amtrak's participation.

New York's Long Island Rail Road (LIRR) is the nation's busiest rail carrier, handling close to 75 million passengers annually on a 319-route-mile system. Its daily volume is so huge that during rush hour the railroad carries one thousand people in and out of Manhattan's Penn Station *every ninety seconds*—that's the capacity of three 747 aircraft. Most of its lines are electrified and multiple-track, required for high-density operations. The LIRR has extended its electrification and is putting in service new double-decker passenger coaches for nonelectrified lines. For those cars, management made a great effort to seek rider opinion about seat design, color schemes, and other issues and included its findings in the design. Non–New Yorkers might find this difficult to believe, but the LIRR is making great efforts to be close to its customers.

The railroad's management is taking the long view to improving services. It has enrolled all professional employees in the Harvard Business School's Breakthrough Customer Service Program, an effort that has resulted in cleaner trains and more courteous employees. The LIRR is exploring ways to provide direct access to Manhattan's East Side by bringing its trains to Grand Central Terminal. Also, management has privatized its freight business through a concession to the New York & Atlantic Railway Co., an affiliate of the Anacostia & Pacific Company Inc.

Metro-North, the LIRR's sister agency, also a unit of the New York Metropolitan Transportation Authority but with added support from Connecticut, has its operation centered on Grand Central Terminal. (A little-known fact is that Grand Central *Station* is the name of the adjacent subway stop.) Mostly electrified, it serves nearly 63 million passengers annually on a 338-route-mile system and has set post–World War II ridership records. Its reputation continues to soar as Metro-North routinely operates with an on-time factor close to 96 percent, performance that is elusive to Amtrak.

In 1983 the agency took over decrepit commuter routes that were long neglected by their ailing owners, the New York Central and the New Haven Railroads and later the bankrupt Penn Central. Metro-North has continually improved service ever since. Its latest project is to build an additional track between New York and Poughkeepsie for increased train frequency (needed to meet demand) as well to extend lines farther into outlying areas. Metro-North also has undertaken the tough job of rebuilding the Park Avenue Viaduct, built between 1892 and 1897, while maintaining train service over it.

All in all, the LIRR and Metro-North managements do an excellent job, considering the immensity and complexity of operations, the antiquated nature of infrastructure they inherited, the simple wear and tear from intensive customer use, and New York's demanding political and social environment. Amtrak could never run the LIRR or Metro-North trains as well.

Also funneling passengers into New York is a system operated by New Jersey Transit (NJT). It serves more than 45 million commuters annually and is growing, as a new link named the Kearny Connection allows trains to operate to Manhattan's Penn Station instead of to Hoboken. Further, a new transfer station at Secaucus, part of a $448 million project to connect NJT's tracks with Amtrak's Northeast Corridor, will permit passengers to take many previously unavailable routings. The agency may also restore passenger service on a route owned by the New York, Susquehanna & Western Railroad.

Rail writer Scott Hartley concluded in *Trains* that "since taking over passenger service from Conrail . . . NJ Transit has shown a lot of improvement. It is spending hundreds of millions of dollars on long-overdue projects, and passengers who soon will be able to enjoy single-seat trips to and from work will find those dollars very well spent." Its capital program includes purchasing new commuter coaches.

To illustrate how complicated commuter rail contractual relations can become, consider the line to Port Jervis, New York. For those trains, the NJT provides the employees, Conrail owns the tracks, and Metro-North owns the stations that lie in the New York State portion of the route. Both the NJT and Metro-North contribute cars and locomotives to an equipment pool. Where Amtrak plays a role is as owner of most the Northeast Corridor line. In this case, the NJT pays fees to Amtrak to operate over segments of its line, a reversal of the typical situation, in which Amtrak pays to operate over tracks owned by freight railroads or public agencies.

The Southeastern Pennsylvania Transportation Authority (SEPTA) is Philadelphia's commuter train operator, and some of its trains operate over Amtrak-owned track, while others run on track it owns. This agency, which handles more than 22 million trips annually, has had to initiate major infrastructure renewal projects, including complex track, signaling, catenary, and bridge replacement projects.

Chicago's Metra commuter rail system, operating on twelve routes and constituting the nation's second-busiest commuter carrier after the LIRR, is outstanding. Its advertising program—"Think of Us as Your Second Car"—builds identity among potential users.

In some instances the freight railroads retain ownership and control of the lines, with Metra reimbursing them for track use and upgrading. These railroads dispatch a high frequency of passenger trains under a stringent five-minute on-time performance tolerance. On other lines, Metra owns the tracks and infrastructure. Metra's contracts vary, with the agency directly employing staff on some trains and contracting with freight railroads for others. It also cooperates with the Northern Indiana Commuter Transportation District to run an interstate service to South Bend. In effect, whatever works best on a particular line is the choice that Metra makes, making its policies and practices the most flexible in the nation. The value of Metra's capital assets exceeds $6 billion.

Considerable credit for Metra's latest progress is due Jeffrey R. Ladd, the agency's chairman, and Philip A. Pagano, executive director, who launched Chicago's first new rail passenger route in seventy years.

Working with the Wisconsin Central Railroad, Metra has opened a route to Antioch, which eventually will include a direct connection to O'Hare International Airport's people mover. The Metra contract permits the Wisconsin Central to earn performance incentives when certain operating conditions are met. Also, as a freight railroad, the Wisconsin Central had been content with a 50-mph maximum speed on this line. Track improvements were made to allow commuter trains to operate at 60 mph, thereby letting the railroad run container trains at that speed.

Two other railroads that contract with Metra—the Burlington Northern Santa Fe (BNSF) and the Union Pacific (owner of former Chicago & North Western lines)—are so experienced in providing service to Metra that they are positioned to bid for commuter rail contracts in other cities. With freight railroad support, Metra boasts an on-time record that Amtrak cannot match. The agency's popularity is such that several additional line extensions are under consideration.

In South Florida the Tri-County Commuter Rail Authority provides service between Mangonia Park, (about five miles north of West Palm Beach), and Miami. It does not operate the trains itself, nor does Amtrak or freight railroads. Here, Tri-Rail contracts with Herzog Transit Services, Inc., of St. Joseph, Missouri, for operations and maintenance. One problem that Tri-Rail's executive director Gilbert M. Robert must deal with is interference from freight trains, a problem that will be eased by adding tracks. Tri-Rail will also build an extension to the Miami International Airport, an investment that will generate more traffic.

The newest commuter service is in Texas, where Herzog Transit Services was successful in obtaining the contract for Dallas–South Irving commuter trains, a system that will be extended to Fort Worth in 1999 and to Dallas/Fort Worth International Airport in later years. This was the seventh new commuter rail system to begin operating in North America in the last decade. The trains, named the *Trinity Railway Express*, operate on a former Rock Island Railroad line now publicly owned; the BNSF performed the track and signal improvements and is in charge of dispatching on the line.

Amtrak as Commuter Rail Contractor

C ontracts to operate commuter trains and fees from commuter systems using Amtrak's tracks provide Amtrak with its fastest-
growing source of revenue. According to Ken Mead of the General
Accounting Office, these contracts generated more than $270 million
in 1994 and accounted for about 20 percent of Amtrak's revenue. Two
years later commuter revenue grew to $318 million, and 36.7 million
commuters were included in Amtrak system traffic. The commuters,
when added to the 19.7 million Amtrak passengers, give Amtrak a 1996
"ridership" of 56.4 million, helping Amtrak appear to be a more significant carrier than it is.

Yet local commuter agencies that contract with Amtrak for operations pursue agendas that are quite independent of Amtrak. Let's
look at Boston, San Francisco, Los Angeles, San Diego, and Baltimore-
Washington, where Amtrak is the operating contractor.

The Massachusetts Bay Transportation Authority (MBTA), which
owns almost all the tracks it uses, has rejuvenated Boston's system. It
has put in service nearly 350 new cars, upgraded tracks, and remodeled
stations. The public has responded, and traffic has doubled since the
1980s. "This ridership proves we're providing the kind of service people need," said James J. Kerasiotes, MBTA chairman. The agency is
poised for more growth as it rebuilds three lines known as the Old
Colony Railroad southeast from Boston to Plymouth (where the Pil-
grims landed) and other towns and extends several routes to farther-
out points. The MBTA also outsources work to entities other than
Amtrak. An example can be found in Transit Realty Associates, which
handles under contract the MBTA's nearly seven hundred tenants,
develops property, and builds and operates parking garages. In 1997,
Kerasiotes said MBTA may terminate its contract with Amtrak because
of deteriorating service.

The oldest commuter rail system west of the Mississippi, known
as CalTrain, links San Francisco with the San Jose area and has attracted its highest ridership level in four decades. That's remarkable

because this is a "fixer-upper" railroad that needs track work, grade-crossing elimination, and other improvements. Said Jerry Kirzner, rail services director: "We're not the Lexus. We're the Chevy that has been going for 300,000 miles that starts right up when you put the key in the ignition. We're doing the things that you take for granted. We're there when you need us." Marketing successes are due to CalTrain's planning, which now provides service to the San Jose Arena, home of the Sharks hockey team, and to World Cup soccer games at Stanford University. The agency even operates a special Santa train pulled by a steam locomotive. An ambitious CalTrain capital plan calls for extending service to an underground terminal in downtown San Francisco.

In the Los Angeles region, the Southern California Regional Rail Authority began providing commuter rail service in late 1992. Named Metrolink, it serves six counties and has seen ridership gains as commuters seek options to driving on the freeways. Metrolink shined immediately after the 1994 Northridge earthquake, when it built new stations in a matter of days—sometimes with help from the Army Corps of Engineers and Navy SeaBees—and extended its trains to locales newly isolated from the rest of Los Angeles. Ridership skyrocketed, illustrated by traffic on its Santa Clarita line that went from one thousand passengers to about eighteen thousand every weekday. Traffic fell when the freeways reopened, but 25 percent of those who tried Metrolink decided to stay. Generally, Metrolink has brought in projects on time and within budget. That is no small feat in that Metrolink's infrastructure costs have exceeded $1 billion. Further, the investments were designed to get results in a compressed period, in contrast to Amtrak's decades-long Northeast Corridor work.

"The SCRRA has delivered on all the objectives developed by member counties five years ago," said Richard Stanger, Metrolink's executive director. "On the construction side, each Metrolink route has opened on time, and we are virtually on budget. Capping [1995] was the inauguration of our sixth line. . . . Connecting Riverside to Irvine, daily ridership on the country's first 'suburb-to-suburb' commuter railroad already exceeds our projections." Part of the reason is that Metrolink does a decent job answering telephones, achieved by contracting with Commuter Transportation Services, Inc.

Metrolink is an example of an agency that dispatches its own trains, relying on a control center as sophisticated as any in the world. Metrolink even dispatches freight trains over the lines it owns. Its system employs several dozen people in its twenty-four-hour central control facility; they are responsible for the movement of as many as 260 daily trains. About half are passenger trains for Metrolink, Amtrak, and the North [San Diego] County Transit Development Board, and the other half are freight trains for the Union Pacific and BNSF Railroads. This center disseminates information to train stations through a sophisticated communications system and employs a monitoring system linked with CalTech to detect earthquakes.

Farther south, a service named the Coaster links Oceanside with San Diego, and here Amtrak has a contract to provide train employees as well as track and equipment maintenance. Nevertheless, other contractors are getting a piece of the action.

The publicly owned San Diego Northern Railway, over which the Coaster commuter trains operate, signed on with a contractor that has been in the rail business since the 1920s, the Massachusetts Electric Construction Corporation, to upgrade its rail line. An engineering company provided design and procurement services that led to the acquisition of coaches. The Coaster's locomotives and cars are maintained by Motive Power Industries, Inc., and inspections of the cars are conducted at the shops of short-line operator San Diego & Imperial Valley Railroad. Meanwhile, parking lot and right-of-way security has been contracted to Wells Fargo Guard Services.

In the Washington, D.C., area, the Virginia Railway Express service links northern Virginia suburbs with Union Station on Capitol Hill. Stephen T. Roberts, director of operations, said the trains have experienced ridership increases since the service started in 1992. On the other side of the Potomac River, the Maryland Rail Commuter (MARC) agency is striving to keep up with passenger demand into Washington and Baltimore by purchasing new coaches and planning to extend service to the growing community of Frederick, Maryland.

One MARC capital item is the construction of maintenance shops to replace facilities shared with Amtrak.

These trains are performing useful public services, but Amtrak's performance has been uneven.

The dismantling of Amtrak would have little effect on commuter systems. Alternative arrangements would be made, and the trains would continue to run. Remember that the commuter agencies own their trains, conduct marketing programs, plan schedules, and are accountable for their own policies and balance sheets. Some commuter authorities might employ more operating staff, and others would seek a new contractor for operations. Members of the non-Amtrak commuter group, which include the giants of North American passenger rail operations, could advise these operators if necessary. Whatever the choices, commuters should find service unaffected; in some cases service will improve.

Facility Sharing and Joint Operations

Regardless of who operates commuter systems, one typical relationship is that commuter trains share some stations with Amtrak. In New York, for example, the LIRR and New Jersey Transit use Amtrak's Penn Station, paying Amtrak in operating and capital funds to do so.

That brings up a concern: what, for example, happens to Amtrak-owned stations used by commuter trains if Amtrak goes out of business? Well, there are precedents for transferring ownership of publicly owned property from a federal agency to the state or municipality. Through one mechanism or another, critical facilities like Penn Station will survive and indeed could thrive.

With Amtrak's demise, an issue for some agencies in the Northeast will be ownership of and access to the lines now owned by Amtrak. Where Metro-North and Connecticut own the New York–New Haven line, and Boston's MBTA holds title to rail routes, no significant issues arise, because Amtrak already is a tenant. In other areas where Amtrak owns tracks, new institutional arrangements will be required. The last chapter of this book deals with such Amtrak reform and transition concerns.

New Business Relationships

C ompared with Amtrak's intercity system, every commuter rail network in the United States has a better on-time performance record, carries out capital projects that are more likely to be on time and within budget, and is more likely to stay close to its customers. It is fair to reach several conclusions about what would happen to commuter trains if Amtrak were dismantled.

No Change in Legal Responsibility. Nothing in any Amtrak law sparked America's commuter revival, and Amtrak's death would have no bearing on the legal authorizations or appropriations in effect for commuter rail agencies.

Replacement Operators Available. The commuter agencies that have a contractual relationship with Amtrak could find new operators through a competitive bid process. The disappearance of Amtrak would not create any inconvenience that couldn't be solved by management talent and new business relationships.

Continued Commuter Improvements. Commuter rail capital programs are unique to the areas served, involve local public investment, and generally enjoy broad public support. Amtrak's participation isn't germane to improving commuter rail.

Fixed Facility Ownership Issues. Questions exist regarding the disposal of Amtrak facilities. While mechanisms to transfer property are available, it's fair to state that commuter capital budgets will need to be increased on a one-time basis to allow purchase of Amtrak facilities. This can be avoided if Washington treats Amtrak as a sunk cost and donates rail facilities to commuter agencies, city or county governments, or state transportation departments.

Amtrak Rolling Stock Disposition. Amtrak locomotives and some of its intercity passenger coaches should be auctioned off to public commuter agencies. Using such equipment to carry local passengers in crowded urban areas is a wise use of public assets.

While those issues will be sorted out tomorrow, it's clear who the heroes are in American rail passenger service today.

They are Thomas F. Prendergast, president of the Long Island Rail Road; Donald N. Nelson, president, Metro-North; Shirley A. DeLibero, executive director, NJ Transit; Philip Pagano, executive director, Metra; and James Kerasiotes, chairman, MBTA. Their jobs and those of their colleagues are among the toughest in the nation as they face daily challenges in operating heavily used commuter trains.

Existing commuter operations can serve as inspiration to leaders in urban areas who are evaluating new rail programs. Planning commuter train systems is being considered or is underway in Detroit, St. Louis, and Kansas City in the Midwest; in Atlanta and Raleigh-Durham–Chapel Hill in the South; Tampa and Jacksonville in Florida; and in the western communities of Denver, Phoenix, San Jose, and Seattle.

The odd thing is, most rail commuters will fail to cheer or condemn a dissolution of Amtrak. Since Amtrak has been virtually irrelevant to those who are America's most loyal train customers, Amtrak simply won't be missed.

Who Will Run Tomorrow's Trains?

*"In the long run the airlines may end up being owners
and perhaps the biggest backers of these rail systems. They'll need
short-haul rail routes as feeders to their airline operations."*
—the late John Riley, federal railroad administrator

D omestic consumers spend more on transportation than on anything else except housing, and such a large market invariably spurs
development of new providers. The end of Amtrak's monopoly
through its dissolution would open possibilities for others to run intercity and commuter passenger trains. But first laws must change to
permit entrants to offer train service in accordance with market demand.

We've seen how, of all the rail services, commuter trains are the
easiest to remove from Amtrak's operating domain.

The regional and long-distance trains that would survive in a post-
Amtrak environment are more complicated to restructure because they

require a higher level of amenities to satisfy passengers. Here, success in transforming these trains to non-Amtrak status can come from new relationships among freight railroads, public agencies, tour operators, commercial airlines, and entrepreneurs.

The freight railroads are in a unique position. For years prior to the creation of Amtrak, the railroads as a regulated industry suffered passenger-service financial losses, which worsened as the Interstate Commerce Commission required continued operation of trains that had lost much of their common-carrier utility. It has taken the railroads several decades to discard their unpleasant corporate memories and become more positive toward passenger service, but it has happened on some railroads.

Changed Rail Industry Attitudes

Today, some freight railroads seek participation in non-Amtrak passenger proposals, particularly commuter rail. William D. Middleton, who has written about rail issues for decades, outlined in *Railway Age* that "for a growing number of railroads, this passenger train revival is now seen as an opportunity to put underutilized assets to work, and to get back into the passenger business in a significant—and profitable—way." He explained that railroads have granted operational rights to commuter agencies, proposing "turnkey" services whereby the railroad manages all operational details. Moreover, the railroads are willing to sell tracks and rights-of-way that just a few years earlier were off-limits to rail passenger planners. He wrote that piece several years ago, but it remains true today.

An example of a refreshing pitch for new business can be found at the Union Pacific (UP), which has been seeking commuter and regional roles in more than half a dozen locations. It issued a promotional brochure and video that asked, "Why would a railroad that hasn't been in the passenger train business for two decades suddenly sign a major commuter rail contract in California?" The answer: "Union Pacific Railroad owns an existing transportation network that has excess capacity, requiring only modest capital improvements to handle commuter rail services. We want to sell that capacity and increase the return on our assets. . . . We'll not only provide the necessary track, we'll also operate the trains."

With confidence, the railroad stated: "Union Pacific, which ranks first or second in every key measure of financial strength, is committed to quickly arranging commuter rail service wherever needed on UP's lines. Behind this commitment is a railroad that has the strength to do the job." The UP promises that a commuter service on its railroad can typically begin within just eighteen to twenty-four months after initial inquiries, including all governmental paperwork and approvals. Any public agency that has requested Amtrak service and waited years to see it come to fruition will find the UP's promptness a refreshing change.

Frank Malone, writing in *Progressive Railroading*, interpreted that effort: "Commuter trains bring in extra revenue, but the big benefit to the railroad is freight capacity improvement with costs shared by local entities. 'Our shareholders will receive an increased return through more intensive use of the railroad's assets,' the brochure says in its only reference to UP gains."

The UP inherited commuter operating contracts with Chicago's Metra when it merged with the Chicago & North Western Railroad. The initial transition to UP management was troubled, and the UP had to apologize to commuters for train delays, but today it adroitly serves ninety thousand riders daily. The Southern California Regional Rail Authority, or Metrolink system, in Los Angeles obtained rights over UP lines between Riverside and Los Angeles. Under the terms of the $17 million agreement, the UP added more than 30 miles of second track, upgraded its signals, and operates the trains. Experts believe the agreement is a model for many cities. UP-operated Metrolink trains serve thousands of riders daily and traffic continues to grow.

The UP has also solicited commuter rail business in Dallas–Fort Worth, Houston, Seattle–Tacoma, Denver (where trains would link downtown with the new airport in less than a half hour), Salt Lake City, and over California's Altamont Pass to link Stockton, Livermore, and Pleasanton with the Bay Area.

The Southern Pacific, in a significant departure from its antipassenger attitude of previous decades, aggressively pursued a range of commuter, intercity, and even high-speed passenger rail opportunities in various parts of its system prior to its 1996 merger with the Union Pacific.

Another western railroad, the Burlington Northern Santa Fe (BNSF), has operated a Chicago–Aurora commuter line for about 130 years. Its experience running what is considered a premier line gives the company an advantage in its meetings with commuter rail planners in the cities it serves. In Houston, aboard a demonstration train to nearby Webster and Tomball several years ago, BNSF officials pointed to their Chicago commuter operation, where as a way to convey pride in the operation, the railroad insists that conductors wear BNSF uniforms and logos, not Metra's. In submitting a proposal to Houston, a BNSF official said that "we're prepared to do anything you want us to do." That positive attitude paid off in Dallas–Fort Worth as the BNSF won a contract to provide service needed for the Dallas Area Rapid Transit passenger trains to South Irving.

A forward-thinking regional railroad is the Wisconsin Central, whose cooperation was indispensable in launching a new Metra service in Chicago (described in Chapter 5).

In specialized train operations, the Union Pacific and the Ansco Corporation (former owner of the Rio Grande and Southern Pacific Railroads) have agreed to continue operating the ski trains between Denver and Winter Park, Colorado, that have never been part of Amtrak's system. The accord has no expiration date.

Freight railroads also help passenger systems, existing or proposed, through their new policy of selling rights-of-way and other real estate. Railroads in the 1990s have surrendered ownership or rights to record numbers of parcels at staggering purchase prices. In Southern California, counties in the Metrolink commuter rail system purchased track and operating rights from what are now the BNSF and Union Pacific Railroads—435 miles for a total of $462 million. In Northern California the Peninsula Corridor Joint Powers Board paid $242.3 million to the Southern Pacific for the 52-mile San Francisco–San Jose line.

In the late 1980s Florida purchased 81 miles of CSX for Miami commuter trains for $264 million. Novel propositions have come from CP Rail, which offered to sell half its Chicago–Milwaukee right-of-way, and from the BNSF, which is willing to sell its Central Valley line in California, for proposed high-speed passenger systems.

These sales bring railroads numerous advantages—including big boosts in earnings that delight shareholders, and substantial relief from real estate taxes—usually while retaining operating rights for freight trains. In some cases, new station-related commercial development could be built on air rights retained by the railroad companies.

The Challenge of Providing Amenities

Intercity passenger train characteristics are different from those of commuter trains and have a bearing on railroad involvement.

Commuter train riders demand little in the way of personal amenities: a parking space at the train station, a clean and reasonably comfortable seat, good lighting to read the newspaper, and on-time arrivals are expected. It's possible for any freight railroad so inclined to operate these rather utilitarian trains.

Freight railroads, even with more positive attitudes today, will nonetheless face challenges in providing intercity passenger train service. The longer the trip, the greater the requirement to provide checked baggage, food and beverage service, pillows and blankets, or tour guides to comment on the passing scenery.

Only one "full service railroad" still provides all that on an intercity train independent of Amtrak: the Alaska Railroad. "Passenger ridership increased to an all-time high as we became the travel mode of choice for independent adventure travelers," said railroad president Robert S. Hatfield, Jr., reporting that the line carried nearly half a million passengers in 1995. That's a 10 percent increase over the year before and more than the previous high set in 1992. The Alaska Railroad is upgrading tracks near Denali Park, a capital project related to its passenger operations.

The major freight railroads in the Lower 48, however, aren't prepared to provide such service to what is a *retail* market. The railroad industry's contemporary role is as a *wholesale* provider of transportation. The wholesale mentality has extended to the movement of intermodal ("piggyback") service; J. B. Hunt Company, a leading trucking line, markets freight movement by rail and has contributed to an explosion of such traffic.

Asking a railroad today to begin marketing passenger trains, or to provide services aboard them, would be a mistake. A railroad can move passenger trains over its lines, but someone else should be selling the tickets, serving drinks, and fluffing pillows for passengers.

The way to develop passenger train possibilities is to team willing railroads with companies that provide services to individuals—to create an "operator–service provider" team. In such an arrangement, the railroad's role would be limited to operating responsibilities, such as providing dispatching services (which railroads do today for Amtrak anyway), engineers to move the trains, and conductors (whose job would be limited to operational and mechanical details).

Partners who are experts in the retail travel market would constitute the other half of the operator–service provider team, the ones to take train reservations, serve food, and fluff pillows. These partners could come from the commercial airline, group tour–operator, cruise-line, hotel, and restaurant-chain businesses. Their millions of employees have the skills necessary to please train passengers, and their executives have the expertise to enter joint ventures, form subsidiaries, and provide services under contract.

With proper leadership and synergy, excellent service could result.

A variety of operator–service provider teams is possible through consortiums or joint ventures. It's reasonable that the Union Pacific and the American Orient Express could operate trains to the national parks. The BNSF could team with Greyhound Lines to run regional train-bus service between Minneapolis and North Dakota points. In fact, with intercity bus companies serving five thousand communities in the United States (nearly nine times the number of stops Amtrak makes), the industry could extend the marketing reach of those who would run trains in place of Amtrak.

Airlines as Potential Partners

The most complicated arrangements will be in new high-speed train systems, where companies building them would look to others to run them. It's possible, say, for a Dallas–Houston high-speed line to be built by Bechtel, which would contract with the BNSF–American Airlines or some other team to run the trains and provide related services.

Airline-rail operations were contemplated by Robert Clarke Brown, who as a senior vice president for Lehman Brothers, said that when it comes to high-speed rail, "airlines might find it a profitable business, both because it's a business they already know, transportation, and because it would be a way to collect customers for their air service and funnel them to airports—a multi-modal elaboration of the current hub system the large carriers all now use."

"Shrewd airlines," according to Bruce D. Nordwall, a writer for *Aviation Week,* "might seize the opportunity to invest in high-speed trains to expand their feeder network." That view was echoed by John Riley, a federal railroad administrator in the Reagan Administration, whose heart was in the visionary high-speed rail camp.

As airport congestion has worsened, aviation visionaries have dipped their corporate toes in rail waters. Although only a few definitive arrangements have been made, airlines are interested in both intercity trains and short-distance trains to connect city centers with airports. Several international airlines have taken larger actions, notably Virgin Atlantic, Lufthansa, Alitalia, Swissair, and Japan Air Lines. Domestic participation has come from United Airlines, Midwest Express, Delta Air Lines, USAirways, and American Airlines.

Great Britain's Virgin Atlantic Airways has been involved in local, regional, and high-speed trains. For several years Richard Branson, chairman of Virgin Atlantic, evaluated plans to operate trains, telling the *Financial Times* that "our idea is to be basically in the long-distance airline industry and in railway in Europe." In 1996, as part of Britain's privatization effort, Virgin Atlantic won a fifteen-year franchise to operate intercity train service from a Birmingham hub to more than 130 stations. Branson considers this a high-growth franchise and said that his company would spend $419.7 million on new trains and increased services. Further, the airline is participating in high-speed rail as part of the consortium named the London & Continental Railways. This group was awarded a long-term contract to build and operate the high-speed line connecting London and the Channel Tunnel, which, when completed, will cut *Eurostar* London–Paris travel time by thirty minutes to two and a half hours. Finally, Virgin Atlantic lost a franchise bid for the local London–Gatwick Airport trains, but its bid demonstrates that the airline has also sought to provide rail service at the local level.

Lufthansa Airlines was a modern-day pioneer in integrating its flights with train service. This German airline books its passengers on numerous *Lufthansa Intercity Express* trains to Düsseldorf and Stuttgart that operate directly out of the Frankfurt air terminal; it also provides rail ticketing and other services. Alitalia Airlines has experimented with operating nonstop intercity trains from Rome's airport to Florence and Naples.

Swissair and Swiss Rail have integrated their operations at the Zurich and Geneva airports to such an extent that travelers easily transfer between trains and planes. At distant railroad stations airline passengers check their luggage to the airports, where Swissair puts them on the proper flight.

A unit of Swissair, Gate Gourmet International, an airline catering company, has adapted its expertise to rail passenger service in Spain. Meanwhile, French airline caterer Servair now supplies two hundred TGV trains daily while supplying three hundred aircraft every day.

In the luxury land-cruise train business, East-West Airlines in India won the franchise for a "tourist sector" train in the southwest portion of the country. It will run on a horseshoe-shaped route between Hospet, Bangalore, Mettupalayam, Mangalore, and Goa.

On a developmental basis, no fewer than five airlines have been involved in high-speed maglev train efforts. It started overseas with

Japan Air Lines' making long-term investments in the HSST (High Speed Surface Transport) technology, at one point spinning it off, only to later retake a shareholder interest. In Germany Lufthansa has participated in planning and testing the Transrapid maglev. The most recent airline entry in maglev is Swissair, which officially joined the effort to support an ambitious Zurich–Berne train proposal.

Two airlines in the United States have indicated an interest in maglev: Delta Air Lines and USAirways.

Delta's involvement came in 1996, when it signed a preliminary agreement with the Maglev Consortium, Inc., which competed for a franchise to build and operate a Miami–Orlando–St. Petersburg line. Had the effort succeeded, its 300-mph trains—allowing a Miami–Orlando trip time of one hour—would have entered service by 2005. It's likely that Delta would have handled the system's reservations, passenger services, and baggage-handling duties. The team lost to a steel-wheel competitor whose technology has been proved in Europe.

The involvement by USAirways began earlier. It started when former USAirways chairman Ed Colodny agreed that high-speed trains could help reduce aviation congestion in the crowded Northeast Corridor. Later, the airline became an equity partner in Pittsburgh's Maglev Incorporated. This consortium has considered building a Transrapid train to connect the city's downtown with the airport to provide a ten-minute trip. Considering that airline crews would be appropriate caretakers of the high-technology maglev trains, it's possible that USAirways would provide operating and maintenance functions in addition to passenger services. The participation by the Company was significant, as it is the sixth-largest domestic commercial airline (based on passenger-miles).

Airlines already have contracted to provide some services to rail operators.

American Airlines designed a computer reservations system and pricing program for the French TGV and Eurotunnel trains. The contract fit in nicely with parent company AMR Corporation's goals to expand its nonairline businesses in consulting, data processing, training, and transportation services.

The Texas TGV team had quiet discussions with American Airlines regarding a joint operation, had the train system been built. That partnership made sense because American is a major carrier at the Dallas–Fort Worth International Airport, a planned stop for the trains. Bob Crandall, the airline's chairman, when asked by *Financial World* about high-speed rail, replied, "We're in the transportation business. . . . If I can participate in running a train and make some money, it's okay with me."

United Airlines cooperates with Amtrak in a program in which passengers travel by train one way and by air the other in a one-price package deal. Although advance purchase is required and "other restrictions may apply," the plan has proved popular enough that it has lasted several years. Meanwhile, Midwest Express offers credit in its frequent-flyer program to passengers aboard Amtrak's Chicago–Milwaukee trains.

Airport-Rail Cooperation

Not only air carriers have an interest in rail; airport planners do, too. According to the *Salk International Airport Transit Guide,* a growing number of airports worldwide have added train links. In 1995 there were fifty-eight airports with direct rail service, compared with forty-eight two years earlier. Now, the BAA, the international airport operator, along with at least two railways, has formed the International Rail-Air Organization. According to the BAA's Andrew Sharp, "The proposal was the brainchild of Rod Hoare, until recently the managing director of the *Heathrow Express* (he is now BAA group rail strategy manager). He saw a niche for an organization to share ideas and best practice, and to encourage technical visits and academic research. . . . We have identified over eighty actual or planned rail links to airports worldwide."

In some instances, the rail links are viewed as intercity in nature, ways to add to airport capacity without building another runway. Executives at airports in Miami, Orlando, Pittsburgh, and Boston are interested in intercity train service. At one point the Orlando International Airport petitioned the state to make its facility a stop on a proposed Miami–Orlando–Tampa system and requested twenty-four-hour-a-day train service, more than the rail planners had in mind.

Rail service can be part of the equation for the construction of new airports. Throughout the United States, new airports will come about only if they are located significant distances from crowded urban areas. Thus, a new airport for Phoenix, if built, may be located in the desert halfway to Tucson; a new southern California airport might be built at one of several locations far removed from the city. The only way such sites can be realistic is by being connected to cities by high-speed trains.

Aviation interest means that a trade group, the International Air Transport Association (IATA), has endorsed rail service. Pierre Jeanniot, IATAs director-general, said, "I am generally in favor of the high-speed train. One may ask, 'How the devil can a man who devoted his lifelong career to the aerial domain start promoting the train?' Well, I do not perceive the high-speed train as a rival of the plane but more as a complement to our North American environment. . . . Train-plane intermodality has already been proven elsewhere in the world."

Thomas Stephen Windmuller of the IATA, a former airline vice president, said, "Even to the extent that high-speed rail does take customers from airlines on individual, relatively short-haul routes, in doing so valuable slots are freed up for airlines to devote to the relatively more profitable longer-haul routes." The group represents airlines that carry 98 percent of all scheduled international traffic.

Having the airlines involved as joint partners in rail service would ease one problem created by Amtrak's breakup—making a train reservation. Although independent train operators today rely on their own systems, there are virtues in using the airline industry's automatic reservation networks. These systems, such as Apollo, Sabre, Galileo, and Worldspan, would employ yield management methods to control train inventory. Travel agents use these systems everyday.

Myths About Aviation Influence at Amtrak

Curiously, some railroad enthusiasts would oppose joint rail-airline operations. A myth exists that Amtrak in its early days had a management team drawn largely from the airlines, and this notion has permitted railroad buffs to blame airline people "who didn't know what they were doing" for Amtrak's rocky beginning. In fact, what successes Amtrak had in its early days were due largely to its fresh-thinking airline types.

The managers from the airlines almost exclusively were recruited for the marketing department, then headed by the late Harold Graham, a jolly former Pan American executive. Little known was that several of his staff had extensive railroad passenger experience prior to joining aviation. They were returning to their roots, so to speak.

The marketing department was Amtrak's center for innovation. Over time it developed a simplified fare structure, snazzy advertising, the USA Rail Pass (similar to the Eurail Pass), "memory schedules" for the Northeast, and a badly needed reservation system. This group created widespread public interest in Amtrak through actions ranging from new color schemes for coach interiors (they had the nerve to use purple cloth for seat covers, but it *was* the early 1970s) to putting young people aboard trains as passenger service representatives, whose primary duty was to be pleasant and help travelers.

The truth is, only a few people came to Amtrak from the airline industry. Most came from the railroad industry, and those with power in Amtrak's early days were the railroaders. The breakdowns that infuriated passengers were largely attributable to the way old-line railroaders did business.

Amtrak's early operating, engineering, maintenance, finance, and procurement departments—each much larger than Marketing—were staffed with pure-blooded railroaders. Many came from bankrupt or otherwise hapless railroads, such as the Penn Central, Milwaukee Road, and Southern Pacific—places where managers had not had an opportunity to try a new idea in years. The best talent on America's best-operated railroads in the early 1970s, like the Union Pacific and Santa Fe, rarely went to Amtrak. It was difficult to lure employees from healthy railroads to join a shaky enterprise.

The old guard lost little time beating the enthusiasm out of the recruits. Conductors and station managers incessantly lectured their prodigies that the old ways were the best ways. These crusty railroad men scowled and barked their way through the day, contributing to poor morale, a lack of team spirit, ineffective communication, questionable maintenance practices, and very late trains. These factors, of course, led to unhappy passengers. The railroaders needed a scapegoat: the marketing department, with its few airline "outsiders," became a target. The railroaders even decried Marketing's request to change a train schedule that hadn't been changed in a decade.

Because the rail-enthusiast community often takes a seasoned railroader's word over that of someone outside the industry, the railroaders' claims were believed and an enduring myth about Amtrak's aviation talent was created. The moral to this story is that America needs to look past myths to consider how forward-thinking airline management, working with competent rail experts today, could boost prospects for operation of non-Amtrak trains.

Air-rail cooperation has existed before. Dan Cupper, in his book *Crossroads of Commerce,* tells how Charles Lindbergh and Amelia Earhart helped the Pennsylvania and Santa Fe Railroads start a joint service with Transcontinental Air Transport, a company "formed [in 1929] to develop a coast-to-coast rail-air system that could ferry passengers across the continent in 48 hours, approximately half the time needed for an all-rail trip. . . . The arrangement was this: Passengers rode trains by night and planes by day." Although not the only air-rail service then offered, it was the most famous. Incidentally, TAT later became Trans World Airlines.

State and Regional Authorities

Don't expect miracles for some trains, regardless of which organizations emerge to replace Amtrak. New ventures will avoid Amtrak's worst performers. Yet for a few places where alternative transportation is minimal, keeping a regional-type train service may be better than discontinuing service altogether. One example is the *Empire Builder*, a train that loses money but serves small communities that become isolated during severe winter storms. If train service is to be kept in such a case, regional operation supported by state governments is the answer.

The idea has support. Anthony Haswell now believes that creating Amtrak was a mistake and, on reflection, that establishing regional entities would have been the better choice. Others echo his view.

Timothy R. Jorgenson, a transportation consultant, set forth in *Trains* that "everything under the sun has a time and season. Those of us who endorse publicly subsidized intercity passenger rail service in America must ask ourselves whether a national rail corporation is a good vehicle to actually develop intercity passenger services over the next 25 years. Isn't America about due for intercity service *development*?" He then mused on "whether America ought to devolve passenger service development to the states or regions."

Addressing the issue more specifically, Johann Fink, a U.S.-based director of information for the German railroad, in another *Trains* column, called for creation of state rail passenger corporations, or "Babytraks." Under his proposal, Wisconsin and Illinois, for example, would cooperate to run Madison–Chicago trains. Babytraks, which would understand local needs, could help communities that "otherwise are far down a priority list" for new service at Amtrak.

Another useful mechanism is the interstate compact. Let's assume that North Dakota and Minnesota want to keep the *Empire Builder* running as a regional train to Minneapolis. Federal law permits states to form interstate compacts with certain rights and powers. Compacts exist for many reasons—e.g., when two states agree to share water, they form a compact. Continuance of a portion of the *Empire Builder* is tantamount to providing a social service. Thus, these states could jointly subsidize a regional train through a compact.

Whatever mechanism is selected, the transformation of the *Empire Builder* into a two-state regional train would cut costs because the expensive sleeping and full dining cars needed for Amtrak's lengthy

The *American Orient Express* is a land-cruise train offering deluxe accommodations. A private company restored this 1950s streamliner and runs it on various itineraries across the United States. (AMERICAN ORIENT EXPRESS RAILWAY CO., SEATTLE)

The *Northern Parks Limited* consists of restored vintage equipment, including a Pullman dome car. This entrepreneurial effort focuses on Livingston and Paradise, Montana, serving tourists who visit Glacier and Yellowstone National Parks. (JOEL P. KING)

Locomotives from Montana Rail Link, Inc., a freight line, pull the *Montana Daylight* (at right) past the *Northern Parks Limited*. The trains run through the Rockies along rivers navigated by Lewis and Clark. The route was served by Amtrak's *North Coast Hiawatha*, a Chicago–Seattle train that died in 1979. (JOEL P. KING)

Visitors can leave their automobiles in Williams, Arizona, and ride the privately operated Grand Canyon Railway to its namesake national park. The station, a National Historic Landmark, is situated near the Canyon's South Rim and is the only log depot in the United States still serving an operating railroad.

(GRAND CANYON RAILWAY, FLAGSTAFF, ARIZONA, BY PAUL KING)

More than a quarter of a million passengers annually take *The Midnight Sun Express,* a joint venture of the Alaska Railroad and tour companies, to Denali (Mount McKinley) National Park.
(HOLLAND AMERICA WESTOURS, SEATTLE, BY DON WILSON)

RIGHT: Billing itself as the "most spectacular train trip in the world," the *Rocky Mountaineer* carries tourists between British Columbia and Banff and Calgary, Alberta. It set a record in late 1996, running with thirty-seven cars——the longest passenger train in Canada's history——and carried more than eleven hundred passengers. The private operator is succeeding on a route where government-sponsored VIA Rail failed.
(ROCKY MOUNTAINEER RAILTOURS, VANCOUVER, B.C.)

California purchased locomotives and passenger cars for Amtrak's use, as have Pennsylvania, Washington, and North Carolina, a prerequisite to obtaining more Amtrak service. Owning such assets will make it easier for these states to keep passenger trains running in a post-Amtrak environment. (JOSEPH ZUCKER)

Amtrak operates new Genesis locomotives built by General Electric, which in an Amtrak breakup could be sold to commuter railroads. New York's Metro-North system uses the model on some of its commuter trains.
(MTA METRO-NORTH RAILROAD BY FRANK ENGLISH)

The Long Island Rail Road's prototype double-deck coaches incorporate suggestions from passengers. During rush hours the railroad carries one thousand people in and out of Manhattan's Penn Station *every ninety seconds,* equivalent to three 747s. This railroad alone carries far more passengers than Amtrak's nationwide system. (MTA LONG ISLAND RAIL ROAD BY ILENE MESSINA)

CalTrain, the commuter agency for the San Francisco–San Jose line, tries new marketing approaches such as this *Sun Tan Special* to the Santa Cruz Beach Boardwalk. (CALTRAIN, SAN FRANCISCO)

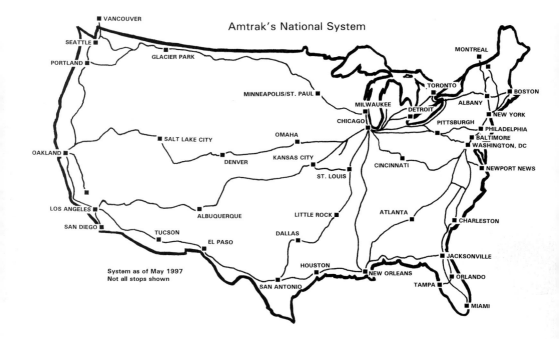

Amtrak "national" network is deceptive because many points are served only three times per week, including big cities like Dallas and Houston, or only in the middle of the night. Vast swaths of the nation are nowhere near Amtrak.

This Amtrak train, equipped with Superliner coaches and sleeping cars, is a throwback to another era. Long-distance trains in a common carrier role serve an infinitesimal share of the U.S. travel market, are declining in popularity in train-dependent Europe, and have been discontinued en masse in South America when railroads have been privatized. (JOSEPH ZUCKER)

Virgin Atlantic Airways through subsidiaries has won three franchises in British Rail's privatization process. Included is the *Eurostar,* linking London with Paris and Brussels (THIS PAGE), and conventional trains (OPPOSITE), now painted in Virgin's livery. The Virgin Rail Group plans to outfit British trains with new equipment and is looking to become involved in rail elsewhere in the world.
(*THIS PAGE:* SNCF-CAV/EUROSTAR/JJD; *OPPOSITE:* VIRGIN CROSSCOUNTRY/CHRIS DIXON)

Lufthansa Airlines was a pioneer in integrating rail with aviation, starting with the *Lufthansa Airport Express,* shown here along the Rhine River. The service crews were airline employees, while the engineer and conductor worked for the railroad, a formula for post-Amtrak arrangements in the United States. The air-rail venture today designates compartments on frequent trains as *Lufthansa Intercity Expresses.* (LUFTHANSA AIRLINES)

Lufthansa, interested in the Transrapid maglev as a way to relieve airport congestion, has helped evaluate the train in this Emsland, Germany, test center. USAirways is an equity partner in a Pittsburgh, Pennsylvania, maglev project, and Delta Air Lines was interested in a Florida maglev plan.

Japan Air Lines holds equity in the High Speed Surface Transport (HSST) train. An earlier version of this HSST-100L maglev vehicle carried more than a million and a half passengers in demonstration service in Yokohama, Japan.
(HSST DEVELOPMENT CORPORATION, TOKYO)

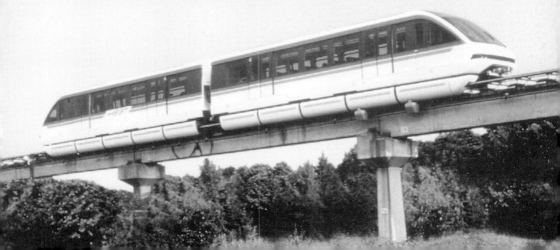

This double-deck TGV is the latest French rail advance. These trains run on high-speed tracks built with significant amounts of private financing lured through a government-guaranteed loan process. (RAIL EUROPE, INC., NEW YORK)

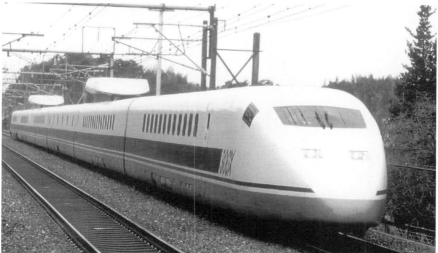

Privatization has sparked a Japanese Bullet Train design boom. JR East is serving Tokyo with new double-deck Bullet Trains (TOP). JR Central is testing the 300X (MIDDLE). JR West put new Series 500 trains in service at 187 mph (BOTTOM), a speed needed to compete with improved air and highway competition. For many years, trains in Japan, France, Germany, Spain, and Italy have run faster than Amtrak trains will in the year 2000 after Amtrak completes its Northeast Corridor project. (JR EAST, JR CENTRAL, JR WEST, JAPAN)

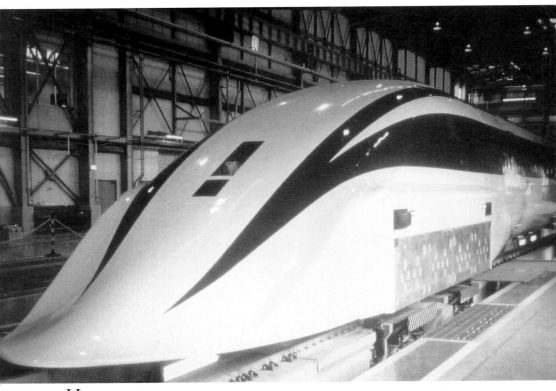

High-tech maglev trains like this Japanese MLX01 superconducting model are beyond Amtrak's distinctive competence to operate, market, or maintain. Future U.S. maglev systems should remain completely separate from Amtrak. (JR CENTRAL, JAPAN)

Chicago–Seattle route would no longer be necessary. Also, with no Amtrak involvement, overhead costs could be reduced.

In some cases, modifying the charter for an existing agency to perform such work may be a good alternative. Here, we again find Haswell developing a useful perspective. He stated in a Wisconsin speech that Amtrak should not be the operator of Chicago–Milwaukee trains, reasoning that "Amtrak has done no long-range planning for improvement and expansion. Further, Amtrak's operating performance is not up to the standard necessary to attract large numbers of people out of their automobiles. . . . We must face the fact that short- to medium-distance services like Chicago–Milwaukee are a low priority for Amtrak. We will never get the train service we want and need in this region so long as we are dependent upon an organization based in Washington, D.C., whose primary concerns are long-distance train service and the Northeast Corridor."

Haswell suggested that an agency be organized along the lines of the Illinois Regional Transportation Authority (RTA) to replace Amtrak in southeastern Wisconsin: "This new agency would then negotiate with the RTA for operation of the Chicago–Milwaukee service by Metra, the RTA's rail service operating division. The RTA is already involved in a similar arrangement with Indiana for operation of the South Shore Line commuter trains, under which RTA and the Northern Indiana Commuter Transportation District fund their respective shares of the service on each side of the border. In addition to funding and overseeing operations, the new regional agency would develop a capital improvement plan."

In other cases, the task would be easier because a state already owns the right-of-way and tracks. New Jersey owns the former Erie–Lackawanna rail line as far west as Stroudsburg, Pennsylvania (nearly two-thirds of the New York–Scranton route), making it possible for some organization or other to start an intercity passenger train between those points if so desired.

In Pennsylvania Amtrak patronage has declined on a rail route between its largest city and the state capital: Philadelphia–Harrisburg. It's no wonder that one report suggested that the Southeastern Pennsylvania Transportation Authority, Philadelphia's commuter agency, take over the route. That would be easier than ever, considering that in late 1996 the state placed an order for railcars for the line. If Pennsylvania, like several other states, must buy the trains Amtrak needs in order to provide service, why not eliminate Amtrak as the middleman?

California has begun the "localization" process because its Caltrans-Amtrak partnership has been unsatisfactory. Assemblyman Tom Hannigan and Senators David Kelley and Jim Costa introduced legislation to move the jurisdiction for Amtrak trains from Caltrans to three regional joint powers boards. Amtrak will continue to operate the trains until its contract expires, at which time the boards could seek competitive bids. Supporting the shift were Quentin Kopp, chairman of the Senate Transportation Committee, and Governor Pete Wilson, who signed the bill into law. One of the new agencies, the San Joaquin Regional Rail Commission, in late 1996 ordered eight new bi-level passenger rail cars for use between San Jose and Stockton.

One state—Illinois—threatened to "pull out" of Amtrak and seek contract operators. State transportation officials caused a stir in late 1996 when they sought changes in state law to permit them to solicit competitive bids for the operation of intrastate Amtrak trains. The action was motivated by Amtrak's sharply escalating costs, and comments in the media suggested that Chicago's Metra commuter rail system should take over the trains. The issue died as Illinois and Amtrak agreed to a three-year continuance plan. Under the new arrangement, Amtrak will pay financial penalties when trains leave origin points more than thirty minutes late, a loose standard that would draw incredulous looks on European and Japanese railways.

More definitive steps to exclude Amtrak from passenger service are certain to come. One long-term development deserves a brief look: maglev trains. Officials at the Pennsylvania Turnpike and New York Thruway have expressed interest in developing maglev. They have discussed raising the financing through bonds, building the lines, and franchising train operations. The word *Amtrak* doesn't even appear in their planning documents.

Contract and Independent Operators

P rivate-sector contractors are ready to work with state and regional agencies, and their number will grow if Amtrak is dismantled.

Herzog Transit Services, which won commuter rail agreements in Miami and Dallas, is prepared to compete "head-to-head against Amtrak" for such pacts. The ATE Management & Service Company, a subsidiary of Ryder Public Transportation Services, has experience serving as a contract operator for bus transit systems; although it failed in a competition for a rail commuter contract, the company has the management and resources to try for future agreements. Organizations as diverse as Chicago's Metra system, the BNSF, Union Pacific, Wisconsin Central, Herzog, and the San Diego & Imperial Valley Railroad have taken or are prepared to take a greater role as contractors in the rail passenger arena.

Florida officials several years ago asked Congress to refuse to extend Amtrak's monopoly to include new high-speed rail lines. The state wanted to lure non-Amtrak bidders in a franchise process, which it did. Also in the Sunshine State, First American Railways, in its Securities and Exchange Commission filing, positioned itself as a potential high-speed train operator, stating: "The company would compete with Amtrak, and other prospective railway service providers, principally on the basis of the quality of service, including convenience of stops, timeliness, entertainment and other amenities, as well as price."

Long-distance trains—reconfigured to seasonal service suitable to passenger demand—could be managed by an expanded American Orient Express or Rocky Mountaineer Railtours, by major travel companies such as Princess Tours or Carnival Cruise Lines, by expanded local concerns like the Grand Canyon Railway, or by companies that would bear a resemblance to the *Florida Fun Train*. Such trains, free from old common-carrier obligations, could enjoy a proverbial land-office business. The market for *Auto-Train* service, largely untapped by Amtrak, could induce new carriers to start service in several parts of the nation.

A Fun Train on CSX

A word is in order about freight railroads that are known to object to the operation of passenger trains—in particular, the CSX, which has imposed liability requirements so high that excursion trains had to be canceled and angered Maryland officials by forcing earlier commuter train departures to minimize interference with freight trains.

Yet even this railroad will help plan a passenger operation where its lines are not saturated with freight trains. In Florida the CSX signed a memorandum of understanding with First American Railways, which wants to operate the *Florida Fun Train* on the railroad's Orlando–West Palm Beach line. The agreement specified that the *Fun Train* must obtain liability coverage, provide meaningful compensation, and agree to schedules developed by the CSX. The railroad would permit speeds up to 79 mph, but the passenger company must understand that the *Fun Train*s must not interfere with freight operations or with Amtrak's intercity passenger trains.

Further, the CSX holds a seat on the board of directors, and Albert B. Aftoora, its vice president for corridor development, was elected in early 1997; also, the CSX can be issued warrants to permit it to purchase stock in the company. The CSX even went so far as to help facilitate the *Fun Train* operation by promising certain financing for capital improvements, with First American Railways reimbursing the railroad over a five-year term.

Monetary issues were resolved when First American Railways agreed to compensate the CSX for access at an initial rate of $20 per train-mile, which will be increased by an agreed-upon inflation index at the beginning of each subsequent year. This payment appears to be reasonable from the railroad's point of view, considering that railroads pay one another between $9 and $22 per train-mile, plus charges for crews, fuel, and locomotive rental when detouring over one another's lines because of floods or other circumstances. This amount would give the CSX a profit on the contract since it would not provide the engineers and other services to the *Fun Train* that it must to a detouring freight train. This demonstrates that even an "anti-Amtrak" railroad is open to a reasonable proposal to run passenger trains when it has the track capacity and when it can earn a reasonable profit.

The companies mentioned here are not necessarily the ones that will someday provide rail passenger service in Amtrak's place. After all, the business, political, and social environment of the United States is not static. A company interested in the rail passenger market today may not be tomorrow. Yet an imperative exists—the situation must change because of Amtrak's unstoppable decline in market share outside a few routes.

While the absence of Amtrak will cause short-run dislocations, where there is a will and a market, there is a way. If the CSX will sign an agreement with a passenger train company that specializes in entertainment, there's hope. If Dallas and Miami can start new commuter services without contracting with Amtrak, so can other cities. If Florida can structure a high-speed franchise that interested Delta Air Lines, then surely Washington has options to consider. If Great Britain can induce Virgin Atlantic Airways and other companies to compete for passenger rail franchises, America can, too.

America's Booming
Freight Railroads

*"Our industry has gone from the brink of nationalization to a Wall Street
success story. Today, we're a growth industry,
and market share is increasing after having declined
for more than fifty years."*

—Robert D. Krebs, president, Burlington Northern Santa Fe

A renaissance is under way on America's freight railroads, brought
about by significant changes in the way the industry does business.
Anyone proposing new passenger service to be operated over freight
railroad lines must understand today's overall rail environment.

One generality stands out: most railroad managers will be fair in
considering the operation of passenger trains on lines that have excess
capacity. Under certain conditions, a freight railroad can add black ink
to its bottom line with passenger train operators paying to run over a
freight line.

In other instances—when dense freight traffic is moving over
tracks that are near capacity—the nature of costs change and opera-

tional headaches mount. The railroad may want nothing to do with a new passenger operation.

The success of the American railroad industry today has bred a more optimistic and confident railroad manager than has been seen in years. For the first time in decades, rail executives can take their place among the top leaders in business. Railroads are improving service to customers, implementing cost-effective technological advances, and expanding capacity to meet growing customer requirements. Railroaders who lived through the post–World War II downturn, railroad bankruptcies, deteriorating track conditions (so bad that trains derailed while standing still), and plummeting traffic can hardly believe the robust rail environment today.

A major reason for this success was the 1980 Staggers Rail Act, which largely deregulated the railroads and permitted them to compete more effectively with trucking and waterway carriers. The law wiped out a hundred years of regulations and bureaucratic ineptitude by the Interstate Commerce Commission (ICC), which was abolished in 1996 (with of its duties transferred to the new Surface Transportation Board).

Another reason for today's rail prosperity is the federal rescue of the Penn Central and five other bankrupt railroads through the creation of Conrail. At first, it was thought that the February 1, 1968, merger of the ailing Pennsylvania and New York Central Railroads into the Penn Central was enough to bring about a healthier rail system. Such was not to be, and on June 21, 1970, the Penn Central became the largest single bankruptcy in the history of the nation. After much planning, the government created Conrail and invested $6.5 billion in it, roughly $3 billion for rebuilding important routes and another $3.5 billion for other costs, including liquidating labor agreements. Moreover, based on a plan by the U.S. Railway Association, Conrail was not saddled with several thousand miles of lightly used, unprofitable track.

These factors helped lure to railroad management people who are generally more open-minded than their predecessors and more willing to contest competitors for freight traffic. Railroads are moving an all-time record level of ton-miles, more than during World War II, and doing so with only a fraction of employees, locomotives, cars, and track. Meanwhile, the companies are safer places to work than at any point in history. They achieved these gains while paying more than $400 million annually in property taxes on their rights-of-way and track. Their trucking and waterway competitors use facilities subsidized by the public, paying taxes and user fees that cover only a small percentage of their share of infrastructure costs.

The railroad story today is nothing less than astonishing. The condition of freight tracks is the best in the nation's history. Rates of return are at acceptable levels (difficult to achieve in the capital-intensive railroad industry), and railroads have lowered their debt-to-equity ratios. The industry has gone from having excess capacity to one that is capacity-constrained on main lines, from initiating large-scale layoffs to hiring hundreds of train crews in the last few years, and from filing bankruptcies to setting traffic-volume and revenue records.

American railroads in the 1990s are examples of what re-engineering an entire industry is all about. Some have called it "a new golden age of railroading," or as Gus Welty, senior editor of *Railway Age*, declared, "It's sunrise for America's railroads."

Railroads Rebuilt for Freight Traffic

R ailroad investment programs are targeted at obtaining new freight business, and they're getting results.

In an example of how one railroad has aggressively sought more traffic, Conrail and the Commonwealth of Pennsylvania launched a three-year project to ease height restrictions on its main line to accommodate double-stack container trains. With the work completed in 1996, overhead clearances on Conrail were increased at more than 130 locations; the railroad funded more than $64 million and the state supplied the remainder of the $97 million cost. Later, a joint Conrail-Massachusetts program accomplished the same objective on the Boston–Albany line. These programs were good for Conrail, the cities of Philadelphia and Boston, and railroads across the nation, as they could more easily compete against truckers for shipments to those ports. Improved freight service operating at a lower cost is also good for consumers, who eventually pay shipping costs as part of product prices.

There's more. Conrail launched a freight service named Press Runner to speed shipments from Maine paper mills to virtually any point in the nation. Conrail also cut shipping costs by two-thirds for various foods and beverages with aggressive pricing designed to fill cars returning west that otherwise would run empty. Conrail is considered a reliable railroad by demanding shippers like United Parcel Service.

All railroads are carrying a wide variety of commodities. Customer-dedicated "unit trains" a hundred cars long filled with one commodity (usually coal or grain) have allowed railroads to post major tonnage gains. The carriers have gone after auto parts, lumber, chemicals, and metals with great success. Overall, railroads have captured 70 percent of the motor vehicle market, in part by using better cushioning systems on auto-carrier cars to help reduce in-transit damage.

Railroad managers now display entrepreneurial attitudes. Wisconsin Central cut operating costs by reducing the size of train crews; it regained lost traffic by showering shippers with good service. Now shippers like Schneider National Incorporated, a major trucking concern that ships via rail, praise the attitude and flexibility found on the railroad. Small shippers are sought out by a sales manager who tries to develop nontraditional business; as a result, the railroad carries containers of vodka destined for Russia.

In the short-line arena, companies like RailTex, based in San Antonio, purchase lines that major railroads spin off; give local management considerable autonomy; and through intensive marketing and personal service, bring about striking increases in rail shipments.

Need for More Track

C arrying record levels of freight affects capacity. In railroading's lean years, downsizing was inevitable. However, as Dean Wise and Dwight Gertz of Mercer Management Consulting wrote in *Progressive Railroading,* "A business cannot shrink its way to greatness. The waves of restructuring, divesting, downsizing, and re-engineering that America's railroads have instituted to become more competitive may have been necessary, but they are not the ultimate solution to achieving lasting prosperity. . . . Growth is an activity that requires skills that in many companies may have atrophied."

Railroads have learned the word *upsize* and are expanding capacity to meet demand. Critical civil engineering projects are underway that are helping railroads cope with surging traffic. "Around the country, freight trains are sweeping the rust from many lines once considered surplus," wrote Don Phillips in *Trains.* "Rail lines once declared surplus by a shrinking industry have become important links in a growing industry." That point is dramatically illustrated in Washington State, where the BNSF revived an abandoned main line through Stampede Pass in a $125 million program. The BNSF has also constructed 138 miles of second main line track between California and the Midwest because the single track could no longer handle the volumes of traffic. This railroad will also install more than a hundred solar-powered switches at a new freight classification yard it is building in Kansas City.

The BNSF has had numerous record-setting performances, but one stands out. For fifty-eight consecutive days that ended in early 1996, it carried 43,709 trailers for United Parcel Service, and every one arrived at its UPS hub on schedule. The streak was broken only when a portion of the railroad in the Midwest became snowbound.

The Union Pacific is adding a third track to its historic main line in Nebraska, believed to be the busiest stretch of freight railroad in the nation, with about 120 trains per day. Railroaders occasionally call this freight line a "super railroad," a term not even used for Amtrak's passenger-busy Northeast Corridor. After the Union Pacific merged with the Southern Pacific, it began a $221 million program to add 100 miles of double track between El Paso and Los Angeles, part of an overall $1.3 billion capital plan to enhance capacity.

The Union Pacific and the BNSF recently installed double track on their joint line to the Powder River Basin low-sulfur coalfield in Wyoming. Here is where the Union Pacific in 1966 set a tonnage record by moving nearly 110 million tons of coal, and traffic on the line is expected to increase every year through at least 2005.

In response to the North American Free Trade Agreement, the Canadian National Railway built the new $200 million Sarnia Tunnel under the St. Clair River at Port Huron, Michigan, and CP Rail enlarged its Detroit–Windsor tunnel. Both projects permit double-stack container trains where only single-level ones were possible before. These railroads, by reducing transit times and improving efficiencies, experienced double-digit-percentage increases in the amount of freight moving through the tunnels.

Rolling Stock Advances

Trains need more than track; they need locomotives. The progress in locomotive design contributes to railroad efficiencies. The latest development is a 6,000-horsepower diesel locomotive, permitting one new unit to replace two old ones. Some designs feature alternating-current motors, which are more powerful than traditional direct-current technology. The new units save fuel, require less maintenance, and offer lower life-cycle costs than direct-current types. Some locomotives are now equipped with radial trucks that conform to curves and help reduce costly wear on rails and wheels. Radio use aboard locomotives is more sophisticated than ever before; dispatchers in Union Pacific's Omaha control center can talk with each locomotive engineer on any train in its system.

The railroads have added many new cars to their fleets. Railway suppliers are busier than they have been for years, as freight car deliveries topped sixty thousand in 1995 for the first time in twenty-five years. Some of these cars employ new technologies in ways that serve customers better at lower costs.

Wonders of the microprocessor and digital communications age have affected every aspect of train operations. For example, telemetry equipment in the form of a small flashing device hooked onto the ends of trains has replaced the red caboose and the employees in them.

Railroads can determine the location of cars better than at any time in history through an automated system installed on more than a million cars. Small data tags are mounted on railcars to transmit information to sensors as trains roll by. Since 1995 no human intervention is required to make a complete record of the cars in a train.

Thanks to the Global Positioning System, satellite-based systems communicating with sensors can pinpoint the location of entire trains, report their speeds, and help monitor the distance between trains. This is the basis for the Positive Train Separation program, which helps establish train locations with great accuracy and reduce collisions by warning engineers *before* they violate a signal or get too near other trains. The newer program literally has predictive powers and, in conjunction with an onboard computer, can take control of a train under a variety of circumstances. Positive Train Separation systems offer safety benefits so great that the National Transportation Safety Board strongly recommends their use, as has rail labor. This is superior to a reactive system, such as Amtrak's Automatic Train Stop system on the New York–Washington line, which provides emergency braking only *after* an engineer fails to comply with signals.

In addition, the Positive Train Control system can increase efficiencies by permitting trains to run closer together, allowing more trains per hour over any given track and allowing railroads to scrap expensive trackside signal systems. Thus, railroads are benefiting from technology developed in the aerospace industry.

Advances in a type of brake system long used on transit cars are found in freight service. Electronically controlled pneumatic brakes can slow trains faster than can traditional braking and allow shorter stopping distances. Typically, when brakes on a long train are applied, they are set on the first car and move car by car toward the back, often taking more than a minute for the brakes to set on the last car of a long train. When a train is one hundred cars long, this requires skillful handling by the engineer to avoid derailments and damage to freight. With electronic braking, the brakes on every car in the train are applied at virtually the same time.

These improvements are being put in place at a cost, of course. Railroad capital spending in recent years has increased from about $3.6

billion in 1990 to $6 billion in 1995. To a casual observer, however, a train at a railroad crossing can look more or less similar to one of twenty years ago. The improvements are not visible, yet they're there: fuel-efficient and more powerful locomotives, satellite tracking, automatic controls, and electronic brakes all add up to astonishing progress. The American public, which usually thinks of railroads in terms of passenger trains, is unaware of the dimension of progress on the freight railroads.

Passenger-Freight Interference

G rowing freight traffic is causing delays to Amtrak passenger service. The intermingling of passenger trains and freight trains creates a conflict: railroads want to keep profitable freight trains moving, while Amtrak wants freights to take sidings and wait for passenger trains to pass. Amtrak has the force of law on its side. Rip Watson, a reporter for the *Journal of Commerce,* wrote that mixing passenger and freight trains leads to "a relationship that resembles a family that strives to look united to the outside world, but smashes furniture behind closed doors."

Dissatisfaction isn't being kept behind closed doors anymore. Amtrak has threatened lawsuits when railroads fail to run its trains on time. A Conrail spokesman decried one public bashing by Amtrak as "a declaration of war on the freight industry and its shippers."

Want Amtrak to run more trains? Not all railroads will welcome the idea. The Norfolk Southern points out that its most congested routes were built originally as single-track lines, so adding capacity is very expensive. The company wants such lines to remain freight-only so that passenger service doesn't cause delays. They deserve credit for being honest about it.

Amtrak's threat to seek legal remedies for late trains caused a CSX spokesman to attack Amtrak's very being, suggesting that Washington "take a hard look at the need for heavily subsidized rail passenger service. The CSX is required by law to play a somewhat reluctant host not justified by public demand." In a speech to the Railway Supply

Association, CSX president A. R. "Pete" Carpenter said, "There are serious, fundamental issues that must be addressed in order to protect the integrity of our freight transportation system. One obstacle is the commingling of passenger services on the nation's freight rail network."

Albro Martin in *Railroads Triumphant* asks whether the railroads faced this passenger-freight operational conflict back when they ran a much higher volume of passenger trains. "The answer is, No, because the freights today run on much tighter, faster schedules, are far longer, and consist of much heavier cars, and—most important of all—they are straining to compete for high-rated traffic that demands delivery on time 'or else!' " He then describes an impressive St. Louis–Detroit unit train carrying auto parts operating over the old Wabash line of Norfolk Southern Railroad and how it fits into "just in time" inventory management at several Detroit auto plants. Considering that most of the line is single-track, "a single overnight Amtrak train on this route would knock the entire operation into a cocked hat."

In essence, on the major freight corridors, train "slots" are as valued as gates and departure times at major airports. What railroad manager would want to sideline half a dozen freights, carrying perhaps more than $100 million worth of goods, so that an Amtrak train can slip by? The freight trains earn medium to large profits that are absolutely necessary to the enterprise. Consider the other modes: air freight isn't expected to gather dust while passengers take priority; truck traffic isn't pushed off the interstate highways during heavy periods of auto travel. Why should the railroads suffer under a standard that isn't imposed on their competitors?

The most important person the railroads could have for a passenger is the President of the United States, and for the first time in history a President had to change his itinerary because of rail-capacity problems. Bill Clinton campaigned for re-election aboard his highly publicized *Twenty-First Century Express* through Ohio, Michigan, and Indiana. But a thorny problem with his journey was fitting the train into Chicago's busy rail network. Thus, Clinton's whistle-stop trip ended east of Chicago because running his train farther would have delayed innumerable freight and commuter trains. Clinton switched to a helicopter for the last part of the trip, and the train limped into the city hours later. That conveys how serious railroad capacity problems are today.

Railroads in the West have been less vocal about Amtrak interference with their freight operations. One reason is that public agencies purchased the rail lines (e.g., most of the line between San Diego and Los Angeles) or invested public funds in upgrading the tracks (e.g., Seattle–Portland) when increasing Amtrak frequency. Further, serious proposals to increase Amtrak service are rare on the busiest western freight lines.

Passenger Train Costs on Freight Railroads

Amtrak believes it has an advantage over non-Amtrak operators because of the provisions it has in its contracts with the freight railroads. To a degree, Amtrak has a point because newcomers would be hard-pressed to obtain the liability provisions and methods of calculating payments that Amtrak negotiated during its start-up.

According to the General Accounting Office, Amtrak depends heavily on freight railroads in operating its passenger trains. Freight railroads own about 97 percent of the track over which Amtrak operates and provide essential services, such as dispatching trains, making emergency repairs to Amtrak trains, and maintaining some station structures. However, the overall financial impact on a railroad of passenger trains' operating over its lines is far different than before 1971, when railroads were saddled with all the direct costs of running passenger trains. Railroads paid for everything back then—all ticket agents, passenger train engineers, dining car cooks, and so forth. Passenger train deficits were at intolerable levels, particularly on bankrupt or ailing railroads in the East and Midwest.

Today, passenger train operators, not freight railroads, cover the directly related wage-and-fuel costs to run passenger trains, maintenance and depreciation costs for passenger cars and locomotives, most station expenses, and "comfort costs" related to the care and feeding of passengers.

Union Pacific's president, for example, no longer spends time on passenger-related marketing, advertising, information, reservations, ticketing, dining cars, sleeping cars, stations, or baggage service issues. Those functions, to the degree present, are financed by Amtrak, the American Orient Express, commuter rail operators, or whoever else is providing the passenger service. Passenger-only organizations have pulled these expenses out of the freight railroads' cost structure and onto their own ledgers. That is why, under some circumstances and with appropriate compensation, passenger trains are welcome on some railroads.

The primary work performed by railroads when Amtrak operates over their lines is management-related. For example, dispatchers overseeing the movement of a hundred freight trains in Pennsylvania admittedly spend some time dealing with the four Amtrak trains sharing the route. Yet how costly is this? After all, if the passenger trains didn't exist, the dispatcher would still be needed anyway.

It is good to turn again to John W. Barriger's book *Super-Railroads for a Dynamic American Economy* to consider cogent explanations about the financial aspects of railroading. According to Barriger, a railroad's operating costs are mostly indirect expenses associated with infrastructure, and capital outlays are largely determined by how much of available capacity is used.

In his argument, *if surplus capacity exists* on a freight line, then adding a conventional passenger train only slightly increases costs for fixed facilities like tracks and signals because the facilities would be there anyway, even if the passenger trains were not in operation; the added passenger train movement earns extra revenue for the freight railroad. Yet, this added revenue is worthwhile only if the number of trains operating on that particular line is *below* track capacity.

Consistent with Barriger's thesis, Amtrak has long compensated freight railroads for the "avoidable costs" of letting Amtrak trains use their lines, meaning costs that would not exist if the passenger trains did not run. The problem is that many lines today are operating at or near capacity, and railroads are experiencing costs that are not compensated properly by Amtrak.

Late Freight Train Costs

The cost of freight train interference is an example. Amtrak does not pay for the costs railroads incur when passenger trains interfere with freight trains, despite the fact that Amtrak contributes to freight train delays. This is a sore point with the railroads. Railroads understand that service reliability is often ahead of price when a shipper decides whether to opt for rail or truck. When railroads can't deliver on time, shippers don't hesitate to switch to common-carrier or privately owned trucks. In some instances, shippers can levy financial penalties on railroads for late deliveries.

Amtrak trains can run late for numerous reasons, which many times are Amtrak's own fault. When Amtrak runs "out of its time slot," the rhythm of a railroad can be disrupted, causing freight train delays. No wonder railroad managers bristle when late-running Amtrak trains disrupt their operations or cause them to miss budget targets.

Amtrak does not compensate the railroads for such expenses even though the indirect costs of freight train delays are significant. Randolph R. Resor, vice president of costing and economic analysis at Zeta-Tech, a consulting firm, explains that Amtrak trains generally operate at higher speeds than do freight trains. Therefore, Amtrak trains may overtake as well as meet oncoming freight trains, causing dispatching problems. The rigid schedules of passenger trains interfere with track maintenance, but unlike freights, the passenger trains cannot be held and then "fleeted" through maintenance locations. Further, dispatcher knowledge of reprimands for poor Amtrak performance often results in extra caution, causing excessive delays to freight trains, which may be held for hours awaiting the arrival of an Amtrak train. The result, in the words of CSX president Pete Carpenter, is a "logistical nightmare."

"Railroads are not currently compensated for any of these costs," said Resor. "Delay to trains does have a cost, however, and that cost can be quantified. A study for Class I railroads in 1989 calculated delay costs for four categories of freight trains. These costs include an hourly ownership cost for locomotives and cars, plus a cost for lading based on market price and perishability. These costs do *not* include any allowance for crew wages, since crews are generally not paid by the hour. Using these costs in an analysis of train delays resulting from Amtrak operations produced some surprising results. Based on a two-week sampling of train delays on a large North American railroad, the annual cost of freight train delays due to Amtrak operation was estimated at nearly $6 million."

That isn't all. Zeta-Tech's analysis showed that to this amount must be added the costs of delays to the work of track-maintenance crews: "Each delay incident, by the railroad's calculation, cost a bit more than $1,000. Using the same one-week sample periods, the annual cost of gang delay (lost productivity, equipment rental, wages, etc.) was estimated at about $1.8 million."

Of course, operating long-distance trains on the land-cruise philosophy at speeds equal to priority freight trains means such trains could be easier to dispatch, thereby minimizing costs and disruption to freight railroads.

Track-Maintenance Costs

A cost problem has been worked out in one area. The railroads have long complained that avoidable-costs methods fail to properly recognize differences in track maintenance required when passenger trains run over freight lines.

Consider one issue—"superelevation" of tracks. A Transportation Research Board study pointed out that superelevation—the difference in height on a curve between the two rails—is a problem. Superelevation requirements vary in critical ways between the optimum desired for freight trains and that for passenger trains. Complex lateral forces of freight trains apply weight to the rails in a different manner than does a faster passenger train. The bottom line is that maintenance standards must be higher in direct proportion to the speed differential between passenger and freight trains. These higher standards mean higher costs.

The railroads and Amtrak agreed to include the cost of maintaining tracks for passenger trains at a standard different than what is needed for freight. They resolved the problem by agreeing to use an ICC-approved "weighted system average cost model" (WSAC) cost-allocation formula. Now Amtrak makes additional payments to some railroads for extra track maintenance required for passenger trains. It could be said that Amtrak still pays on an "avoidable cost" basis, but the costs are defined in a more acceptable manner to the freight railroads.

Further, under incentive contracts, Amtrak pays most railroads a premium for on-time performance. This means that of the about $100 million Amtrak pays freight railroads annually for services, about $20 million is in incentives. Under the new 1996 Amtrak contracts, which include the WSAC payments as well as incentive payments, the cost to Amtrak for operating over the freight railroads increased by about $25 million annually.

It appears that Amtrak today more fairly compensates railroads for services provided, but there is still room for disagreement. According to Resor, "The proper allocation of common costs in rail transportation is one of those classic problems for which there will never be a permanent solution." Zeta-Tech helped develop the WSAC model for the Association of American Railroads (AAR).

Passenger Liability Problems

To some railroads, a problem worse than passenger trains delaying freight trains is liability exposure from passenger train accidents. For this reason, the CSX is apprehensive about Amtrak. The CSX owns the Alabama line on which forty-seven people died in the *Sunset Lim-*

ited wreck in 1993, the worst in Amtrak history. The following year, on CSX tracks near Raleigh, North Carolina, Amtrak's *Silver Meteor* derailed after hitting a passing freight train. In 1996 an eastbound Maryland commuter train operating on a CSX line hit Amtrak's westbound *Capitol Limited*, killing eleven aboard the commuter train.

Liability is an industry-wide concern. In 1993 the AAR issued a policy statement that said, "Freight railroads must be indemnified and insured against any and all financial liability arising from accidents affecting passenger services." Some have pointed to liability as being so insurmountable that it will doom any proposed non-Amtrak operation. Indeed, that may be true for incremental high-speed train operations over freight tracks because intermingling such trains with slower freight trains can be unsafe.

But the severity of this concern depends on the proposed service and the financial wherewithal of the operator. When it comes to freight trains, railroads have no problem with one another. According to Chicago attorney Michael W. Blaszak writing in *Trains,* the railroads in 1906 adopted a detour agreement that, although amended, remains in use today. The detouring railroad "assumes all risks of liability arising out of the detour operations. Its responsibility is absolute, even if the [railroad over which it is operating] is at fault."

Public agencies whose commuter trains operate over private railroads have solved liability problems, although the contractual details vary from city to city. Before it would agree to a new Boston–Worcester commuter rail service, Conrail demanded that the Massachusetts Bay Transportation Authority purchase a minimum of $75 million of liability insurance, with Conrail included as a named insured. The agency agreed, and the trains began.

Yet even the CSX has agreed to a passenger operation if the conditions and terms are right, the route can accommodate it, and liability coverage has been arranged. First American Railways and the CSX solved the problem with the passenger carrier agreeing to a rather hefty $300 million liability policy. When the company's treasurer writes the check for that insurance policy, some of the "fun" will go out of the *Florida Fun Train.*

Freight Railroads and a
Post-Amtrak Environment

I t's clear that the railroad industry will continue to attract new customers and bring about still more freight traffic growth. The industry's ability to squeeze more trains on busy lines will be limited at the very time new operators will surface in a post-Amtrak era. Alternative providers would include public agencies wishing to operate commuter or regional trains, joint ventures planning seasonal land-cruise trains or auto trains, and high-speed rail planners wanting to purchase available rights-of-way for passenger-only tracks.

The railroads should publicly pledge that they will cooperate with any such organization, provided that legitimate concerns are addressed. A willingness to explore options with passenger carriers would have public relations benefits but could also represent worthwhile new revenue.

Where land-cruise passenger trains operate, the industry could enhance track capacity by running them at speeds no faster than for priority freight trains. Operations at the same speed can reduce the frequency of sidetracking freight and passenger trains. This practice is now found in Europe, where some nighttime passenger trains blend with freight traffic. These steps, combined with eliminating Amtrak's stops at intermediate points, could reduce dispatching conflicts. Critics will scoff that passenger train speeds should be lowered, particularly after the drubbing given Amtrak in this book for its slow schedules. Remember, however, that land-cruise passengers represent a less time-sensitive market, and a modest slowdown would be offset by fewer stops and improved punctuality. The *American Orient Express* runs this way and is most often sold out, verifying that land-cruise trains can be leisurely and popular at the same time.

The Future of Freight

Despite this glowing chapter about railroads' moving record amounts of freight—worth $39 billion in revenues last year—problems exist.

"The freight railroads are rolling . . . with record traffic volumes, strong earnings, the warm approval of Wall Street—and the uneasy feeling that if they aren't careful, they could lose it all." That surprising statement came from Luther Miller, editor of *Railway Age,* who was writing about policy changes in Washington that could negatively affect freight railroading. The railroads are concerned about a push in Congress for "open access," which would require railroads to open their lines to competitors, and threats of reregulation.

And not all shippers are happy. One estimate is that rail freight traffic will climb to $50 billion within seven years, but only if the railroads fight for traffic and perform in ways to keep it. Gus Welty, also writing in *Railway Age,* reported that "in customer survey after customer survey, railroads come in a poor second to motor carriers when it comes to reliability and dependability of service, speed of service as reflected in transit times, and the simple matter of ease of doing business with the carrier."

New technologies and business interests are certain to present challenges.

American railroads could lose some coast-to-coast intermodal container traffic if an international consortium builds a planned rail link across the Central American isthmus in Nicaragua. The rail line would provide a five-hour schedule between the Atlantic and Pacific Oceans, offering a new option for transshipments of containers between ocean-going vessels.

The railroad coal market may be threatened in places. Engineers at the University of Missouri have developed a method for processing coal into logs that can be moved by water through pipes. Designers claim that the system uses less water to move coal than do earlier coal-slurry designs. The new technology interests executives at coal companies, some of whom are indignant over rate-setting methods used by railroads.

Railroads over the years have lost much of the highest-value merchandise traffic to air-freight services, and record amounts are being palletized and flown on overnight schedules. United Parcel Service is spending several billion dollars to purchase all-cargo aircraft (as are its competitors), and a growing number of air-freight carriers will inject more competition into the priority-shipment field. Some cargo aircraft are so large that they transport intact railway locomotives between continents.

Of course, trucking companies and barge lines will remain tough competitors for all types of traffic.

As railroads prepare for the challenges of the next century, it will do them good to reflect on a vision from the past: "No other means of transportation can haul so much, so far, for such little expenditure of man-hours, of fuel, and of capital; and, by so doing, confer benefits on so many people," wrote John Barriger four decades ago. "It is a paradox that there should be super-highways and super-markets and super-everything-else that is a part of modern America's burgeoning economic life, while there are no super-railroads."

America finally has super-railroads—super freight railroads. John Barriger would be proud of America's railroads today.

Washington Spins
Its Wheels

*"This is a dying system and a sick system that needs
some major surgery, not just tinkering around the edges."*

—Congressman John L. Mica of Florida,
speaking about Amtrak

S olving the problem of the U.S. government debt is the single issue
that will override concerns about Amtrak and other federal programs in the future. The nation is bequeathing to its future generations
a debt that is approaching $5 trillion.

Amtrak advocates will staunchly claim that Amtrak is but a small
contributor to the national debt. Considering that total federal expenditures for Amtrak will soon exceed $21 billion, however, Amtrak is
indeed a part of the problem. Consider these issues:

True Cost of Amtrak. The funds appropriated to Amtrak by
Washington do not represent the total paid by taxpayers once state

and local expenditures are included. Thus, Amtrak's burden to taxpayers is actually higher than $21 billion.

Shadow Price of Amtrak. Economists refer to the "shadow price" on each unit of government spending—a dollar in taxation creates losses and distortions elsewhere in the economy because of either the tax itself or the costs of collecting the tax.

Fiscal Payback Absent. If public expenditures would have made Amtrak profitable, it would have happened by now. Instead, there is no end in sight to Amtrak subsidies.

Amtrak as Microcosm. What is true of Amtrak is true of just about every government program: it represents pork-barrel spending and vested-interest politics. Economist Robert Samuelson was referring to Amtrak, among other programs, when he wrote in *Newsweek* that "the symbolic importance of ending these unjustified programs overshadows their size. If they enjoy immortality, then the political process is captive to past commitments, no matter how dubious."

Washington Reform Commissions

Federal programs across the board are in trouble, according to the National Performance Review, commonly known as the Gore Report on Reinventing Government. "Public confidence in the federal government has never been lower," it begins. "The average American believes we waste 48 cents of every tax dollar. Five of every six want 'fundamental change' in Washington. Only 20 percent of Americans trust the federal government to do the right thing most of the time—down from 76 percent 30 years ago."

The report continues: "We all know why. Washington's failures are large and obvious. For a decade, the deficit has run out of control. . . . The federal government seems unable to abandon the obsolete. . . . It is almost as if federal programs were *designed* not to work. In truth, few are 'designed' at all; the legislative process simply churns them out, one after another, year after year." The result is a budget deficit and a "performance deficit."

Over the years various commissions have tried to change government. In 1987 President Ronald Reagan established the Commission on Privatization, and its report contains "78 recommendations for sweeping reforms" based on concerns that "the federal government has become too large, too expensive, and too intrusive in our lives." The commission examined Amtrak and concluded that "private sector initiative in the provision of intercity passenger rail service should be encouraged. The federal government should adopt a multi-year plan to move Amtrak or major portions of its operations to the private sector, in conjunction with repealing Amtrak's exclusive rights to provide intercity rail service. As part of the multi-year plan, federal subsidies should be incrementally reduced, and a deadline should be set for the Department of Transportation to decide whether Amtrak or portions of its operations should be continued."

It isn't surprising that such recommendations are ignored. After all, similar calls to restructure government have fallen on deaf ears. In January 1984 the Private Sector Survey on Cost Control, also known as the Grace Commission Report, warned that if government programs were not cut, the deficit would continue to grow. "Taxes can no longer fill the budget gap . . . the way to end deficits is to cut wasteful spending."

Washington is not doing that with Amtrak.

Don Phillips, writing in *Trains* in early 1997 after another Amtrak fight for survival, concluded that "once again, Congress has proved itself incapable of dealing with the Amtrak problem. After two decades of debate, nothing has been decided on any rational basis. Amtrak was not shut down; it was not given a half-penny of the gasoline tax; it wasn't given new flexibility to cut its own costs—nothing except hot air." That followed an earlier column in which he wrote, "Amtrak is still living a perils-of-Pauline existence. There is no assured source of capital funding, and each year brings yet another silly season of smoke and mirrors as Congress tries to give Amtrak just enough money to keep running through every Congressional district possible."

Calls to Kill Amtrak

Two years earlier, Jonathan Yardley of the *Washington Post*, an admitted "railroad sentimentalist" and former Amtrak proponent, wrote a rather blunt article. He declared that "the nationalized public railroad has become one of the fattest pork barrels around. . . . The truth is that the 'constituency' for nationalized passenger rail service to which Congress so routinely capitulates is a chimera." Yardley pointed out that travel on Amtrak is a barely visible blip in the overall travel picture and that Washington has proved beyond any reasonable doubt that it has no idea how to run a railroad. Concluded Yardley: "Put Amtrak on the block. Private interests will buy it, kill the unprofitable routes and bring the workable ones up to speed. Privatization is hardly the answer to all of government's programs, but in [Amtrak's] case it's the only answer."

Such views have been building for some time. Many politicians and pundits gave Amtrak the 1970s to improve service and establish itself in the marketplace. Views hardened after Amtrak failed, and by 1985 the Reagan Administration was trying to kill Amtrak. Reagan's budget director, David Stockman, declared Amtrak a "litmus test" of budget-cutting sentiment. At that time, *Wall Street Journal* transportation reporters Christopher Conte and Daniel Machalaba wrote what can now be viewed as prophecy: "With its hard-line position, the Reagan administration risks complete rejection of any Amtrak budget cuts in Congress. Amtrak, by failing to press for cost-cutting alternatives . . . leaves itself open to renewed assault in the future. And that damages the railroad itself, since continued uncertainty hurts its chances of attracting good management, luring new passengers and perhaps even raising capital privately to secure its future."

Uncertainty surrounds Amtrak. In a 1995 congressional hearing, Amtrak's Tom Downs said, "At Amtrak we are all afraid. We are all afraid for our future. Whether it is management, whether it is employees, even whether it is our customers, this is a very uncertain time. People are even afraid to book trips for the summer because they are not sure we are going to be here. People are afraid to be a contractor for us, about whether or not we are going to be here long enough to live out the contract terms. People are afraid at the union level about entering into longer-term labor contracts, about whether or not we are going to be here or the contract terms themselves will be modified. So it is a time of great uncertainty for us all."

Lessons Learned from Conrail and the Alaska Railroad

What should Washington do?
Privatize Amtrak?
Devolve Amtrak to state governments?
Answer: Both.

Washington has demonstrated that it can privatize a railroad; it did so with the Consolidated Rail Corporation (Conrail). The federal government owned 85 percent of the railroad prior to privatizing it as required by the 1981 Northeast Rail Services Act. It took six years, but the Department of Transportation sold its interest in Conrail for $1.6 billion, which at the time was the largest initial public stock offering in the nation's history. The March 26, 1987, transaction, with added payments from Conrail to the U.S. Treasury, produced about $1.9 billion for the taxpayers. The revival and "spin-off" was exactly what Congress had envisioned when it created Conrail.

Few recognized in the early 1970s that the six bankrupt railroads that eventually became Conrail*—all of which suffered from deferred maintenance, freight train derailments, and a declining market share—

*Penn Central, Central Railroad of New Jersey, Erie–Lackawanna, Lehigh & Hudson River, Lehigh Valley, and Reading. Earlier, the Penn Central resulted from a merger of three ailing railroads—the Pennsylvania Railroad, New York Central, and New York, New Haven & Hartford.

would someday become successful. Conrail had required $7 billion in public aid to finance operating losses, severance pay for thousands of employees, and capital expenditures for new rolling stock and track rehabilitation. For about a third of what taxpayers have paid in Amtrak subsidies, the nation has a robust Conrail that plays a vital role in the national economy.

Conrail's value steadily increased, to the point where the CSX and Norfolk Southern Railroads made competing $10.3 billion merger offers to Conrail shareholders. The outcome of the takeover battle was that CSX and Norfolk Southern will divide Conrail between them. The Conrail privatization lesson is that what may appear to be impossible or improbable may be simply difficult.

Washington also demonstrated that it can transfer a rail asset to a more logical public owner by devolving the Alaska Railroad. It was in 1914 that Congress agreed to fund construction of the railroad, and the federal government remained involved for the following seven decades. But on January 14, 1983, Congress enacted legislation that authorized its transfer to the state of Alaska. It took two additional years for the state to pass companion legislation, complete negotiations, and finalize the conveyance process. The transfer may have been slow by Wall Street's standards, but it proved that such changes are possible.

Increasingly, calls are heard to denationalize Amtrak, disassemble it, and transfer useful portions to state or regional agencies. Revamped trains could be operated on other lines by private interests attempting to earn a profit.

Washington Paralyzed by Institutional Inertia

This is where controversy intensifies and action is stalled in Washington.

Washington's problems include bureaucracies suffering from institutional inertia, and a Congress that undertakes cosmetic changes to programs like Amtrak and heralds them as major reorganizations. Worse, special interests favoring the status quo continue to build strength. A highly acclaimed book by Jonathan Rauch, *Demosclerosis:*

The Silent Killer of American Government, shows how year after year the American public forms more interest groups—so much so that gradually government has calcified. He defines *demosclerosis* as the "government's progressive loss of the ability to adapt."

Rauch, a contributing editor of the Washington-based *National Journal,* demonstrates that no program can be cut without incurring the wrath of one group or another, and special interest groups care more about saving a program that the general public cares about killing it. "Can't you at least get rid of the programs that fail?" he asks. "One problem is that people disagree about which programs have failed, and even about what 'failing' means."

Then there is the power wielded by a handful of senators and representatives. Wrote Rauch: "Consider that as few as three or four well-placed congressmen (sometimes even one or two) can create a new subsidy program, if they're careful not to step on the wrong toes. . . . But once a subsidy program or an anti-competitive deal is in place, three or four congressmen can almost *never* get rid of it, because the people enjoying the subsidy can always line up ten or twenty congressmen to defend it."

That is why it seems every government program lasts forever.

He argues that when it comes to Amtrak, government shouldn't do things "just because they seem nice." He asks, "Is the main justification for a program sentimental? Does a program 'protect a way of life' (agriculture subsidies) or 'save a treasured institution' (Amtrak passenger-train subsidies)? . . . That's not a reason to fund it."

Pro-Amtrak interest groups would have America think otherwise. Railroad equipment suppliers, labor unions, civic boosters, rail fans, and others will fight tooth and nail for federal subsidies to Amtrak.

Complicating the lobbying process is Congress's hearing arguments from organizations that are living in the past. An example is the National Association of Railroad Passengers (NARP). What was a visionary organization when formed in the late 1960s by Anthony Haswell has become a preservationist society today. When I was a regional director, and later executive director, for the NARP in the early 1970s, the organization filed lawsuits and initiated action before regulatory bodies on behalf of rail service consumers. In Amtrak's early days, the association maintained an arm's-length relationship with Amtrak just as Consumers Union does today with manufacturers of consumer goods. In short, the NARP was a watchdog concerned with true progress in rail service.

Today, the NARP is little more than an Amtrak booster club, and it's difficult to untangle the relationship between the two organizations. Amtrak's employee publication has promoted the idea that its staff become NARP members. Amtrak's Internet page offers glowing comments about the association, a favor the NARP returns with every minor Amtrak action. When the association bestowed its Golden Spike Award on Senator Bill Roth of Delaware for working for Amtrak subsidies, an Amtrak news release issued at taxpayer expense gushed with praise for the NARP and the senator. Also, many NARP members appear indifferent to the need for marketable high-speed trains on busy corridors, instead offering vehement defenses of hopeless long-distance Amtrak trains. This growth-repressing activity is harmful to the future of rail service in America.

Perhaps such behavior isn't surprising, because railroading has a mystique about it that attracts hobbyists and sentimentalists. I, too, am a rail sentimentalist—how fondly I recall youthful rides on the friendly Baltimore & Ohio—but the difference is, I no longer expect the taxpayers to subsidize my travels down memory lane. I'm not alone in thinking that the NARP board of directors has an optimism about Amtrak bordering on folly and that the organization suffers from interest-group barnacles.

"It seems to me that NARP has become part of the problem, not part of the solution," wrote alternate NARP board member William Lindley of Mesa, Arizona, to fellow members. "The actions of passenger rail advocates in recent years remind me of a doctor treating a severely bleeding patient who instead of stopping the cause of the bleeding complains that the nurse isn't pumping blood in fast enough. Amtrak doesn't merely need more money. We need to treat the disease, not the symptoms."

Such interest-group behavior is not all that unusual. Management expert Tom Peters has pointed out that "I'm really struck by the degree to which most activities—particularly when you think of lobbying—are amazingly defensive as opposed to offensive. It's sort of, how to protect what we had in the 1980s or Seventies or Sixties, rather than, how can we really help position this industry for the year 2005 or 2007 or 2008."

It would be unfair to single out the NARP as the only organization with a too-blind-for-comfort position regarding Amtrak, nor is it the only one with which Amtrak curries favor. Amtrak officials are cozy with leaders in many organizations; examples include the National Association of Counties, Association of Metropolitan Planning Organizations, American Public Transit Association, National Council of State Legislatures, and others.

Clinton's Broken Rail Promises

Bill Clinton's 1992 election was supposed to change Washington. *The New York Times* said, "Twelve days before the Inauguration, we may be able to predict the fate of Bill Clinton's promise to free American government from the grip of special interests: Broken by Day One."

Kevin Phillips relies on that quote in his book *Arrogant Capital* to convey that Washington is now dominated by ninety thousand lobbyists, sixty thousand lawyers, and "the largest concentration of special interests the world has ever seen." Phillips, a political analyst and commentator, refers to an "iron triangle" of politicians, interest groups, and media who in one way or another complement one another in maintaining the status quo. He declares that "the Washington that now approaches the twenty-first century is an interest-group fortress."

Rail groups concerned more with the status quo than with growth have captured Clinton and his lieutenants.

During the 1992 campaign Clinton declared, "I strongly support the development of high-speed rail because we need to ensure that we possess a transportation system that boosts American productivity and international competitiveness." Notice that he didn't say Amtrak, he said high-speed rail, and at the time every such effort except for the Northeast Corridor project was completely independent of Amtrak. Interviewed on CBS's *This Morning,* Clinton emphasized building high-speed rail to "create an unbelievable number of jobs and really help our economy." He also promoted non-Amtrak-style "bullet trains" in speeches at Harvard and the Wharton School. His running mate, Al Gore, in his book *Earth in the Balance,* supports development of "attractive and efficient" maglev train systems.

After his inauguration, Clinton appointed Jolene M. Molitoris to the post of federal railroad administrator partly because of her experiences in an Ohio rail agency and as a vice president for the High Speed Rail Association. Observers naturally expected that she would begin the process of realizing high-speed rail.

What happened is that high-speed rail degenerated into an incremental program to help Amtrak. Distressing to planners of new systems was that Molitoris appeared to go from the visionary camp to the incrementalist camp virtually overnight. Worse, under her leadership, the FRA fatally damaged non-Amtrak proposals.

The Death of Texas TGV

The privately financed Texas TGV Corporation needed the Federal Railroad Administration (FRA) to start the safety-certification process for all-new trains slated for the Dallas–Houston route. After fruitless meetings with FRA staff, the company pleaded for help in a letter to Molitoris: "The need by a project developer to know the safety criteria for the purposes of design and cost estimation is essential. Also, the ability to represent to prospective investors that a product meets U.S. operating safety standards is critical." The company also was in dire need of a statement that the FRA would seek changes in federal law to permit TGVs to run faster than 110 mph without having to obtain FRA waivers. Such documents were considered vital to persuade Wall Street that Washington would no longer stifle private investments in high-speed rail.

Molitoris and the FRA failed to provide such statements, thus helping suffocate a progressive non-Amtrak effort. On August 14, 1994, the Texas TGV group gave up hopes of building a system under its state franchise, saying that among the reasons for failure were FRA delays. Clearly, the FRA failed to help a rail consortium that had invested $40 million in private capital to develop a system that would be far superior to anything that could be found on Amtrak's drawing boards, then or now.

Rail Development Legislation Is Inadequate

M eanwhile, the Clinton Administration announced a five-year high-speed rail legislative package which failed to recognize that government resources are limited and that private financing must be part of such a capital-intensive program. While Molitoris trumpeted the effort, the editor of *Public Works Financing*, William G. Reinhardt, pointed out that the modest plan "does little to encourage private investment in high-speed rail. . . . It takes a low-budget, incremental approach that ignores public-private efforts to develop 150-mph-plus systems that can attract high volumes of new ridership and returns for private investors." The modest bill was renamed the Swift Rail Development Act (for then-retiring Congressman Al Swift of Washington State, the bill's chief sponsor). Although the amiable Swift is well liked in Washington, he received a dubious honor since the law will primarily improve Amtrak in minor ways.

Washington's promises of fresh starts in rail become rehashes of old programs because the forces working to defend old programs are stronger than the forces advocating change and advances. The result is a Clinton Administration program for second- and third-rate rail projects and no program at all for first-rate rail development.

Perhaps the FRA's behavior was to be expected for another reason. As other Clinton legislative programs were being watered down or stalling outright, Clinton began complaining about his administration's members failing to be bold. According to Bob Woodward's book *The*

Agenda: Inside the Clinton White House, "Clinton had even called them 'incrementalists' who didn't understand his vision."

Stalled Federal Maglev Initiative

Another non-Amtrak train project also skidded to a stop, thanks to the FRA. Consortiums of high-technology and aerospace companies were prepared to launch a program to design a domestic maglev train to compete with German and Japanese models already setting speed records on test tracks. The development effort needed a cost-sharing arrangement with the federal government if American designers were to have any hope of challenging foreign-subsidized competitors. The public-private partnership died when the administration shifted nearly $20 million in maglev funding to California earthquake relief. Aid to California may have been justified, yet the FRA still found resources to increase appropriations for Amtrak. Molitoris retreated as a maglev advocate, betraying what many had perceived to be a Clinton-Gore promise to help put aerospace employees displaced by defense cutbacks to work on high-technology trains. The nation will feel the sting of this program termination when someday it finds itself unable to compete in the international market for maglev trains.

It is no wonder that then–Lieutenant Governor Stan Lundine of New York, a Democrat, said, "I'm disappointed the Clinton Administration is not following through with the visionary commitment to high-speed surface transportation articulated during [the] campaign." Lundine, in language usually reserved for members of the opposing Republican Party, called Clinton's decision to kill maglev "outrageous" and suggested that the administration had not been forthright with him. By early 1997, as the Japanese completed a second test track for their superconducting maglev and the Germans were moving to build a commercial line, the FRA tried to repair its image by establishing another maglev advisory committee. While other countries build, Washington talks.

One change that Washington must make is to move jurisdiction for maglev out of the FRA, an agency ill-equipped to deal with high-technology issues. Oversight should shift to an agency accustomed to dealing with technological challenges, such as the National Aeronautics and Space Administration, or with major infrastructure construction, such as the Army Corps of Engineers, or some such combination. Senator Daniel Patrick Moynihan of New York said several years ago that "the FRA is not the best equipped organization institutionally" to take on a maglev program, and that remains true.

Many believe that Molitoris contributed to the collapse of the Texas TGV and American maglev technology programs, but obscured these failures by effusively praising Amtrak's Northeast Corridor program. Molitoris and her Amtrak colleagues fail to note that when passengers board Amtrak's fastest Northeast Corridor trains in 2000, they will be riding trains with average speeds that are slower than what Spain operated in the early 1990s, France in the 1980s, and Japan in the 1970s.

As Clinton ran for re-election in 1996, the FRA issued its long-awaited high-speed rail commercial feasibility study. It discussed—surprise!—the importance of public-private partnerships, the very types represented by the Texas TGV and maglev consortiums that died during Clinton's first term.

Role Played by the Republicans

The Republicans also contribute to preserving Amtrak. Early in 1995, when the Republicans took control of Congress, many believed Amtrak would be killed or severely slashed. The House of Representatives' leadership named Congressman Scott Klug of Wisconsin to be point man on privatization, and he in turn supported Colorado Representative Joel Hefley's bill to eliminate subsides to Amtrak.

The effort failed because Congress has as members people like Robert Walker of Pennsylvania, a fierce Republican critic of Amtrak who demanded an end to its subsidies—well, almost. Albert R. Karr of the *Wall Street Journal* reported that "Amtrak recently said it would eliminate service on the *Keystone* train that runs through Lancaster, Pennsylvania, in Mr. Walker's district. The lawmaker responded by firing off an angry letter charging, 'What Amtrak has done is outrageous, unnecessary and thoroughly incompetent.' He clearly wants to keep his train. . . . 'It's a classic political problem—everybody values their train, and they want to preserve it, but they want to zero out other people's trains,' says Republican Representative Susan Molinari of New York, chairwoman of the House railroads subcommittee, who considers her own Amtrak Northeast Corridor trains to be vital."

Amtrak also dangles purchasing contracts before railway suppliers, and doing so counts with elected officials. Consider the case of Governor Tom Ridge of Pennsylvania, a Republican, who during the 1996 budget fight appealed to Congress to continue funding Amtrak at current levels. The action came a month after Ridge announced that Amtrak had placed a $235 million order for ninety-eight diesel locomotives from General Electric Transportation Systems, based in Erie.

Through early 1997, when it came to Amtrak, the "Republican revolution" looked more like a retreat.

What is a congressman like Bud Shuster to do? Shuster's district includes Altoona, Pennsylvania, which has more active and retired railroad employees than any community in the country. For that reason alone, he should be in favor of Amtrak service. Yet, Shuster knows a bottomless pit when he sees one. He said in a congressional hearing, "I think you are going to see elephants flying before this Congress is going to approve another $4 billion [for Amtrak]."

Shuster and Molinari tried to enact Amtrak reforms but were blocked by most Democrats, some Republicans, and the general squad of status quo advocates who reside in Washington. With growing frustration, Frank Wolf, a northern Virginia Republican, chairman of the House Transportation Appropriations Subcommittee, began asking witnesses for their views about setting up an Amtrak route-closing commission similar to the military base-closing commission.

It wasn't surprising that Republican reformers were stymied in their Amtrak efforts. Remember that changes in Washington—while not impossible—are difficult because of the tight grip by special interests. Thus, as Democrats and their labor allies fight for the status quo on Amtrak, and as Republicans see Amtrak creating jobs in their districts, Washington's political bias toward inaction is reinforced.

A Ballot Box Irrelevancy

I t's time someone asked Congress what it is afraid of.

Let's assume the "worst," from the perspective of a member of Congress—Amtrak will be dismantled, and train service to his or her town will end. If I were scripting the reaction for a Hollywood scene, here's what I would tell a congressman to do.

First, in a speech on the floor of Congress when the C-SPAN cameras are turned on, express "shock and dismay" while exaggerating the importance of Amtrak. In a news conference later with local reporters, express serious concern over impaired mobility back home, but be sure to ignore highway, bus, air, and sometimes even other train alternatives. In an appearance at which a taxpayer says killing Amtrak is a "good idea," distract everyone by attacking some Republican if you are a Democrat, or vice versa. If a congressional hearing is held, squander hours on minor issues like "If they painted the station, more people would ride the train." Finally, as Amtrak runs out of money and gets ready to terminate trains, vote more money for Amtrak and rush home to claim a vital role in solving an "emergency."

As Amtrak creeps toward its thirtieth birthday, the public's patience has run out on this show. A reality that never gets mentioned is this: *Not a single member of Congress will lose his or her seat as a result of Amtrak's demise or because trains to a particular district or state are discontinued. Amtrak is a ballot-box irrelevancy.*

Over time Amtrak has stopped service on routes in twenty-nine states and no evidence exists that any public official ever lost a seat for "failing" to save a train. That was true when Amtrak discontinued the Chicago–Florida *Floridian,* Chicago–Seattle *North Coast Hiawatha,* Chicago–Houston *Lone Star,* Chicago–Norfolk *Mountaineer,* and New York–Kansas City *National Limited.* When these and other trains came off or service ended at particular stations, 127 communities were stricken from Amtrak's map. (See Table 8.1.)

TABLE 8.1. Communities No Longer Served Directly by Amtrak Trains Because of Changes in Train Routings, Discontinued Stops, or Train Discontinuances

Alabama: Decatur, Dothan, Montgomery

Arizona: Coolidge, Phoenix, Tempe

California: Pasadena

Colorado: Greeley

Florida: Clearwater, St. Petersburg

Georgia: Thomasville, Valdosta, Waycross

Idaho: Boise, Nampa, Pocatello, Shoshone

Illinois: Chillicothe, East Dubuque, Elmhurst, Freeport, Galena, Rockford, Streator, Warren

Indiana: Bloomington, Fort Wayne, Garrett, Lafayette, Logansport, Marion, Muncie, Nappanee, Peru, Richmond, Terre Haute

Iowa: Dubuque

Kansas: Arkansas City, Wichita

Kentucky: Bowling Green, Louisville

Minnesota: Cambridge, Breckenridge, Duluth, Morris, Sandstone, Willmar

Mississippi: Batesville, Canton, Durant, Grenada, Winona

Montana: Billings, Bozeman, Butte, Deer Lodge, Forsyth, Glendive, Livingston, Miles City, Missoula, Paradise

Nevada: Caliente, Las Vegas

North Dakota: Bismarck, Dickinson, Jamestown, Mandan, Valley City

Ohio: Akron, Athens, Canton, Chillicothe, Columbus, Crestline, Dayton, Lima, Youngstown

Oklahoma: Ardmore, Guthrie, Norman, Oklahoma City, Pauls Valley, Perry, Ponca City, Purcell

Oregon: Baker City, Hinkle-Hermiston, Hood River, La Grande, Ontario, Pendleton, The Dalles

Pennsylvania: McKeesport

Tennessee: Nashville

Texas: Brenham, Gainesville, Laredo

Utah: Milford, Ogden

Virginia: Crew, Bedford, Christiansburg, Farmville, Narrows, Norfolk, Roanoke, Suffolk

Washington: East Auburn, Ellensburg, Yakima

West Virginia: Bluefield, Clarksburg, Grafton, Keyser, Oakland, Parkersburg, Rowlesburg, Welch, Williamson

Wisconsin: Superior

Wyoming: Cheyenne, Evanston, Green River, Laramie, Rawlins, Rock Springs

As of May 1997.

Perhaps Amtrak was not an issue because community leaders said, "Okay, at least we're not being singled out—other places are losing Amtrak, too." This theory is weak because Amtrak has rerouted trains and abandoned communities one at a time or in small clusters. In such instances, big cities and small towns indeed cried foul as other places kept their Amtrak service. Yet, again, no congressman, mayor, or city council member lost an election in any community, whether Amtrak disappeared in a city as large as Phoenix or one as small as Bowling Green, Kentucky.

Also, communities have prospered or withered for reasons that have nothing to do with Amtrak's presence or absence. Amtrak's economic relevance to most places is microscopic.

At some unknown future time, when more Amtrak trains make their last runs, political egos will be bruised and community pride hurt. Rail aficionados will bellyache, especially when the media run stories that induce nostalgia for passenger trains. However, every single elected official holding office when the trains are running will still hold office after the trains stop. This message is important because in Washington perceptions are often more important than reality.

The public is smart enough to know that common-carrier alternatives will remain even with Amtrak gone.

A few Amtrak-served points would retain rail service provided by non-Amtrak entities. For example, more people ride Maryland's commuter trains that serve Harpers Ferry and Martinsburg, West Virginia, than ride Amtrak. Those commuter trains will continue to operate after Amtrak disappears. In other areas, new public or private rail operators may emerge to launch regional trains or other service.

Aviation serves many medium-sized cities, almost always at more convenient hours than Amtrak does.

In small towns bus service should not be overlooked. Theodore Knappen, a representative for Greyhound Lines, said in congressional testimony, "If the entire Amtrak system were shut down, there would be exactly fifty-six communities in the country that would be left without any intercity public surface transportation. . . . And what is also true about the fifty-six communities, the vast majority of those are small communities that are closer to a town with bus service than we are to Dulles Airport as we sit here." Knappen said that bus companies would likely begin service to some of the communities, depending on size and location, if Amtrak trains stopped running.

Highways will remain open for those wishing to travel by automobile, as most rural Americans do.

Without corrective action, Amtrak's subsidy drain will persist. On February 18, 1970, as policy makers were discussing the formation of what later would become Amtrak, Undersecretary of Transportation James M. Beggs warned in a letter to the Nixon White House that "political pressure may be placed on [Amtrak] to continue uneconomic routes." That prediction came true.

Where rail passenger service is important, regional, state, or private initiatives could keep it operating. Such changes are feasible because, after all, politics remains the art of the possible. That's why Washington succeeded with programs to privatize Conrail and denationalize and devolve the Alaska Railroad. It's Amtrak's turn.

NINE

Should Amtrak
Be Privatized?

"The Japanese government is planning several new lines. . . . As an
independent, investor-owned organization, JR East will cooperate
only to the degree that the company's performance is not
adversely affected. We will not be pressured or swayed
by outside agencies."

—Shuichiro Yamanouchi, chairman, and Masatake Matsuda, president,
East Japan Railway Company, in 1996 annual report

I t is now acceptable in policy circles to raise the prospect of privatizing Amtrak. Although privatization isn't the exclusive way to solve
the nation's problems with Amtrak, it can make a significant contribution to reducing federal government subsidy requirements for intercity passenger trains.

Privatizing Amtrak is possible, but it won't be easy. Those who
are wedded to the status quo are trying to discredit the idea. For example, in a 1995 hearing before Congress, Amtrak president Thomas
Downs said, "We are probably the most privatized passenger railroad
in the world."

That's misleading, as we shall see.

Immediately after Downs's statement, the National Association of Railroad Passengers' newsletter claimed that a privatized intercity passenger rail system "does not exist anywhere else in the world."

That's also misleading.

It is true that governments worldwide generally are not attempting to privatize entire rail passenger systems, which are costly dinosaurs with no appeal to private investors. Instead, they are electing to abandon long-distance routes and privatize other routes.

In any country, three elements should be in place for a successful rail privatization to occur. First, it is helpful if privatization in other domestic industries or denationalization of other assets is under way, carried out by a cadre of professionals who know how to privatize within their country's social, political, financial, and legal framework. Next, other countries' experience in privatizing rail service has to have been studied to see what applies to the particular privatization at hand. Last, the government must be committed to creating and maintaining an institutional framework that provides a reasonable opportunity for well-run private operators to make a profit running passenger trains.

Such an environment is building today in the United States. Let's begin by examining activity here, which shows that an unprecedented era of privatization is underway. After that comes a summary of rail privatization activity around the world.

United States

Hundreds of books about privatization have been published in the United States, yet many people are unclear about just what it means.

The first use of the term *privatization,* which occurred about three decades ago, is credited to management expert Peter F. Drucker. One definition is that privatization enables government to *provide* a service without *producing* that service. Another, according to E. S. "Steve" Savas, is that "privatization is the act of reducing the role of government, or increasing the role of the private sector, in an activity or in the ownership of assets." Savas is regarded as a privatization guru, having dealt with the issue in 1969 while serving as a city administrator under New York Mayor John Lindsay. Today he is director of the Privatization Research Organization at New York City's Barauch College.

Savas wrote in his book *Privatization: The Key to Better Government* that "selling off or denationalizing a state-owned airline, factory, or coal mine is privatization." Other forms of privatization include using private financing to build infrastructure, contracting or outsourcing with private vendors to provide services previously provided by public agencies, or establishing franchise operators when long-term or special circumstances dictate doing so. A difference between contracting and franchising is that a contractor usually is paid by the government, but a franchise holder generally earns revenues from consumers.

"Several major forces, or pressures, are behind the privatization movement: pragmatic, ideological, commercial, and populist," wrote Savas. "The goal of the pragmatists is better government, in the sense of a more cost-effective one. The goal of those who approach the matter ideologically is less government, one that plays a smaller role vis-à-vis private institutions. The goal of commercial interests is to get more business by having more of government's spending redirected toward them. And the goal of the populists is to achieve a better society by giving people greater power to satisfy their common needs, while diminishing that of large public and private bureaucracies." He adds that countries try to denationalize industries or assets, a form of privatization, because the new entities will innovate far more than the old entities did.

In April 1992 President George Bush signed an executive order encouraging privatization for state and local government infrastructure. By 1994 President Clinton began talking about privatizing the Federal Aviation Administration, a Navy-run oil field, and other entities. Clinton signed an executive order that allows projects built with federal money to be sold to private entities. Meanwhile, international privatization became so popular that *The Economist* called it a "global economic revolution."

The Reason Foundation, of Los Angeles, founded in 1978 as a

research organization with a "market-based approach and outside-Washington perspective," advocates divestiture of government assets and enterprises to private parties as well as issuing franchises to private enterprise to design, finance, build, and operate facilities. Robert W. Poole, Jr., its president, wrote that selling state-owned enterprises has major financial benefits to government—the sale is a one-time windfall, and the sale ends a budgetary drain in the form of subsidies. Says Poole, "With its endless stream of budget deficits and soaring national debt, the United States is long overdue for a sustained, long-term program of downsizing government."

The savings can be impressive. Another Reason Foundation report, by John C. Hilke, a Federal Trade Commission economist, concluded that "more than 100 studies over the course of the last 20 years have demonstrated privatization-competition cost savings in service areas from airport operation to weather forecasting." He gave as reasons for the cost savings better management techniques, use of more productive equipment, greater incentives to innovate, use of incentive pay, and more efficient deployment of workers. The value of the savings was estimated at between 20 percent and 50 percent, depending upon the type of service and methods used to privatize the service.

Hilke's conclusions are important because he reviewed studies conducted on a mind-boggling array of public services, of which the following is but a sampling: airline operation and airplane maintenance, airports, bus service, cleaning services, electric utilities, fire protection, forestry, health services, highways, hospitals, housing and community development, legal services, libraries, liquor stores, military support services, nursing homes, parking, parks and recreation, postal service, prisons, public welfare, refuse collection, schools, ship repair, street cleaning, and water utilities.

Consider the capabilities of Comarco, Inc., which provides services to Washington National Airport and others. There is no need to hire government staff for airports when this company provides "around-the-clock, seven-days-a-week services for aircraft fueling, operations and maintenance of airport terminals and grounds, aircraft rescue and firefighting services, environmental compliance, marketing, development, and lease negotiations." It also provides construction project management, Skycap services, snow removal, and public relations services.

Richard C. Loomis, a Comarco senior vice president, speaking on behalf of the Contract Services Association of America, noted that "what is different today is that services never considered for 'privatization' earlier are being scrutinized (e.g., airports, highways, police, fire) and many governments which never before considered the options are being forced to consider them. Events outside the United States, where government enterprises are being sold off, are also adding to the potential and pressures."

In 1984 the Grace Commission Report proposed more privatization of government activities, but such a recommendation goes back further—the Hoover Commission issued a report in 1955 recommending that agencies performing significant public services be required to finance themselves instead of relying on subsidies. The commission didn't use the word *privatization* because it didn't exist then.

Federal Agency Privatization

American perceptions are changing about what should remain public and what properly belongs in the private sector. See Table 9.1 for a sampling of federal privatization activity.

Few could have predicted that in 1996 the National Aeronautics and Space Administration would partially privatize the space shuttle by contracting with United Space Alliance, a joint venture of Rockwell and Lockheed Martin, to take over management of most shuttle operations. NASA administrator Daniel Goldin declared it "a very, very, major turning point for this agency." Goldin sees the move as reducing shuttle operating costs by at least $400 million over six years, cutting launch costs and allowing America to compete against rivals such as Europe's Arianespace S.A. A new space vehicle, the VentureStar, will emerge from the arrangement. The craft will be the first space shuttle designed, built, and maintained by private industry.

TABLE 9.1. Examples of Federal Privatization Proposals for
Services and Assets

Amtrak

Beltsville Agricultural Research Station

Bonneville Power Administration

College Construction Loan Insurance Association (Connie Lee) (1996)

Federal Home Loan Mortgage Corporation (Freddie Mac)

Federal National Mortgage Association (Fannie Mae)

Federal Aviation Administration, air traffic control system

Food and Drug Administration (section that approves new food and medicines)

General Services Administration

Idaho National Engineering Laboratory

Medicare

National Aeronautics and Space Administration, space shuttle program (1996)

National Helium Reserve

National Institute of Standards & Technology

National Technical Information Service

Naval Petroleum Reserves

Oak Ridge National Laboratory

Public Broadcasting Service

Social Security

Student Loan Marketing Association (Sallie Mae) (1997)

Tennessee Valley Authority

U.S. Coast Guard Vessel Traffic Information System

U.S. Enrichment Corporation (uranium-enrichment operations)

U.S. Geological Survey

U.S. Postal Service

Year is shown when privatization became an accomplished fact.

Aviation industry leaders like Ron Allen, chairman of Delta Air Lines, support creation of a nongovernmental corporation to manage the air traffic control system, which is by far the Federal Aviation Administration's largest function. Transportation Secretary Federico Peña campaigned for the change as a way to upgrade the computer and radar systems so critical to air traffic safety. A corporation could achieve such objectives while saving as much as $18 billion over a decade. FAA administrator David R. Hinson said, "It would be a lot better if we had a board of directors that had the authority to manage the chief executive and run it like a business. We don't need the government to run a business. They don't know how."

Several airports are privatizing by contracting for services as permitted under a 1996 federal law. "Why are U.S. airports suddenly ripe for privatization?" asked *World Airport Week*. "Three reasons: lack of public money for infrastructure improvements, sweeping changes in management philosophy throughout the service sector of the U.S. economy, and an emerging private sector capability to provide first-class airport management services." The Indianapolis Airport Authority projects savings upward of $100 million as a result of a ten-year contract for operations and maintenance with a private firm, BAA USA Inc. (The parent company was the British Airports Authority when owned by the British government from 1966 until its privatization in 1987.)

Public transit services with operating losses can be privatized, generally by contracting out to increase efficiency and lower costs, selling development rights near stations, and shifting more responsibility to the private sector for owning and financing transit assets. Contracting is the most common form of transit privatization. "We know that you can't provide public transportation at a profit," said Massachusetts Transportation Secretary James Kerasiotes of Boston's system, "but we don't want to continue spending the kind of dollars we've been spending." According to Savas, "Where private firms in the United States, selected by competitive bidding, were awarded contracts to take over the provision of public transit service, cost reductions of 50 to 60 percent or more were achieved, meaning that public costs were close to twice the private costs."

Jose A. Gómez-Ibáñez and John R. Meyer found somewhat lower cost savings but wrote in their book, *Going Private: The International Experience with Transport Privatization,* that the savings were long-term: "The U.S. experience . . . indicates that the savings generally do not disappear over time." School districts have long understood this, which is why more than a thousand privately run school bus companies across the nation collectively earn $3.3 billion in annual revenues.

When it comes to financing assets, look to northern Virginia, where a commercial real estate company will privately fund a $20 million subway station. The arrangement is part of a plan to manage traffic around a development to be built at the abandoned Potomac railroad yard in Arlington.

Whatever the privatization, not all proposals come from Republicans. Senator John Breaux of Louisiana and the Progressive Policy Institute, considered a think tank for centrist Democrats, released a plan to privatize Medicare; some Democrats favor privatizing the Social Security system.

None of this surprises Poole, who told the *Michigan Privatization Report*, "This has become a nationwide phenomenon, with governors and mayors and city councils of all political persuasions, in all parts of the country, and of all sizes of government, actively embracing and starting to implement privatization."

Unfortunately, Congress has stopped many privatization proposals. The Grace Commission reported that "so powerful are the special interests pressuring Congress to continue its policy of spend and tax that it will take an equally insistent counter-force—the taxpayers of this land—to overcome those pressures and make Congress fiscally responsible." Thus, privatization of Amtrak may be difficult, but certainly not impossible.

International Developments

Amtrak and its boosters believe it would be unwise to dismantle America's rail passenger system and transfer it to private interests, or to state, regional, or local authorities. Yet, a survey of developments internationally shows that is exactly what countries around the world are doing.

Other nations are privatizing extensively with the approval of public officials across the political spectrum. "Although many associate privatization with conservative leaders such as Britain's Margaret Thatcher, privatization has been embraced enthusiastically by leaders

TABLE 9.2. **Examples of Railroad Privatization**

Various Forms Employed, Including Sale of All Properties, Concession Awards, and Private-Sector Ownership of New Railroad Facilities

Asia/Far Pacific: Australia, China, Japan, Malaysia, New Zealand, South Korea, Taiwan, Thailand, Vietnam

Africa: Cameroon, Ivory Coast, Zimbabwe

Central America: Costa Rica, Guatemala, Panama

Europe: Austria, Channel Tunnel, Czech Republic, Estonia, France, Germany, Italy, Russia, United Kingdom

North America: Canada, Mexico, United States

South America: Argentina, Bolivia, Brazil, Chile, Colombia, Ecuador, Peru

of many ideologies, including Spain's Socialist Felipe Gonzalez, New Zealand's Labourite Roger Douglas, and Argentina's Perónist Carlos Saul Menem," said Poole.

Divestiture of state-owned enterprises is the most common form of privatization, with Poole saying in congressional testimony that "some one hundred countries have organized programs to divest assets, and over the past decade the sale of state-owned assets and enterprises has generated over $445 billion."

That divestiture includes railroads—their passenger and freight operations as well as infrastructure. Although hardly anyone predicted it just a few years ago, officials are relying on new strategies to discard hopelessly uneconomic services while finding private capital necessary to upgrade promising ones. For unprofitable rail service that must remain for social reasons, planners are finding ways to lower subsidies through franchising (Europeans tend to use the word *concessioning*), and spinoffs to regional or local governments.

In some cases, countries are retaining ownership of rail rights-of-way, similar to the public ownership of highways, but are franchising the movement of traffic over them. Elsewhere, railroads are sold as complete units. Various types of railroad privatization are presented below.

Europe

Great Britain

Prime Minister Margaret Thatcher's government made the sale of government commercial entities one of the principal themes of her administration, and to this day the country carries out a daring divestiture and privatization program. The World Bank reported that the sales of British Telecom and National Freight were major successes, and privatized British Airways has become one of the world's most profitable airlines. Also sold were British Aerospace, Rolls-Royce, Jaguar, and Heathrow and Gatwick Airports.

It's British Rail's turn. To carry out the task, the British government created the Office of Passenger Rail Franchising and other entities.

The government has completed selling components of British Rail as sixty separate businesses. For example, the process created three passenger rolling stock leasing companies with ownership of eleven thousand pieces of British Rail passenger equipment. Late in 1995 the government sold the rolling stock companies for $2.85 billion to Angel Train Contracts, Eversholt Leasing, and Porterbrook Leasing—Britain's largest-ever privatization by direct sale.

British Rail train operations has been divided into twenty-five passenger and six freight companies, all of which have become franchises that lured numerous bidders.

Virgin Rail Group won two British Rail franchises, one of which is for the CrossCountry trains based in Birmingham. "Virgin believes that it can be built into one of the prime rail franchises serving several markets," said Virgin's chairman, Richard Branson. "Exciting times are ahead." Virgin said the subsidies for such service were $213.2 million in 1996–97, but they will decline over the fifteen-year term of the franchise to an annual average of $61.1 million, and in the final year Virgin Rail will make a $16.9 million payment to the government. The company plans to replace many CrossCountry trains with new equipment between 2000 and May 2004.

Other organizations that have won passenger franchisees include:

- Connex Rail, a subsidiary of *Cie. Générale d'Enterprise Auto*, for London's southeastern and south-central suburban routes. The French-based company is Europe's second-largest private-sector passenger transport operator and manages various forms of public transport.

- Stagecoach PLC, a bus operator, for London's southwest trains.

- National Express PLC, another bus operator, for the *Gatwick Express* between London and Gatwick Airport and the Midland Main Line trains linking London with Derby and Nottingham.

- Great North Eastern Railway Company, a subsidiary of Sea Containers, Limited, for the east coast route between Edinburgh, Leeds, and London. (Sea Containers owns the Venice–Simplon *Orient Express* luxury trains.) The railway's 1996 revenues of $413 million exceeded expectations, and operating profits are up strongly because of cost reductions and revenue growth.

Depending on circumstances, some bidders may operate routes with equipment that was assigned to the service in the past, while others face a mandatory requirement to purchase hundreds of new passenger cars.

By March 1997 the government had awarded all twenty-five regional passenger rail franchises. Mike Knutton, editor of *International Railway Journal,* reported that franchisees are showing "strong performance in terms of punctuality and reliability" and that new marketing initiatives are underway. Knutton, concerned about ticket prices and convenience when a trip includes two or more franchisees, wrote that more coordination is necessary, but "the benefits of privatization so far do outweigh the disadvantages."

Nothing is sacred in the sell-off process. Late in 1995 a consortium led by the Wisconsin Central purchased Rail Express Systems, which operates the queen of England's *Royal Train* and Royal Mail services. "For the first time since the 1940s privately operated trains will be running the length and breadth of Britain," said John Watts, a transport minister. The consortium paid the British government $39.9 million for the company, which has annual revenues of nearly $88 million. The Wisconsin Central consortium also submitted the winning bid for four freight companies—Loadhaul, Mainline Freight, Transrail, and Railfreight Distribution (which operates freight trains through the Eurotunnel). The group paid about $350 million for the companies, which had combined revenues of $865 million in the twelve months ended March 1995. The company is now known as the English, Welsh & Scottish Railway Ltd.

Private investment is moving into British railroad infrastructure for conventional services, airport connectors, and high-speed train links.

One new creation is Railtrack, which now owns railroad track and related infrastructure. Railtrack was privatized through a stock offering, and as Britain issued additional franchises, Railtrack's shares hit an all-time high, rising 118 percent in January 1997 from the May 1996 issue price.

A British airport operator, BAA, has participated in financing the construction of a $396 million electrified rail line to Heathrow Airport, over which the *London–Heathrow Fast Train* should begin operating by mid-1998.

A consortium named the London & Continental Railways, which includes the Virgin Group, Bechtel, and others, was awarded a contract to build a $4.6 billion high-speed rail line connecting London and the Channel Tunnel. The new line will cut rail travel time from Britain to Paris by thirty minutes—to two and a half hours—when completed about 2003. The consortium will receive some British government subsidy to build the 68-mile link from London to Dover, but private funds must be part of the package. For its investment, the consortium will get ownership of European Passenger Services, part of the company that holds a long-term concession for the service and runs the *Eurostar* that links London with Paris and Brussels. The award provides Virgin Atlantic with an opportunity to expand into all areas of the European travel industry.

Eurotunnel Franchise

Eurotunnel, both the company and the tunnel itself, is a private venture that has always been separate from British Rail. The tunnel, which permits trains to operate under the English Channel between England and France, is the largest privately financed engineering project in history. In return for building the tunnel and related infrastructure, Eurotunnel S.A., a Franco-British company, holds a fifty-five-year concession, meaning it will operate the tunnel up to July 2052. The tunnel was built for $15 billion (double the original estimate); costs rose with contractors blaming the increase on inflation, design changes, construction problems, and excessive government delays in approvals. Funds were raised by arranging bank loans on commercial terms and by selling shares to more than 650,000 shareholders.

The tunnel was ceremonially opened by Britain's Queen Elizabeth II and French President François Mitterrand on May 5, 1994. The organization has been hampered in attempts to boost revenues because of equipment breakdowns when the service began and by French railway workers' strikes. As traffic and revenues failed to reach projections, Eurotunnel's finances suffered and it defaulted on its loans. The company was trying to restructure debt with its 225-strong banking syndicate by giving the banks a higher level of equity in the company, but the situation worsened late in 1996 when a fire seriously damaged the westbound tunnel.

Despite fire-related disruptions, Eurotunnel released traffic figures for 1996 showing that the number of passengers using *Eurostar* trains as well as shuttle trains rose 62.5 percent to 13 million passengers, from 8 million in 1995. Early in 1997 the company also published the results of a Gallup survey that found 77 percent of French and 68 percent of British people questioned believed the tunnel was safe. The public confidence was strong enough to lead officials to predict that it will again see traffic growth.

The lessons with Great Britain and Eurotunnel are that private interests can take over existing services as well as build new facilities, although financial problems can and will arise from miscalculation and government delay.

France

Privatization in France has been under way since March 1986 when Jacques Chirac became prime minister and the country transformed numerous public entities into private ones. France now plans to privatize Air France. *Aviation Week* correspondent Pierre Sparaco reported in early 1997 that Air France chairman Christian Blanc said, "Air France must be quickly privatized. . . . The government is unable to determine and implement a strategic plan and is an incompetent shareholder in state-owned companies."

The French National Railway is losing substantial sums on freight and non-high-speed passenger operations. In an attempt to reorganize, the railway has been relieved of about $44.5 billion in debt, which is about two-thirds of its total debt, and of the burden of financing new infrastructure. Also, the government has created an infrastructure authority named the French Rail Network to assume responsibility for tracks, with the railroad paying access fees. The railway wants to regionalize money-losing local passenger service, which is bitterly opposed by several rail unions.

The TGVs operate at a profit. The southeast line, which includes Paris–Lyon, earns an annual profit of more than $300 million, and the Atlantic line, Paris–Brittany–Bordeaux, about $150 million. The profits have enabled the railroad to raise private financing for TGV infrastructure through a government-guaranteed loan process.

Private funds paid for 100 percent of the TGV southeast line's construction cost, possible because of its 15 percent rate of return. The

Atlantic line had lower traffic forecasts and a 12 percent rate-of-return estimate. Thus, the government financed 30 percent of the Atlantic line construction costs, and private investors paid for the rest. The railroad's loans were paid on time—indeed, in some cases ahead of schedule.

Future TGV extensions, if built, are intended to reach areas with lower demand. The regions benefited will join the national government and private investors to work out "optimal financing solutions." Whatever the formula, private-sector financing certainly will remain an essential part of the French equation for new line construction and other parts of the railway system.

Germany

Major changes have occurred in Germany since reunification, with privatization near the top of the list. The government has sold more than eight thousand companies (most were small), especially in the former East Germany, where it inherited a state-owned economy. Germany privatized Lufthansa Airlines, and the company has been weaned from direct subsidizes.

The government has announced plans to privatize the German Federal Railway, stating, "The railways in their present structure carrying out state duties cannot perform the role of a successful competitor in the transport market."

First, however, it had to merge West Germany's railway with East Germany's run-down system. A study concluded that the subsidies required to sustain the merged railways would rise to intolerable levels if nothing were changed. Thus, after the 1994 merger, the railroad was split into commercial and public sector functions and released from debts. The commercial portion became a joint-stock company, Deutsche Bahn AG, and organized so that passenger, freight, and infrastructure will eventually become separate businesses. The government owns all the stock, but privatization will follow after the railroad proves it can attract private capital. What has been satisfying to planners is that in 1995 and 1996 the restructured company earned operating profits.

A part of railway reform, not expected to be completed until after 2000, is the regionalization of rail traffic. This will give regional and local governments the power to decide local rail issues, for which they will hold financial responsibility.

A major development in the passenger arena is that Germany is planning to build a high-speed Transrapid maglev line between Hamburg and Berlin, which may be operational by 2005. It is a public-private venture in which the government will finance $5.6 billion and private-sector partners another $2.1 billion in construction costs. The government is willing to share the costs of Transrapid commercialization to give the technology a boost against foreign rivals in the international market, while private companies see value in owning a part of the technology.

Germany is demonstrating that it can merge a strong railroad with a weak one, reorganize the resulting entity into units that can be sold to private interests, and use private-sector financing to help build one of the world's most advanced trains.

Many countries are restructuring their railroads in line with European Union directives, which call for separating infrastructure from operations. Sweden has done so, and it appears that Austria, Denmark, Italy, Spain, the Netherlands, and others will follow. Some will rely on privatized companies for future operations.

Eastern Europe

Russia

Reforms swept over Russia after the downfall of the Soviet Union. Entrepreneurs took over tens of thousands of state operations and converted them into commercial enterprises. Although privatization started slowly in strategic industries, today the process is seen as the most significant and successful of the Russian reforms.

Boris E. Lukov, an international relations expert for the Russian

Ministry of Railways, reported that the Soviet Railway has become nineteen railroads in Russia, six in the Ukraine, three in Kazakhstan, and one each in a dozen independent counties.* The system remains in public hands, but a World Bank study reports that it is in terrible shape. Its breakup has hurt delivery times, equipment availability, and revenues. The situation worsened as rail lines into neighboring states were severed by ethnic conflicts and acts of war.

Russia's Minister of Railways sets policy for the railroads as well as exercising authority over the construction of new rail lines. Despite all of Russia's railroad problems, the office supports construction of a visionary high-speed system. A new Moscow–St. Petersburg rail line is being built at a cost of $7 billion by the Russian High Speed Railways Shareholding Company. The line will have a top speed of 186 mph, although it isn't expected to be open along its entire route until 2005.

The shareholding company was founded in 1991 by decree from Russian President Boris Yeltsin. Serving as deputy director-general of the company is Eugeney Sotnikov, who said planners would seek to obtain "unconventional financing" by issuing stock, by taking on long-term loans with repayment from operating revenues, and through project financing by participating foreign firms.

This is less a privatized entity than a state corporation because the Russian government holds 51 percent of the equity, and other shareholders include city governments. "Founder shareholders were the city administrations of Moscow and St. Petersburg, the Russian government, the government of the Leningrad area, and the October Railway," reported *Railway Gazette International* editor Murray Hughes. "Capital took various forms, including land and property, and other shareholders included Systra of France, Lonrho, and Nalex, a civil engineering company."

Bonds also are employed as a financing mechanism, with the company raising $23 million from such sales in 1996 and planning additional sales annually for five more years. With support from the Russian

---

*Armenia, Azerbaijan, Belarus, Estonia, Georgia, Kyrgyzstan, Latvia, Lithuania, Moldova, Tajikistan, Turkmenistan, and Uzbekistan.

Finance Ministry and the Central Bank, they are in effect government-guaranteed bonds.

Elsewhere in Russia, public and private entities hold shares in another hybrid corporation, Gelleflint. *Railway Gazette International* called it "the first privately promoted railway to open in Russia for over 80 years" as it completes its line in Karelia, which lies east of Finland. It will carry freight between northeast Russia and Finnish ports in the Gulf of Bothnia.

Russia is demonstrating that it can induce private investment in a visionary high-speed rail project as well as in a new freight line. Clearly, the nation is beginning to lure private capital for rail projects. That is remarkable for what was once the center of Communist power. Russia's efforts are being watched by the Czech Republic and Estonia as they seek ways to privatize their railways.

South America

Argentina

After Carlos Menem was elected president of Argentina in 1989, the government passed laws that forced privatization of its telephone and electric-power systems and many other institutions. In aviation, Aerolineas Argentinas was sold, and the nation is moving to privatize fifty-nine airports.

Argentina had serious problems with its national railroad, the Ferrocarriles Argentinos (FA), a money-losing operation that suffered from deferred maintenance, weak management, and a loss in market share. According to Jorge H. Kogan and Louis S. Thompson, writing in *Japan Railway and Transport Review*, "There was no further hope for a company that was mainly a provider of surplus employment and uneconomic services, subject to political pressure, and strongly influenced by workers' unions, suppliers, and local authorities. There were two options: let the situation continue until FA collapsed, or do something drastic."

Kogan helped develop the general strategy for restructuring the Argentine railways, and Thompson holds the position of railway advisor to the World Bank, where he is involved with railway lending activities. In 1991 Argentina's railway system received a $300 million loan from the World Bank to invest in rail facilities and make severance payments, actions designed to attract buyers.

Planners separated the railroad into smaller units offered as thirty-year concessions to those willing to pay fees to the government and to finance capital improvements. In return, the concessionaire would receive contracts to operate over state-owned tracks, obtain a set number of cars and locomotives, and of course have the opportunity to profit from operations. The objectives were to reduce the railroad's financial burden on the public treasury, improve service, rebuild run-down facilities, and develop a nucleus of private-sector rail managers.

The first concession was issued in 1991; the new operators showed that demand for rail service existed, and freight traffic returned. Within two years, four additional freight concessions were issued.

The concession process was used for local passenger service, but was altered to include subsidies. Now four concessionaires run the large Buenos Aires commuter and subway networks, which carry more traffic than the systems in New York City. One concession is held by a team that includes the Burlington Northern Santa Fe Railroad.* Ridership is up in Buenos Aires, as is on-time performance.

Most long-distance passenger trains in Argentina were struggling to survive in a common-carrier mode and incurred large deficits. The national government stopped all subsidies for them, and about 70 percent of the passenger trains were discontinued. Those worth saving devolved to the provinces, which now pay fees to the freight lines to keep them operating.

There was an opportunity, however, to franchise one intercity

---

*Other North American railroads have been active as bidders, advisors, or operators in Argentina, namely Conrail, Iowa Interstate Railroad, Montana Rail Link, and Canadian National.

passenger operation. Frank Richter in *Progressive Railroading* reported on the route between Buenos Aires and the coastal city of Mar del Plata: "That is one of the two higher-density passenger corridors in the country. It has the largest patronage to and from both ends of the 325-mile distance. There also is a potential to obtain a larger share of the market with better equipment and faster schedules." The route carries 1.8 million passengers annually, and according to South American rail expert Enrique Garibotto, writing in *Railway Gazette International,* "Additional revenue is generated on this line from the car-carrying train used by thousands of motorists wishing to avoid driving on Route 2, considered to be Argentina's most dangerous highway." Those factors made the line attractive for concession.

By 1995 *International Railway Journal* reported that Ferrobaires, the company set up to take over those passenger trains, "has turned a heavily loss-making run-down operation into a growing business which no longer requires a subsidy. As a result, the government now plans to privatize it. . . . Astonishingly, Ferrobaires is now financially self-sufficient, requiring no subsidy from the central government. It has even been able to introduce new passenger services."

Argentina's rail privatization program has saved the government more than $300 million a year, has terminated useless services, reduced freight transport costs, and has improved rail passenger service in an area where running passenger trains makes sense. Indeed, a rather conventional corridor passenger service combined with auto-ferry service is operating at a profit.

Elsewhere, Brazil has approved railway privatization. The government is carving the system into six segments available as thirty-year concessions. In 1996 two consortiums won concessions, and each time RailTex of San Antonio, Texas, was a member of the winning team. A third franchise was awarded to a group that will construct a new freight railroad, making it the first Brazilian railway in this century to be built with private financing. The countries of Bolivia, Chile, Colombia, Costa Rica, Guatemala, and Peru are beginning the rail privatization process; Paraguay, Uruguay, and Venezuela may follow suit. Meanwhile, a joint venture that includes the Kansas City Southern Railway won a concession to run the Panama Railroad Company.

Asia/Far Pacific

New Zealand

In 1990 New Zealand privatized its petroleum, telecom, and banking companies. The transformation was primarily achieved by a Labour government caught in a financial crisis brought on by too many state subsidies. In transportation, the government sold Air New Zealand and New Zealand Rail to international consortiums.

The railroad sale brought $220 million from Tranz Rail Ltd., a group whose members include the Wisconsin Central, Berkshire Finance (a U.S. investment firm), and Fay, Richwhite & Co., Ltd. (a New Zealand bank). The national government continues to own the railway's land.

"Tranz Rail's revenues have increased by 15 percent in the two years since privatization, a sea change from the long-term decline in revenues experienced for many previous years," said Wisconsin Central president Edward A. Burkhardt in *Railway Gazette International.* "Tranz Rail shares will be floated within the next few years. After a market in the stock is established, we will start an employee stock purchase program similar to that used by WC." Moreover, in its first year as a privatized entity, the railroad showed a net profit of $23 million, a little more than double the result for the previous year.

About passenger service, Burkhardt said, "The railroad operates commuter services in Wellington and Auckland under contract to the local regional councils, and one of the few unsubsidized and profitable fleets of long-distance passenger trains in the world." Of course, "long distance" in tiny New Zealand would be short distance in the United States.

Australia

Australia sold its national air carrier, Qantas Airways Ltd., in 1995 and reaped $1.07 billion for its treasury. Finance Minister Kim Beazley said, "The completion of the sale would help the government achieve its target of a budget surplus of $531 million for the financial year to June 1996"—note that this government is privatizing transport companies to achieve a budget *surplus*.

In rail privatization, Australia plans to keep right-of-way ownership in the public domain but privatize operations through "open access," whereby qualified parties can run trains over tracks for a fee. Australia appears intent on breaking up Australian National Railway (which really isn't national in scope); to facilitate privatization, the government has agreed to acquire rail debts. The privatization proposal has attracted the interest of U.S. companies—Burlington Northern Santa Fe, CSX, Kansas City Southern, RailTex, and Western Rail.

Australia wants private-sector financing for a new high-speed passenger rail line between Sydney and Melbourne via Canberra. One proposal, called the VFT for "very fast train," failed several years ago when the government declined to grant tax concessions. Subsequently five consortia are competing to build the rail link. Meanwhile the future of Australia's famous long-distance trains—the Sydney–Perth *Indian Pacific*, Adelaide–Alice Springs *Ghan*, and Adelaide–Melbourne *Overland*—is open to question.

Australia is demonstrating that it will privatize existing and new rail facilities, an interesting development in a country with freight and passenger traffic that is comparatively light when judged against volumes in the United States.

China

Even Communists can privatize in a limited way, as long as it's called "economic liberalization." Instead of selling enterprises outright, China has sold minority stakes in many industries. Privatization headway was evident late in 1996 when two companies, Hainan Airlines and China Eastern Airlines, announced they planned to offer stock on the Shanghai, Hong Kong, and New York exchanges.

China's Ministry of Railways drafted a plan in 1994 to allow commercial railroads to be operated independently by joint ventures. Wrote Mike Knutton of *International Railway Journal*: "One of the boldest moves in using market mechanisms has been the establishment of autonomous railways such as the Guangzhou–Shenzhen Railway Corporation and the Sanshui–Maoming Railway Corporation. Both tailor freight rates and passenger fares to prevailing market conditions and generate sufficient funds to qualify for loans and part-finance developments such as the Guangzhou–Shenzhen quasi-high-speed railway."

The lesson from China is that it recognizes the importance of private-sector financing, so much so that it is planning its first rail public offering—a part-interest in the Guangzhou–Shenzhen Railway. As with developments in Russia, a decade ago no one could have predicted this would happen.

Japan

Rail privatization in Japan is nothing short of astonishing. Former Prime Minister Yasuhiro Nakasone initiated the privatization of the Japanese National Railroad (JNR), a mixture of profitable high-speed lines built to standard gauge and money-losing services on narrow-gauge lines.

Japan privatizes differently than does Europe and South America, where national systems generally are put through a vertical separation, which means track and infrastructure ownership is assigned to one entity while operations go to others. In Japan the privatization is horizontal; the JNR was divided by geographical region, with infrastructure and operations retained in the same entity.

That choice probably was influenced by the existence for years prior to the breakup of the JNR of more than one hundred private railway companies, fifteen of which are major operations. Each manages infrastructure and operations quite well through a single management structure. Because most of these companies operate at a profit, a bias existed in favor of keeping infrastructure and operations together in Japan's privatization process.

What is convenient about examining Japan is that same-country comparisons can be made between public and private railroad operations. In 1985, for example, JNR personnel expenses amounted to 78 percent of total revenues, compared with about 40 percent for private railways. This was a remarkable level of efficiency for the private railways because some of them operate many labor-intensive commuter trains in the Tokyo, Osaka, and Nagoya metropolitan areas.

"Privately owned railways flourish in the metropolitan areas, where captive commuter traffic at high densities makes them quite profitable," maintain Professors Tony Ridley and Francis Terry. "Many of them are owned [by] or allied with diversified businesses, though it does not appear that there is more than a marginal element of cross-subsidy. The Tobu Railway, for example, operating in the northern Tokyo region, is part of a group of eighty-plus companies. . . . It is a leader in triple track construction in which it has invested to cope with tidal commuter flows." The Tobu Railway operates at a profit.

Other examples of successful private railways are the Keihin Electric Express Railway (with an annual patronage of an astonishing 440 million commuter trips in the Tokyo area); the passenger-only Hanshin Electric Railway in the Osaka-Kobe region (carrying 250 million passengers annually); the Kobe Electric Railway, which develops housing communities and provides railway services to them; and the Odakyu Electric Railway, which lures businesses to locate along its line (which ensures a steady rise in passengers).

The Odakyu Electric Railway carries 1.95 million customers *daily*, and its business continues to grow. It has renovated stations to permit longer and higher-capacity express trains, put new commuter equipment in service, increased train frequency, converted single tracks to double tracks in suburban areas, and acquired land for a new line—all since 1993.

Ridley and Terry report that passengers help pay for capacity expansion because "fare rises are specifically permitted to help finance certain large future projects; the additional revenue is kept in a Specific Urban Railway Fund, where it earns interest tax free for ten years. Four major private railways have already started construction of additional double track lines using this arrangement." The central and local governments also contribute varying amounts to new line construction, depending on circumstances, but private investment is a major force.

Japan created a Provisional Committee on Administrative Reform that in the early 1980s proposed JNR privatization. This was a giant step for Japan because the railroad had been nationalized since 1906 and was accustomed to running trains for an undefined "public benefit." Moreover, the JNR as an entity was established in 1949, and over time it grew into Japan's largest employer. Its privatization appeared to be an impossible task.

"The committee concluded that restoring JNR's financial health was impossible as long as it was operated as a centralized, nationwide public corporation," wrote Koichiro Fukui in the World Bank's *Japanese National Railways Privatization Study*. "By 1987, JNR was broken up into six regionally based railroad passenger companies and a seventh company to handle freight transportation for the entire country. The major portion of JNR's debt, which had reached $286 billion by the end of 1986 (greater than the combined national debts of Brazil and Mexico), was reassigned to the newly created JNR Settlement Corporation along with any surplus real estate of JNR and the shares of the newly created [regional companies]."

The JNR Settlement Corporation has made little progress in liquidating its debt as scheduled, partially because Japan tries to sell stocks in privatized companies at unrealistically high prices. The early 1990s economic slowdown and depressed state of the Japanese stock market also have been factors. Other revenues failed to materialize when the corporation was unable to sell land, because of excessive political interference. These factors contribute to troubles at the JNR, which may have to be rescued through a government bailout.

Of the six regional railroads that were created, the three largest are named, simply, JR East, JR Central, and JR West and are located on the main island of Honshu. Three others are known for the islands they are located on: JR Hokkaido to the north, and JR Shikoku and JR Kyushu in the south. Also, the Japan Freight Railway Company was established and pays fees to operate over the six railroads.

The three on the main island are operating at a profit. Successes are somewhat limited on the smaller island lines because they carry less traffic in their rural areas. Thus, government subsidies continue for these lines, but at a lower rate than the JNR needed. JR Freight also operates at a loss, and government officials are considering selling it to trucking companies.

The good news far outweighs the bad news.

The World Bank study concluded that the restructuring resulted in passenger and cargo traffic increases; a drastic drop in the number of employees, from 414,000 to 191,000 (a 53.9 percent reduction); improved efficiency; and reduced subsidies. The three main JR railways (East, Central, and West) improved passenger service by increasing the number of Bullet Trains operated per day from what the JNR offered in its final year.

"Before restructuring, the annual subsidy from the government to JNR reached $4.9 billion on average," wrote Fukui. "After restructuring, the annual subsidy to JR companies has been drastically reduced. In 1990, for example, the subsidy to JR companies was only $48 million, and $1.2 billion including the JNR Settlement Corporation. [In 1992] profitable JRs paid $1.2 billion in corporate tax to the government. . . . The privatization process of JNR can be judged to have been successful." Some of the inherited liabilities of the JNR Settlement Corporation are expected to be borne by the public; hence, the subsidies.

Privatization has reinvigorated independent development efforts so much that *International Railway Journal* headlined one story JAPANESE DEVELOP NEW TRAINS GALORE. The new JR companies designed a variety of experimental trains—a JR East train was named STAR 21, an acronym for "Superior Train for Advanced Railways of the Twenty-First Century." This train is expected to lead to a model that can run faster than the French TGV. Not to be outdone, JR Central ran its experimental Series 300X Bullet Train at 274.6 mph on July 26, 1996, setting a new Japanese rail speed record. JR West meanwhile launched its WIN 350 experimental train.

Planners would not let privatization impinge upon Japanese railway's commitment to technological advances. Research efforts were shifted to a Railway Technical Research Institute (RTRI), formed as a foundation authorized by the Ministry of Transport. According to Kai-nen Watanabe, the RTRI executive director, most of the operating funds come from the JR railways in proportion to their transport revenues.

Rail passenger traffic growth is healthy, especially considering that Japan has been in a recession. The average growth in passenger traffic in the JNR's last five years averaged 1 percent, but each of the JR railways has shown growth ranging from 2.3 percent to 7.2 percent in their first four years of operation. Another index is that the peak in JNR passenger traffic of 215.6 billion passenger-kilometers in 1974 was quickly exceeded by the six new companies in only their second year of operation.

According to a report by the Japan Transport Economics Research Center, "Passengers seem to be happy with the services offered, because, among other reasons, service frequencies have increased, the attitude of employees towards passengers has been considerably improved, and stations and the trains themselves are kept cleaner." Every railway had made passenger advances:

- JR West put newer *Nozomi* ("Hope") high-speed trains in service, which cut another twenty minutes from already fast Tokyo–Osaka schedules.

- JR East inaugurated the *Narita Express*, which links Tokyo with Narita International Airport, where passenger demand is soaring; introduced new double-decker Bullet Trains; and will start high-speed train service to Nagano in time for the 1998 Winter Olympic Games.

- JR Central increased train frequency on the Tokyo–Osaka *Shinkansen,* the world's busiest high-speed intercity rail line, and in 1995 its Bullet Train ridership was at an all-time high of 128 million passengers. The railroad also extended electrification on a conventional line and rolled out an experimental superconducting maglev train onto a just-completed test track.

With revenues up and costs down, JR East, JR Central, and JR West have become commercial successes.

JR East is Japan's largest railway company, serving more than 16 million passengers daily on more than twelve thousand daily high-speed, conventional, and commuter trains. Its operations are near-flawless, and *Fortune* found cause to praise its business sense. Since 1990 the railway has made a profit of about $500 million a year, achieved through productivity increases and higher passenger revenues, without raising fares. In the process, it also reduced its debt.

In its seventh year of privatization, JR East applied to list its stock on four domestic exchanges. It planned to sell half of the 4 million shares held by the JNR Settlement Corporation, with the first 600,000 to be auctioned off, and the remaining 1.4 million to be sold at a fixed price. Analysts praised the railroad for being so much more efficient that its JNR predecessor and recommended the stock as a "buy and hold" because of the company's expected solid if unspectacular growth.

Meeting the listing requirements of the stock exchange in terms of net assets, net profit, and dividends, JR East was listed on October 26, 1993. Shares were offered at $3,655 but immediately skyrocketed in value 57.8 percent. Within hours trading was suspended because the volume overloaded exchange computers. This was Japan's biggest listing in six years, and the JNR Settlement Corporation had to release another half million shares for sale to ease the mismatch between sellers and buyers. The public offering for JR East netted nearly $10.1 billion for a 63 percent ownership interest—more than twice the $4.7 billion achieved in a public offering for 100 percent of Japan Air Lines.

By January 1995 JR Central and JR West were profitable and wanted to launch public offerings. That was not to be, however, as a major earthquake in the Kobe area damaged the Japanese economy, wrecked railroad facilities, and reduced railroad earnings. By summer the Tokyo Stock Market was in the doldrums as the Japanese economy suffered the fourth year of its worst postwar slump. Stock prices were flat.

In October 1996 JR West went public. Analysts called the sale the making of a "blue-chip stock." The reasons? The company operates "lucrative" Bullet Train routes, offers an attractive price-earnings multiple, and holds promise of a dividend yield above Japan's market average. Sales were reasonable considering that overall Japanese investor demand remained weak.

Even in Japan not all passenger trains survived the privatization process; some trains continued running only with support from local governments.

"JNR abolished eighty-three local lines," said Yasushi Tanahashi, president of the Japan Railway Construction Public Corporation. "More than half of them were changed to bus lines and the rest were placed under the management of third-sector railway companies funded by local governments."

Japanese rail privatization is working out well. To commemorate JR East's tenth anniversary in 1997, company president Masatake Matsuda said, "From the standpoint of business results, I think all of the JR Group companies have generated results that have far exceeded initial plans. . . . [We have a] determination never again to return to the dark memories of JNR's final years, when the organization was, in effect, bankrupt. Government-owned corporations and other national agencies have only vague objectives. . . . When the government comes to us with a request, we ask for measures to ensure the profitability of any undertaking. If necessary, we can even refuse requests. For example, we have more than once refused requests to construct a [new line] because studies show it would not be profitable for decades. However, government agencies and corporations do not have the freedom to turn down such projects or to declare bankruptcy. Therefore, our reorganization as a private-sector company has given us an extremely well-defined objective."

Japan has served as an inspiration to Taiwan, which hopes to raise significant private-sector funds to help finance a new high-speed passenger line; to Malaysia, which sold Malayan Railways to a joint venture made up of companies in construction, finance, communications, and real estate; and to Thailand and Vietnam, now seeking private-sector investment in rail facilities.

North America

Canada

The Canadian National Railway (CN) privatization process began in 1993 when Paul M. Tellier, a former official with Prime Minister Brian Mulroney's government, became the line's president. Soon after, a study concluded that less than 40 percent of the existing Canadian railway network was required to maintain a financially viable rail system that met most transport needs. By 1995 Canadian transport minister Douglas Young presented legislation to Parliament to privatize CN, predicting that it would become "the biggest share issue in Canadian history," which in fact it was. The government retained ownership of many CN real estate assets and allocated funds to help pay down CN debt before privatization. With the stage set, the initial public offering sold 83.8 million shares, with proceeds of approximately $2.3 billion going to the national government.

Tellier's assessment after one year was justifiably upbeat (the following figures are in Canadian dollars): "CN is now investor-owned and investor-driven. But the charges are much more profound than that. We had to improve productivity. Four years ago, we ran 3 million revenue-ton-miles-per-employee. Today, it is over 4 million. We had to improve the bottom line. Four years ago we lost nearly $100 million dollars on $3.9 billion of revenue. Last year we made a profit of $350 million on $4.1 billion. And the price of our shares has doubled in value."

The CN is essentially a freight-only railroad—the only one presented in these examples—but its experience is worth considering. After all, like its passenger-carrying cousins, its success depended on a fundamentally different approach to the way it conducts its business. As a nationalized entity, its service was merely acceptable and it required subsidies. Now its service is greatly improved and it operates at a profit, important gains from privatization.

The well-orchestrated move of Canadian National to the private sector was noted by *Railway Age*. Its editor, Luther Miller, wrote that Paul Tellier was named the magazine's 1997 Railroader of the Year "for his leadership in preparing the railroad for privatization and then guiding it to levels of efficiency and profitability that many thought would take far longer to achieve."

In the passenger arena, Canada has more gumption that the United States for discontinuing financially hopeless trains. Ottawa slashed the route structure of VIA Rail, Canada's equivalent of Amtrak, as officials admitted that its long-distance trains could no longer survive in a common-carrier role. Yet, a private operator, Rocky Mountain Railtours, enjoys continued success with its seasonal land-cruise trains. In late 1996 the company announced that a *Rocky Mountaineer* thirty-seven cars long departed Vancouver with more than eleven hundred passengers—"This is the largest train in our company history, and the largest in the history of passenger train travel in western Canada."

With the CN privatization and VIA Rail discontinuances, evidence is available north of the border about what types of rail reforms work.

Mexico

Mexico has had an urgent need to restructure its economy and has privatized telecom, banking, television, satellites, and ports. In transportation it privatized the airlines *Aeromexico* and *Mexicana* and wants to award concessions to operate more than fifty airports.

Something had to be done about the Mexican National Railway system, which needed hundreds of millions of dollars in capital improvements and annual operating subsidies. Mexican President Ernesto Zedillo's administration drafted changes in the constitution to permit railway privatization, along with a plan to break up the national railroad into parts and offer them as concessions. United States Treasury Secretary Robert Rubin noted in a report to the Congress that Mexico was doing the right thing in carrying out reforms, including legalizing private investment in its railroads.

Mexico issues fifty-year concessions, with the option of fifty-year extensions, to those who will operate regional rail lines. By late 1996 a joint venture that includes the Kansas City Southern Railroad successfully bid $1.41 billion for what became known as Mexico's Northeast Railway. It owns a key line connecting Mexico City with Monterrey and Laredo. Privatization of additional Mexican rail lines is expected to occur through 1998.

Mexico has demonstrated an understanding that it had to ease railroad subsidy demands and also improve railroad efficiency to adapt to the demands shippers would make in light of the North American Free Trade Agreement. Officials knew that a public-sector organization would no longer work.

Amtrak Fails Privatization Tests

Recall that Amtrak president Tom Downs claimed to Congress that "we are probably the most privatized passenger railroad in the world." His assertion not only fails a comparison with the privatization examples outlined above but also fails the test of evidence as outlined below:

> *Stock Ownership Is Very Different.* Shares in companies that serve as rail franchise operators usually are traded on stock exchanges and are held by a wide variety of interests—individual shareholders, retirement funds, mutual funds, holding companies, partnerships, joint ventures, and others. The same could be said for shares in privatized companies that own rail infrastructure; entities like Britain's Railtrack, Japan's JR East, New Zealand's Tranz Rail,

and perhaps even China's Guangzhou–Shenzhen Railway. In comparison, Amtrak's nationalized status is beyond doubt: Amtrak's preferred shares are owned by the U.S. government and held by the U.S. Department of Transportation. Amtrak's common stock is considered by its owners to be worthless. Also, most privatized companies pay dividends to shareholders; Amtrak does not.

Track and Station Ownership. Several nations have privatized ownership of track, rights-of-way, and other rail infrastructure. Others have retained public ownership of the tracks or underlying property but have turned operations over to the private sector. But no rail privatization is leaving intact the structure Amtrak has in the Northeast Corridor, where it is the public owner of track *and* the public operator of the trains.

Maintenance Base Ownership and Operations. The first task many privatized railroads accomplish is to sell their repair facilities. In some cases, they simply shutter the maintenance bases and contract with companies to perform the work. Privatized railroads invariably find that such actions bring about improved equipment availability and declining maintenance costs. Amtrak, in spite of evidence that its maintenance facilities are inefficient, continues to own and operate sizable bases in Beech Grove, Indiana, and Wilmington, Delaware, along with locomotive- and car-servicing facilities in several cities. Amtrak has signed a maintenance agreement for its new *American Flyer* trains, an exception to its standard practice.

Rolling Stock Ownership. The rail privatization process often includes transfer of rolling stock to independent authorities, who then sell it to private interests or to franchise operators. In this category, it could be said that some limited privatization of Amtrak has occurred because its upcoming Northeast Corridor high-speed trainsets, along with other equipment, have been obtained through sale-leasebacks or similar arrangements.

Financing of New Tracks for High-Speed or Conventional Service. Britain, France, Germany, Russia, Japan, China, Taiwan, and Australia have various formulas in effect to induce private-sector underwriting of rail lines. Amtrak still relies on the U.S. Treasury to finance the Northeast Corridor upgrading and on state funds for work elsewhere.

These characteristics evident on foreign railroads are worth emulating in the United States, even though the process can be difficult. Those who have denationalized railroad organizations and commercialized rail functions have found that concessions are difficult to value, performance criteria are hard to formulate, unclear proposals can result in miscalculations by all parties, labor organizations resist change, and planners sometimes have to start the process all over when initial efforts fail.

Yet rail privatization is an unmistakable fact around the world—evident in industrial nations as well as struggling Third World countries. It is remarkable that debt-ridden South American countries as well as former Communist states have found ways to lure private financing into railroad freight and passenger services.

Indicators Support Partial Privatization

It is reasonable to reach these conclusions about a possible privatization of Amtrak.

The Factors That Justify Railway Privatization Exist in Amtrak. The problems of most public-sector railroads before privatization were excessive control by the government, slow reaction to changes in the marketplace, archaic labor practices, insensitivity to local needs, and excessive need for subsidies. Those are also Amtrak's problems.

Private Investment Can Be Lured to Fixed Infrastructure for High-Speed Rail Passenger Services. Other nations have projects that involve private-sector financing of new high-speed passenger facilities; the participants include airlines, banks, construction companies, and the public (through share offerings). Amtrak's operating losses, combined with its poor reputation, serves as a restraint to private financing of new infrastructure for which it will be the operator. Dismantling Amtrak would improve the environment for private-sector investment in passenger-related rail facilities.

Private-Sector Participation Can Be Obtained for Rail Passenger Operation. The range of franchising and concessioning arrangements varies widely between, say, the United Kingdom and Argentina. Yet, concessionaires consistently increase railroad revenues through innovative marketing practices; they also lower costs through improved efficiency. These factors reduce the burden of rail operations on public treasuries; and when subsidies remain, they are lower than they were for public entities. The closest the United States has to rail passenger franchising at this time are independent operators like the *American Orient Express* and the *Napa Valley Wine Train*. An end to Amtrak's monopoly status is essential if we are to expand the role of private operators beyond a few trains.

Americans Are Interested in Rail Privatization. The freight railroads in the United States have demonstrated that they are willing to consider new operating arrangements and bid for railroad franchises. These firms have gotten involved in passenger issues as they meet franchise terms in other countries, sometimes even running the passenger trains. If Americans are interested in rail franchise opportunities overseas, it is logical that some would be interested in similar ones at home.

Finally, two contrasts between privatized railroads and Amtrak are worth considering.

On a grand scale, in Japan the JR East Railway is building a new Bullet Train line to Nagano that will open in time for the 1998 Winter Olympic Games. Amtrak, however, was unable to arrange operation of a few extra passenger trains to Atlanta over existing railroads for the 1996 Summer Olympic Games.

On a more routine scale, in New Zealand a privatized entity is operating conventional passenger trains at a profit. Amtrak, with a much bigger passenger market, does not.

The nationalized Amtrak system is unable to provide the kind of train transportation that America needs at a price America can afford. It's time to start the Amtrak privatization and regionalization process.

An Amtrak Transition and Dissolution Plan

*"The role of government is to steer,
not to man the oars."*

—Steve Savas, privatization expert,
quoted in *The New York Times*

T he issue of Amtrak's dissolution is not *whether* but *how.*

Inducing the private sector and state governments to participate in the defederalization and breakup of Amtrak will require laws
and policies to be changed. The United States dampens innovation in
rail passenger service by preserving Amtrak and maintaining laws as
antiquated as the steam locomotives that were in use when the laws
were passed. We should change or repeal outright these antiquated
statutes, which are remarkably self-defeating, to foster sensible rail
service in areas where it is needed.

Amtrak knows it's headed for more trouble and fears that the power of its congressional life-support system is waning. Simply put, Amtrak fears for its life. A *Forbes* article by James R. Norman in 1995 reported on Amtrak's cash crisis and explored the ins and outs of a possible Amtrak bankruptcy proceeding. At the time, with a congressional stalemate over funding, House Transportation Committee chairman Bud Shuster and Railroad Subcommittee chairwoman Susan Molinari urged the Clinton Administration to develop a contingency plan for an Amtrak shutdown. That was when Amtrak president Thomas Downs admitted that Amtrak could be put in bankruptcy with relative ease.

The crisis passed, and later that year in *Passenger Train Journal* Downs said, "I don't think anyone has the stomach to try and willfully kill us off and dismantle us. . . . I don't think our danger is about someone intentionally killing us off. I think it is easier and far more likely in this environment in Washington to be killed by accident." Downs explained that congressional failure to appropriate subsidies "could easily mean that, by accident, we get lost." The media dubbed this the "Washington train wreck scenario."

The states know that Amtrak may not survive for long. Downs admitted in congressional testimony: "Several states don't want a contract like our 403(b) program anymore [a traditional way that states obtained regional train service from Amtrak]. They want a straight contract as if we were a vendor. They don't want anything other than very explicit costs and terms. They will contract for it, and that is the end of it. They don't want long-term contracts. Many states feel that we are an undependable partner. They don't want to depend on us for passenger rail service, and that is a very strong concern that we have about being a dependable partner for those states."

Downs, in an interview with the *Kansas City Star,* called himself a "public-sectorist." That would explain his notion that Amtrak might die because Washington was botching its job in the political arena instead of Amtrak failing in the commercial arena.

Yet, despite Amtrak's problems and its declining market share, Amtrak will fight any plan to privatize, regionalize, or otherwise dilute the organization. Every Washington bureaucracy fights to survive. A review of public comments by Downs gives an inkling of what some of Amtrak's survival arguments will be.

On March 27, 1996, he told a luncheon meeting at the National Press Club that "Amtrak is a new mode of transportation." How's that again? How can a system where the *majority* of Amtrak routes see trains operating on schedules slower than they were fifty years ago represent something new?

Downs claimed that "Amtrak has made steady progress toward revitalizing passenger train service throughout the United States." How? Where? Putting new coaches in operation is not the same as "revitalizing" a service. Amtrak's dismal revenue and ridership numbers fail to support Downs's assertion, with the exception of routes in New York, Wisconsin, Washington, and California (where the states have taken action) and in the Northeast Corridor (where federal investment has been underway since before Amtrak was born).

Sometimes Downs is more direct. That was evident after some freight railroad executives suggested Amtrak be closed down. William Vantuono of *Railway Age* reported that "Downs is not one to mince words. . . . He had this to say to those who feel that Amtrak doesn't have a right to exist and should drop dead: 'Get out of my face.' "

Amtrak's anxiety about survival is justified. Amtrak is sinking deeper; its losses in early fiscal year 1997 more than doubled over the same period a year earlier. The extra subsidy that Congress had given Amtrak was proving insufficient to cover the deficit. The latest cash crisis would further reduce Amtrak's system, and cutting an already skeletal long-distance network could lead to eventual elimination of the network.

"The railroad may be forced to borrow $60 million to $70 million to 'meet cash flow' needs through the year," according to *Wall Street Journal* reporter Anna Wilde Matthews. "Only twice before in its 27-year history has Amtrak had to borrow for this purpose, and this time it would be doing so when the rest of the travel industry is posting strong results."

Time for Reform and Phaseout

Amtrak is a strong candidate for breakup through privatization of the parts that can be operated profitably; regionalization of unprofitable yet socially desirable services, the fiscal responsibility for which would be transferred to state or regional agencies; and discontinuance of trains so useless that they offer neither profit nor social purpose.

The termination of such a nationalized organization and its disassembly requires congressional action. What follows is a general outline of how such a plan might work.

The first step Washington should take is to place Amtrak under a near-total moratorium on capital spending and to scale down Amtrak's operating subsidies. This plan will not satisfy those with an ideological attachment to privatization (where privatization is the end), but it should prove acceptable to those who believe in a practical application of privatization (where privatization is a means to an end). This plan will temporarily retain some present rail service by creating a transition period to work out problems relating to selling and transferring Amtrak assets.

As part of an Amtrak phaseout, Congress should prohibit additions to its money-losing route system; prohibit Amtrak from placing any further orders for rolling stock; require Amtrak to attempt to cancel orders for new equipment designed for long-distance trains (e.g., its order for diesel locomotives, many of which won't be needed after Amtrak's dissolution); cease capital funding except for safety-related items and Northeast Corridor Projects; and place ceilings on operating subsidies.

The moratorium on most Amtrak capital funding will do more than reduce Amtrak's drain on the public treasury. It will signal to the railroad industry and railway suppliers, potential private operators of passenger service, state and local governments, and federal bureaucracies and interest groups that Washington is serious about closing down Amtrak.

Congress should set a deadline for selling or transferring Amtrak's assets to private entities and nonfederal agencies. A deadline is the best way to overcome foot-dragging by Amtrak's bureaucracy and its friends in the Federal Railroad Administration, or at least compress delaying tactics into a manageable time frame.

Liquidation Questions

This structured phasing out of Amtrak will probably be applauded by those in Congress who are exasperated with Amtrak's never-ending problems. Some already have moved in this direction. In the summer of 1995, during another Amtrak financial crisis, Shuster and Molinari, in a letter to Transportation Secretary Federico Peña, asked the department to provide (1) contingency plans for liquidating Amtrak; (2) a legal analysis of the position of the department and the U.S. government as creditors if Amtrak is liquidated; (3) an assessment of Amtrak's assets and liabilities; and (4) the department's plans for future management and support of commuter and freight rail traffic as owner of the Northeast Corridor.

It isn't surprising that such questions had to be asked. If it's time to set up a new agency in Washington, countless professionals with such experience will step forward to assist. Seek help to dismantle an agency, however, and few people with the necessary expertise can be found. Fortunately, the Treasury Department has set up a new unit to help other federal agencies with privatization. The office seeks to maximize the return to taxpayers when government assets are sold to private interests.

The liquidation of Amtrak raises interesting questions, especially as Amtrak's assets are insufficient to repay everyone because Amtrak has a zero or perhaps a negative net worth.

The first parties to be paid would be the creditors (banks, other financial institutions), who hold more than $1 billion in debt securities on locomotives, passenger cars, and other assets. This equipment and property could be repossessed and sold, but the net from sales probably would be insufficient to repay creditors.

The second in line to be paid would be the federal government because it is a preferred shareholder and the holder of certain liens (including a 999-year lien on the Northeast Corridor). Even if the Northeast Corridor were sold (the Guilford Rail System of New England has offered to buy the line), some of the proceeds may be obligated to private lenders. No one at this time quite knows for sure.

The last to be paid would be the common shareholders, and they certainly would receive nothing. These shareholders (three railroads) are fully aware of this, which is why each has written down the value of their Amtrak shareholdings to one dollar and took tax write-offs years ago.

This wouldn't be the first time the taxpayers got soaked by Amtrak in a financial transaction. The government guaranteed repayment of nearly $900 million in loans to Amtrak in the 1970s, but in 1983 Washington relieved Amtrak of responsibility for repayment. The U.S. government now holds a $1.120 billion note for Amtrak, which matures in 2082. The debt, and the costs related to it, do not appear on Amtrak's books.

Some in Congress want to find a way to package and spin off federal assets. One concept is to create a Spending Reduction Commission, which has been proposed by Senator Connie Mack and Congressmen Dan Miller and David Minge. Regarding Amtrak, Congressmen Frank Wolf and Joe Barton proposed establishing a commission similar to the military base–closing commission that, according to Barton, "would look at all the Amtrak routes, come back to the Congress, and make recommendations on which routes might need to be eliminated."

While this and other proposals may be worthwhile for government assets in general, overseas experience suggests the need for a specific office to grapple with the complexities of privatizing, regionalizing, and terminating railroad services.

Whatever is created should be separate from Amtrak and the FRA, which are staffed by the very people who've made a mess of Amtrak. British privatization experts would warn that permitting such personnel to remain involved could enable Amtrak loyalists to sabotage the restructuring effort. The FRA for many years has failed to develop a meaningful Amtrak restructuring program. If the FRA failed to act constructively when it had the opportunity, then the termination of its jurisdiction over Amtrak is long overdue. In fairness, asking the FRA to be forward-looking probably was asking too much in the first place because its foremost responsibility is to oversee rail safety. Of the 750 employees at the FRA in 1996, about 560 were involved with safety.

Amtrak Transition Board

Washington needs to create an independent agency to carry out the complex mission of dismantling Amtrak. The agency could be modeled after the U.S. Railway Association that created Conrail from the ashes of bankrupt railroads, the British Office of Rail Passenger Franchising, the Japanese Railway Settlement Corporation, or perhaps some hybrid. The law creating the agency should mandate sunset dates for Amtrak and for the agency itself.

The name I propose for the agency is the Amtrak Transition Board (ATB). This office would serve as the Treasury Department's disbursing agent (instead of the FRA) for federal subsidies to Amtrak, be given audit powers over Amtrak similar to what the Transportation Department and General Accounting Office have, be responsible for designing and implementing a transition period in which trains are spun off to private-sector operators or regional agencies, plan and carry out the liquidation of Amtrak's assets, and eventually terminate Amtrak as an entity.

For operational purposes, the organization should have authority to hire staff and contract for services, issue requests for proposals and negotiate with proposers, sell or transfer by reasonable means Amtrak's fixed and rolling assets, and function as an advisor to private-sector or regional entities requiring assistance in taking over existing passenger trains or starting new ones.

The ATB would attempt to liquidate Amtrak's debt by selling Amtrak assets. It would carry out sales through an auction or by whatever means would maximize the return on investments in rolling stock, maintenance facilities, and the Northeast Corridor roadbed, tracks, stations, parking lots, and other property. The portion of private debt not repaid by asset sales, if any, would be financed through federal appropriations—an "Amtrak closing" cost never to be repeated. The latter would represent the federal taxpayers' final payment in a string of Amtrak subsidies that dates back to December 1970, when Washington paid to establish Amtrak's board of incorporators.

The ATB should be mindful of important rail-restructuring experience gained in other countries. Koichiro Fukui in the World Bank's *Japanese National Railways Privatization Study* offers lessons that can be useful to consider in Amtrak's case.

Plan Carefully. The JNR privatization was not carried out hastily; time needs to be available to debate issues, consider various measures, and implement with care.

Divide Short- and Long-Term Problems. The first phase involved reducing subsidies to the JNR. During the second phase, longer-term issues such as debt elimination and sale of surplus real estate were carried out.

Establish an Impartial Planning or Guidance Committee. When politics is involved, or when a fresh outlook is important, the use of dispassionate experts can help build consensus.

Break Up the Monolith and Treat Each of the Constituent Parts on Its Own Merits. The problems and solutions of one rail line are different from those of another, but this was never clear under the JNR structure. The breakup permitted individual entities to find solutions more appropriate to their particular conditions.

Make Replacement Institutions Fit the Market. Most passengers are carried within each of the individual passenger operations. JR

East, for example, is focused on conventional, especially suburban, traffic, while JR Central lives or dies by Bullet Train patronage.

Get the Incentives Right for Efficient Management. Unlike the old structure, each JR railway has incentives to maximize revenues and minimize costs, which serves as a barrier to incessant political interference. "However simple this may seem," wrote Fukui, "this is at the heart of a radical change in the corporate mentality of the railways."

Leave the Sins of the Past in the Past. The debt burden was apportioned so as not to sink any of the new companies. Further, many debts resulted from misbegotten governmental policies, and it seems inappropriate to burden the new companies with a disproportionate share of inherited liabilities.

Attack Problems and Institutions, Not People. The monolithic personnel problem was that the JNR essentially lacked commercial attitudes but had superb strengths in engineering and operating techniques. The transition to new companies was handled in a way that permitted a buildup in commercial attitudes and skills while retaining existing technical strengths.

Make Every Effort to Identify and Compensate the Losers. With few exceptions, those affected adversely by the change were identified early and fairly compensated.

Have the Right People in the Right Places. "With the old JNR management and labor union leaders remaining in the posts, the privatization process could not have been carried out successfully. Prime Minister Nakasone also understood that he had to replace those who could not support his policies. This type of restructuring could easily fail (or almost fail), if opponents to a new system are left in positions of power," concluded Fukui.

Market Demand Issues

Lessons from other nations suggest that certain prerogatives should not be delegated to the ATB. Its powers should *not* include the ability to order continued operation of any portion of an Amtrak route that becomes an "orphan"—a train that no private-sector or regional-government entity will take. If a route fails to show promise of profitability, and many Amtrak routes will, or fails a social-value test as applied by state or regional agencies, then the train would be discontinued. Countries as diverse as Japan and Argentina have discontinued passenger trains that failed to compete with air and road travel; the United States should, too.

Nor should the ATB establish a franchise process (although states will). Simply put, we should open rail passenger operations to the rough-and-tumble of the marketplace and depend on state initiatives—actions sure to horrify traditionalists. Those who elect to become providers of rail passenger service should be able to freely select their routes and price their services in accordance with market demand. Several potential operators will want routes that have a high probability of profit, and states will probably contract for regional operations where social and mobility concerns outweigh profitability.

In any event, the ATB would seek from the states an expression of their willingness to assume any part of Amtrak's operations. The board would order discontinuance of Amtrak service on such routes, but give the states time to establish a transition program. Failure by states to respond would mean that the ATB would order discontinuance of Amtrak service. (The states should not be placed in the politically awkward position of being required to state a refusal to assume responsibility for a service.)

If, for example, the ATB requested every state on the *Sunset Limited* route to express its intent to assume responsibility for the train in some fashion or other, and the states didn't respond, then the train would be discontinued at an early date to stop Amtrak's financial hemorrhaging.

What about railroads that want to obstruct passenger train operations on their lines? Anthony Haswell and many others would argue that railroads still have some obligation to the public because of their unique status. Thus, the U.S. government should retain residual power to compel railroads to be fair to new passenger entities. Perhaps the answer is to give post-Amtrak operators the right to appeal to the Surface Transportation Board those railroad decisions that appear to constitute price gouging or unreasonable denial of access to facilities.

Although it appears that many Amtrak routes are hopeless, no one at this time can say with certainty which routes or *portions* of routes should remain in operation. Ken Mead of the General Accounting Office has testified that "five of the forty-four routes, the ones in the Northeast and Southern California, account for over 50 percent of all riders, 56 percent of revenues, and 40 percent of cost." That's a logical starting point to figure out which parts of Amtrak's system are candidates for privatization.

Results can be surprising. Who would have predicted that Britain's cross-channel hovercraft ferry service, which lost money and was unwanted by the private sector, would become profitable after ownership was transferred (practically given) to employees? How many experts foretold that after Japanese privatization, the Bullet Trains would remain profitable even though fares weren't raised? In this country, how many economists forecasted that bankrupt eastern railroads would someday become a profitable Conrail system?

If a state elected to operate part of a route, then two events would help the state ease into the service. First, the state or its franchisee could be given preference in purchasing Amtrak rolling stock at a discount. Also, a federal subsidy could continue for that portion of the route on a gradually declining basis, a good-faith effort to help the state "buy time" to build ridership and revenue. A subsidized transition period for rail privatization is a procedure being used in Great Britain.

On railroads that are willing to cooperate with new private-sector providers or state transportation departments, initiating passenger rail service in place of Amtrak would involve negotiations over scheduling, liability coverage, and the level of charges the railroad would want for use of its tracks. The bottom line for the railroads is just that—the bottom line. The railroads can work with potential operators to make anything work that is in their mutual interests.

The ATB needn't be involved in proposals for advanced train systems, but without Amtrak, tomorrow's trains show promise. A study done for the California-Nevada Super Train Commission showed that Los Angeles–Las Vegas high-speed trains operating on new infrastructure would be profitable; a Price Waterhouse study concluded that private-sector operation of a high-speed Chicago–St. Louis line is possible, with revenues covering operating and maintenance costs and most investments needed to put the service in place.

Prospects for Selling the Northeast Corridor

The Northeast Corridor rail line is one of the most important transportation assets in the United States. It is the country's most important passenger line because of the high number of intercity and commuter passengers who rely on it—more than 70 million trips (mostly commuter) are taken over the line annually. These tracks also are vital to North American commerce generally and the freight railroad industry specifically, as they serve freight shipments to or from the Lower 48 as well as Canada and Mexico.

A debate will ensue about whether Amtrak's Northeast Corridor can be sold to private interests such as Guilford Rail System or should be transferred to a regional public authority. Yet profit is possible.

In 1993 *Railway Age* editor William C. Vantuono reported that Amtrak trains operating in the corridor are profitable on what is called an "above the rail" basis, even including a portion of maintenance. That was followed some time later by an Amtrak announcement that the *Metroliner* earned a profit. *Progressive Railroading* summarized it best: "It has taken many years and billions of dollars in new equipment and infrastructure, but at least one Amtrak passenger service is finally making money. Amtrak says its Northeast Corridor *Metroliner*s in fiscal

1996 became the first service in the company's 26-year history to post revenues that covered fully allocated costs of operation. *Metroliners* took in $1 for every 93 cents in costs, Amtrak says, to earn a record $155.7 million, 10 percent more than in fiscal year 1995." The *Metroliner* profit was $14 million on a fully allocated cost basis. Amtrak projections show the *Metroliner* will probably operate at a profit in future years as well, and Amtrak is convinced that the *American Flyer* trains will, too.

If Amtrak can achieve that performance, a private-sector operator more attuned to meeting consumer demands while improving efficiency should be able to do even better. Moreover, the property itself provides opportunities for commercial revenues. For example, MCI Communications, AT&T, and several other telecommunications companies have leased parts of Amtrak's right-of-way for placement of fiber optics lines. Washington Union Station, redeveloped and revitalized, has become an upscale shopping and dining "experience" that generates commercial rents considerably above the national average. Proposals by developers have revived talk of selling air rights over other busy terminals.

An objection might be made that privatizing the Northeast Corridor after it has been improved by taxpayers—despite whatever its sales price might be—is unwise because the line might become profitable in ways we're unable to visualize today. In such an eventuality, mechanisms exist to protect the public interest. Henry Gibbon wrote in *A Guide for Divesting Government-Owned Enterprises* that "it is not uncommon to build into sales processes an obligation on the part of the newly privatized company to reimburse the government a portion of any unanticipated profits that accrue from the sale of surplus property. This 'clawback' of gains is used to protect the government (and hence, the taxpayers) against under-valuation of assets."

Gibbon, editor of *Privatisation International*, encourages governments to seek advice on pricing and other aspects of asset sales from investment banks or accounting firms. Gibbon also explores issues such as a government's holding a "golden share" in assets, residual shareholding, and other mechanisms in selling a public asset. The point is that precedents and procedures for such transactions are being refined, making the sale of Amtrak's Northeast Corridor a more interesting proposition today than it would have been ten years ago.

The progress that Great Britain is beginning to experience with its Railtrack privatization is noteworthy. Britain managed to float stock in an enterprise that owns what was money-losing infrastructure, and that stock is increasing in value. One reason is that the government's initiative in improving key lines has enhanced the value of rail assets in the marketplace. That also is what Washington did with bankrupt railroads—Conrail went public only after the taxpayers rebuilt and rejuvenated its infrastructure.

Public Authority

On the other hand, should no buyers be found, or if the proposals to purchase are deficient, the federal government could simply *give* the line to the states (whose seven commuter railroads operate about 91 percent of the passenger trains on the corridor each year). A regional compact could own the Northeast Corridor and develop a service provider through a franchise process. Amtrak-watcher Anthony Haswell believes the Northeast Corridor is a candidate for privatization in the sense of private operations over an Authority-owned track. His view would be supported by European rail privatization experts.

Every major city along the Northeast Corridor line has already invested in the rail line, either by purchasing and improving parts of it or buying railcars that operate over it. The region's cities and states also support public transit authorities that operate commuter trains and carry out substantial rail capital projects. Thus, a cadre of professional talent is in place to deal with the issues relating to the transfer of Amtrak property to state or other public hands. New York is considering new options for financing regional train services and may establish a Tri-State Regional Transportation Authority and a Tri-State Infrastructure Bank or may give more power to existing agencies. Such a move can only further position it to play a key role in the disposition of the Northeast Corridor.

Further Corridor Improvements

Whatever arrangement finally evolves, the federal government's capital investment in the Northeast Corridor should continue until the line's disposition. While this suggestion is sure to agitate regionalists in the South and West who would lose Amtrak service, it is nonetheless a fact that the line is too vital to allow to deteriorate.

Further, national benefits accrue as electrified trains in this populated area help reduce air pollution, and their energy efficiency ranks them as one of the nation's few transport systems that help offset excessive dependence on costly petroleum imports. Moreover, other options to expand transport capacity in the region are few—for example, no new airport will ever be built in the cities of Boston, New York, Philadelphia, and Washington. Simply put, it would be foolhardy to stop Northeast Corridor upgrading at this juncture, an act that would cause more problems than it would solve.

Congressman John Mica said of the Northeast Corridor: "The long-term prospect of course is to turn [it] over to the private sector and to privatize some of these operations, but you can't make that step until you make the investment, until you make the commitment to improve [it]. No one is going to pick up an asset that is not an asset, that is sort of a mess and needs these capital-intensive improvements." That is a responsible perspective, especially because it comes from a congressman who represents not a Northeastern state but Florida.

Rolling Stock Disposition

A clearer case exists with Amtrak rolling stock: its locomotives and passenger cars can be sold. Various types and amounts of equipment will be required for use in the Northeast Corridor by a public authority or privatized franchise holder. States will probably want to purchase Amfleet coaches for regional service. Urban commuter agencies in need of additional capacity might also purchase Amtrak coaches;

sales are possible if the price is right, although the designs are less than ideal for commuter operations. Commuter authorities would want some of Amtrak's locomotives, as might some freight railroads.

Some states already own their own passenger coaches, allowing them to minimize equipment-acquisition problems should they launch independent regional service. Washington State owns Talgo trains; California designed and purchased a significant number of "California cars"; North Carolina and Pennsylvania own or will soon own passenger equipment that Amtrak uses in those states.

The biggest demand may develop for Amtrak's mail and express cars. The value of Amtrak contracts with the U.S. Postal Service in fiscal year 1996 was $66 million, and most of that mail moves on overnight Amtrak trains. The freight railroads could move these shipments on their priority trains, many of which also move mail, and Amtrak's equipment could become an addition to their fleets.

The most difficult portion of Amtrak's fleet to sell will be its sleeping cars. While some could be sold to land-cruise train operators, the disposition of the remainder is a question. Traditionally, some American passenger train equipment was sold in secondhand condition to Mexico and South American countries, but it is unlikely that Amtrak's sleeping cars will follow their ancestors, because the market is evaporating south of the border for long-distance trains. Amtrak's sleeping cars could be transformed into coaches, although at some expense. Quite possibly sleeping cars will be sent to the scrap heap because of a lack of buyers. This is an example of how a moratorium on new car purchases could save American taxpayers from financing procurement of assets with questionable value.

Thorny issues, these. Should an ATB be created, it will face numerous challenges as its sets about its task. It will require a tough staff— one that can resist brickbats motivated by those resistant to change. To succeed, the ATB needs strong support from more than just the executive and legislative branches of government, it needs the backing of American taxpayers who want to see Washington liquidate what needs to be liquidated.

New Rail Passenger Environment

What about passenger trains in a post-Amtrak world?

The United States is faced with two choices:

If Washington leaves outdated laws in place, the result will be a muted effort to run rail passenger service in Amtrak's place. Yes, a Northeast entity in one form or another will continue and will probably improve trains in the region, a few additional land-cruise trains will start, and several states will feel compelled to run regional service.

Or Washington can be bold. Our nation can undertake long-overdue changes in laws and induce a thriving set of private-sector and regional train operations.

Should the latter option be chosen, the most urgent need will be to reduce the costs of operating passenger trains, much of which are labor-related. Amtrak's salaries, wages, and benefits in fiscal year 1995 totaled $1.24 billion, or almost 53.8 percent of its nearly $2.306 billion in total expenses. Remove interest and depreciation, however, and that leaves about $2.028 billion in operating costs, with the percentage of labor-related costs climbing to 61 percent. This amount is surprisingly high considering that in recent years rail labor made some cost-saving concessions though changes in work rules.

Lower labor costs do not necessarily mean lower pay. In an interview dealing with contracting for services, Steve Savas pointed out to Michael Allen of the *Wall Street Journal* that "it is a common fallacy to believe that the savings through competitive contracting come from lower wages. That is simply not true in the general case. A major study by the National Commission on Employment Policy in the late eighties shows that there is little statistical difference between the two. In fact, the real savings from contracting out come from increased productivity, not from lower wages."

Savas points out in *Privatization: The Key to Better Government* that "an examination of Amtrak's labor productivity shows profound differences when compared to that of four private railroads." He cited a study showing that Amtrak track crews installed fewer crossties than private railroad track crews, with the railroads being almost ten times more efficient. In a comparison of rail removal, private railroads were eight times more efficient than Amtrak. Said Savas, "Assuming that all other relevant factors were essentially constant, the private firms were vastly more productive than Amtrak when it came to track maintenance work."

But more than improved efficiency is necessary—much more.

Labor laws boost costs unreasonably to the point that they can be deal-breakers to entrepreneurs interested in replacing Amtrak services. The laws are the Railway Labor Act (its labor-protection provision in particular, and the act overall), the Federal Employers' Liability Act, and the Railroad Retirement Act.

Railway Labor Act—Labor Protection

This law affects the breakup of Amtrak as well as the start-up of new companies.

Dismantling Amtrak under existing laws would set off an employee-severance package that would be absurdly costly to the nation's taxpayers. It is difficult to believe, but a furloughed Amtrak employee is entitled to full wages for as long as six years. Congressmen Joel Hefley of Colorado and Joe Barton of Texas want to change that. Says Hefley: "One of the most onerous regulations imposed on Amtrak is the Railway Labor Act. It requires Amtrak to offer a generous severance package, worth one year's salary for each year worked up to six years, to any employee who is laid off because a route has been discontinued. Further, if Amtrak wants to move a worker more than 30 miles from his or her present job, the employee can refuse to comply and opt instead for the six-year severance package. Needless to say, Amtrak shuts down few train routes even though most of them are big money-losers."

Hefley is correct. These payments are such a significant liability that merely the threat of their kicking in has been used for years as an argument against discontinuing long-distance trains.

Barton is seeking a legislative remedy: "I want to reduce the six-year severance package down to six months. If we terminated all twenty-four thousand Amtrak employees, and we are not advocating that at all, but if that were to happen, it would cost $3 billion in severance. There is no other industry in the world we can find that gives one year of severance pay up to six years. The airline industry for some of their management employees has a six-month severance package. The parcel post system has three months. The aerospace and defense industries average about one and a half months, and bus line employees get no severance at all. So what I want to do is take the severance requirement down to six months, which would still by industry standards be the most generous in the United States." Barton and Hefley also would eliminate the 30-mile rule.

The $3 billion in estimated severance costs is disputed by Amtrak, which gives varying figures. A March 14, 1995, letter from Amtrak to Congress said that "if Amtrak was completely shut down," the liability for all current employees would range from $2.1 billion to $5.2 billion, depending upon circumstances. Amtrak has also warned that "Amtrak's assets would be insufficient to pay the labor protection claims, and Amtrak's employees would look to the federal government for payment. Thus, despite the termination of national rail passenger service, the federal taxpayer would be required to fund a multi-billion dollar bailout for Amtrak."

Such a situation is unacceptable. Not only does it make downsizing Amtrak more difficult, it will also make privatization and regionalization difficult.

These provisions apply to existing services, but rail labor leaders—in one of the most shortsighted actions imaginable—have demanded that these provisions apply to new high-speed rail systems. The demand stunned state officials and private-sector developers and has been a factor in discouraging investment in high-speed lines. In other words, the *creation* of railroad jobs has been stymied because of labor's demand that protection provisions apply, should the job ever be *lost*. This stance has restrained public and private investment in rail in the United States.

State officials active in developing non-Amtrak proposals are alarmed by labor's proposals. Florida Transportation Secretary Ben Watts, in an appeal to Congress, suggested that state or private franchise applicants be exempted from labor-protection requirements. "Florida and thirty-five other states have to varying degrees constitutional or statutory prohibition against guaranteeing labor protection." Charles Smith of Florida's rail office added, "Negotiating with railroads, the franchisee, contractors, and the federal government on this will be horrendous."

Congress did not offer labor protection to the more than 150,000 Defense Department and other federal civil servants who have lost their jobs in downsizings since 1993. Washington has not imposed any labor protection on companies that plan to furlough thousands of workers. Virtually every American, regardless of industry or occupation, has no labor-protection plan. It is appropriate, fair, and reasonable to ask Congress to terminate such absurd protections for Amtrak employees. Congressman Barton's proposal to reduce rail job-protection coverage to six months is more than generous; labor should graciously accept it.

Should this effort fail, another approach is needed. To induce the greatest number of new entrants possible into the rail passenger arena, rail labor-protection provisions should at least be amended to exclude from coverage employees of any new operator. Further, states that wish to launch regional passenger service should also be excluded from the requirements.

Railway Labor Act—General

Railroads and airlines come under the Railway Labor Act (RLA) instead of the National Labor Relations Act, which governs all other industries and labor organizations.

Patrick J. Cleary, prior to his departure from the National Mediation Board, asked in a speech, "Should airlines and railroads be segregated from the rest of U.S. industry in their treatment under labor law?" He questioned the wisdom of the RLA scheme, pointing out that on average about two and a half years are needed to complete the mediation process in railroad industry labor disputes. Cleary's initiative was appropriate because times have changed significantly since Congress passed the law in 1926, a law that has rarely been amended since.

To consider the RLA's deficiencies, note the views of E. Hunter Harrison, president of the Illinois Central Railroad, who wrote in *Progressive Railroading,* "I believe the Railway Labor Act is antiquated and actually hinders the process of reaching timely agreement. While this is a minority opinion among industry's management and labor, the fact that presidential and congressional intervention has become routine and predictable speaks to the failure of the process." He added that the RLA perpetuates adversarial relationships between labor and management and is an impediment to progressive labor relations going forward into the twenty-first century.

Congress should consider exempting new rail operators from the Railway Labor Act and placing them under the National Labor Relations Act.

Federal Employers' Liability Act

Early in this century, when management had a callous attitude toward employee welfare and safety, working on the railroad was an invitation to death and dismemberment. Although the safety records of railroads today are better than ever, an old safety-related law remains on the books.

The law is an anachronism called the Federal Employers' Liability Act (FELA), an injury compensation law. FELA was passed in 1908 and represented major progress in its time, as laws then denied meaningful protection to workers. Railroads have been and remain the only industry subject to its provisions. Since FELA's passage, all fifty states have chosen to enact no-fault workers' compensation laws based upon economic loss. They have shunned FELA because it is an unusually expensive tort-based system.

Data from the Association of American Railroads is disturbing: "Despite shrinking rail employment and fewer injuries, FELA costs keep going up. In 1981, the first full year railroads operated in a competitive environment under the Staggers Act, payout for FELA claims was $399 million; by 1993, payout had grown to $991 million—a 249 percent increase. Meanwhile, employment declined by 51 percent and the number of injuries fell by 68 percent." Under FELA, an injured worker usually must prove the railroad to be at fault before collecting for an injury, and a lower burden of proof exists than under workers' compensation laws. This means that injuries foster mistrust between employees and employers, and simple claims in turn become costly lawyers' battles.

FELA is a costly aberration. In a perfect world it would be repealed and railroad workers would be put under state workers' compensation laws just like everybody else. Unfortunately, Washington experts say there is little likelihood that the statute will be repealed, because of its favored status among special interests—especially FELA-savvy claims lawyers.

This is another counterproductive law because it reduces prospects for inducing investment in rail passenger service. First, the arcane nature of FELA can intimidate nonrailroad businesses. Thus, airlines or tour operators might decline to join a rail venture based on the costs of administering a negligence-based claims program and the unreasonable awards by courts for legitimate claims. Second, the product being offered—in this case, transportation by a passenger train—would be handicapped by a higher cost basis due to FELA, while all the competitors to that train are under more reasonable workers' compensation laws.

Failing repeal of FELA, a necessary option is to rewrite the law so that any organization that replaces Amtrak is exempted from FELA and is placed under workers' compensation laws.

Railroad Retirement

Railroad employees are not covered by Social Security but by the Railroad Retirement Act (RRA). Rail workers and the railroad industry jointly pay per-capita employment taxes that are substantially higher than Social Security payroll taxes, and such payments are put into a dedicated federal trust fund. Revenues from the fund are used to finance benefits paid to retired rail workers, their dependents or survivors, and disabled rail workers. Also, unemployment and sickness benefits are provided under the Railroad Unemployment Insurance Act (RUIA) rather than federal and state laws that cover all other industries. The RUIA benefits are paid from a separate federal trust fund financed exclusively by the railroad companies.

These laws present another problem to non-Amtrak operators. The decline in the number of railroad employees as a result of improved efficiencies on freight lines, or as a result of mergers, has a direct impact on the railroad retirement system. As the workforce shrinks and the retiree rolls balloon, costs increase on railroad companies that have a stable or growing workforce.

Amtrak finds that it is paying disproportionately into the fund. It is paying about $142 million annually in excess of its own retirement needs, which in 1997 are modest because it has a fairly large workforce but a relatively small retiree roster. Amtrak has tried to chip away at the requirement to cover employees under the railroad retirement system, asking Congress to change the law so that part-time station custodians (a growing workforce) should not be considered railroad employees for retirement purposes. Congress has yet to agree.

A new passenger train operator would also pay a disproportionate share of retirement expenses (costs related to employees from a bygone era), an economic anomaly that does not apply to its competitors. Again, to induce new entrants, Congress should amend the law on behalf of those who work on passenger trains in a post-Amtrak environment. They should be shifted to Social Security and related laws that cover all other Americans.

Laws as Obstacles

The RLA, FELA, RRA, and RUIA—abbreviations that would baffle most Americans—are laws that have a bewildering and inhibiting effect on newcomers. (If these stodgy laws had covered employees in America's computer industry, Silicon Valley would still be an agricultural area.) Failing to change these laws would mean that it's acceptable for public policy to blunt new initiatives in an old industry. Thus, future decisions to avoid entering the rail passenger business may have less to do with its prospects as a business and more to do with these costly and byzantine laws. If an entrepreneur or risk-taking company has worked under "normal" labor, injury, and retirement laws, why would it elect to come under these fossilized aberrations?

At a minimum, Congress should legislate a new category of railroad workers for those in private-sector concerns or in public agencies that operate intercity trains as replacements for Amtrak. This law, sweeping in scope, would move these employees out from under the unique railroad laws and put them under the laws that cover all other workers in the United States.

Remember the lessons from the World Bank study on Japanese railway privatization: government must put the proper incentives in place to induce replacements for a nationalized entity. Also, to create an environment for the new organization to succeed, government must leave the sins of the past in the past. The RLA, FELA, RRA, and RUIA laws are not exactly sins of the past—indeed, they were right for their times—but in the realm of post-Amtrak passenger train operations, they will be sins of the future.

Profit Sharing

The duty to improve the bottom line for passenger train operations through labor reforms should do more than simply call for sacrifices from railroad employees. Reforms should also encourage profit sharing by employees. Former federal railroad administrator Gilbert Carmichael believes that "for those services which are candidates for privatization, employee ownership or an equity stake for employees merits consideration."

John O'Leary and William D. Eggers of the Reason Foundation, writing in *Privatization and Public Employees: Guidelines for Fair Treatment,* agree that giving workers an ownership interest in an enterprise is a good idea. They write: "The term employee ownership embraces a number of strategies that result in stock being owned by employees.

Such arrangements are typically structured through Employee Stock Ownership Plans, which give workers a stake in performance. . . . Employee ownership played an important role in Britain's privatization program of the 1980s, especially in the area of bus services." They explain that privatization through employee ownership also has the advantage of offering current workers an economic incentive to privatize, since stock offerings are often free or heavily discounted for workers.

It is true that labor unions often oppose privatization, but if circumstances are right, unionized employees may resist less than reformers fear. Consider two North American experiences, both dealing with railroads.

At Conrail's inception, labor unions agreed to changes in work rules and pay scales below the industry norm. In return, these employees obtained a stake in the new company. Without labor's cooperation, it is doubtful that Conrail could have become the leaner, market-oriented company that has improved service, gained traffic, and produced profits.

At the Canadian National, about 40 percent of its employees have purchased stock in the company. *Progressive Railroading*'s Tom Judge reported, "While CN is not officially an employee-owned company, the employees are shareholders, not just stakeholders. After all, it's a lot easier to be devoted to creating shareholder value when you and your friends and co-workers are shareholders. . . . The attitude exhibited by the employee shareholders [at an annual meeting] gives the railway a definite edge."

Steve Savas would agree for another reason: selling or giving shares to workers of an enterprise that is to be denationalized helps to build support, which is needed because privatization is more a *political* than an *economic* act.

Private Financing for
New Passenger Railroads

The brightest future for intercity rail passenger service in the next century will be in corridors where travel demand will support new high-speed rail lines.

With or without Amtrak, public treasuries will have a tough time financing such lines. Ken Bird of Illinois Rail said public-private partnerships are essential in this emerging business: "The deficit and budget realities at the state and national level and the pressing repair needs of current infrastructure—along with ongoing social program requirements—will continually clash with those who would finance high-speed rail solely from government treasuries. Only through private-public partnerships that provide a return on the investment in real dollars will we be able to afford such systems."

Such ventures have yet to become a reality in the United States. Dan Cupper reported in *Trains* that year after year "the previous year's hot corridor has gone down in flames, the result of political fights, public-relations sabotage, lack of state or private money, or lack of federal resolve to do anything more than pay for more studies. The casualty list of unfulfilled hopes isn't short: California, California-Nevada, Florida, Illinois-Wisconsin, New Mexico, New York, Ohio, Pennsylvania, Texas."

The failure of these projects is a reminder that entrepreneurs do not seek risks, they seek opportunities. Federal and state governments should play a role in helping to build such lines, considering that they offer social benefits, including relief from airport and highway congestion, energy conservation, and abatement of air pollution.

The federal government can induce private investment in such facilities by, again, changing the law. The investment community is innovative, and its interest would be boosted through continuing to use federal authority for tax-exempt bond financing; creating public-benefit bonds with special rules to make them appealing to pension fund investors; providing federal loan guarantees on a highly selective basis; continuing cross-border leasing authority as well as lease-purchase and sale-leaseback transactions; permitting depreciation of high-speed train equipment on an accelerated basis; and using infrastructure banks to form public-private partnerships, which is permitted in a limited fashion under the 1995 National Highway System Designation Act.

How States Can Help

State and local governments could maximize their public powers in eminent domain, establish tax assessment districts, assist with funding environmental assessments (just as they do for highways and airports), grant real estate development rights to franchisees around stations, and provide access to state funding for construction of system infrastructure.

Some states are looking to other revenue streams. Florida will use one cent of its gas tax, about $70 million per year, as part of a package that includes bonds to help finance development of a high-speed rail line. A California report suggests using retail sales taxes and a motor vehicle fuel excise or sales tax to help finance the system. The planners said they want to keep the need for state funds reduced to the greatest extent possible. They recognized, however, that "once the capital debt has been repaid, the system will generate substantial excess revenue that may be returned as income to the state"; so they do see a payback.

New rail infrastructure can come about another way, too. Robert Poole of the Reason Foundation explained in testimony to the U.S. Senate Budget Committee: "A global trend is the use of a long-term franchise by which a private firm or consortium is authorized to design, finance, build, own, and operate a new infrastructure facility. In most such arrangements, at the end of the franchise period (typically, twenty to forty years), the facility is transferred to the government, free and clear. Hence, the common term for such arrangements is *build-operate-transfer* (BOT).

Poole said there are several principal advantages of using long-term franchises for new infrastructure. First, it permits government to tap into new sources of capital at a time when public resources for infrastructure are shrinking. Second, experience shows that private firms are able to develop projects considerably faster than government can—sometimes with time savings of as much as 50 percent. Third, since time is money, the private sector's speedy design-build methods can reduce investment costs; in addition, a firm that will be the owner-operator has strong incentives to design the facility for efficient operation. Fourth, BOT projects transfer a significant degree of risk from government to the private sector, thereby limiting the extent to which resources get spent on white-elephant projects.

Public Ownership of Rights-of-Way and Track

The state governments could boost private-sector involvement in regional and high-speed rail through public ownership of rights-of-way and track. A high-speed developer is at a disadvantage if it has to acquire rights-of-way as well as build all needed capital-intensive facilities with private funds.

The aviation and highway competitors enjoy rights-of-way provided to them at public expense. Gil Carmichael, acknowledging that the government has stacked the deck against rail, said, "Use of these corridors establishes a foundation for the public-private partnership that we've been talking about, in which the state government makes its contribution in the form of its rights-of-ways that it's got billions of dollars invested in [such as along highways]. Securing the right-of-way represents a significant funding issue for these projects."

Precedents exist. The federal government owns Amtrak's Northeast Corridor, but states and local authorities also own rail lines where commuter trains operate. Parts of the Northeast Corridor are owned by Massachusetts, Connecticut, and New York. Commuter trains are running over state- or locally-owned lines in New Jersey, Pennsylvania, Florida, Illinois, Texas, and California.

Regional Trains

State-supported regional trains will evolve in areas where their continuance may be socially desirable but ridership is insufficient for the train to operate at a profit. Savas would say that states should contract for the services at what he calls a "negative price." In other words, the state would evaluate bids and find the lowest subsidy required to operate a particular route while meeting standards set for particular schedules, frequencies, and amenities.

A way to alleviate objections is to modify the Intermodal Surface Transportation Efficiency Act of 1991. The law created flexible funding programs such as the Surface Transportation Program (STP) and the Congestion Mitigation and Air Quality Improvement Program (CMAQ). The STP funds issued as block grants are intended to be used for congestion relief in urban areas; CMAQ funds are designed to fund projects that contribute to the attainment of air-quality standards. States may use such funds for a multitude of projects, but they are prohibited from using the STP funds for intercity trains.

This anomaly needs to be amended to permit states to use the flexible funding provisions for intercity rail passenger service, helping to put them in a position to contract for private-sector operators.

Federal Trust Funds
and New Rail Facilities

Transportation inequities are perpetuated by the existence of federal trust funds for highways and airports, but not rail. This is a disadvantage to private-sector developers of rail passenger service, regardless of the type of service they wish to offer. An articulate case for change came from a high-speed rail advocate.

"Rail companies are the only transportation systems required to 'pay-before-they-go,'" wrote Larry Salci when serving as vice chairman of Texas TGV. "Airlines and highways have been able to use a 'pay-as-you-go' principle, which has accelerated their development. . . . The resulting double standard has held private industry back from building a competitive high-speed rail industry in the United States."

Anthony Haswell would like to see Congress establish an Intercity Public Transportation Fund, with grants made on a matching basis to state and regional agencies for transportation projects without regard to mode. That would allow planners and policy makers to think in terms of moving people by the optimum mode or combination of modes rather than be constrained by the necessity of "preserving" existing service by one mode of transportation or another.

Amtrak is attempting to obtain a halfpenny of the federal gasoline tax for capital projects, a way of leveling the playing field against those who gain from the other trust funds. Amtrak's idea is a bad one simply because the money will go to Amtrak, possibly perpetuating the organization and maintaining long-distance trains that are holdovers from another age. Instead, Congress should make gas tax funds available *only* to organizations that substitute their trains for Amtrak trains. Such funding also should be limited to fixed facilities. While new equipment can be privately financed, the need for high-grade tracks and signals is critical to implementing high-speed train service. Moreover, past government expenditures for the benefit of highway and air services have gone almost entirely into fixed infrastructure rather than into new vehicles.

Also, the provisions of the Intermodal Surface Transportation Efficiency Act should be amended to permit states to utilize block grants for non-Amtrak intercity rail passenger service. This would place rail programs on an equal footing with a multitude of other purposes permitted by the law. Putting equity in the way states may finance projects would boost the prospects for successful intercity rail service.

A Congressional Action Plan

Time has run out for Amtrak. Its future as an organization is irrelevant after one considers the dynamic changes taking place on railroads in numerous foreign lands. If Amtrak were located in *their* lands, governments would be closing down Amtrak.

Congress should initiate the process to phase out and dissolve Amtrak while creating opportunities for new providers. It should enact comprehensive legislation, perhaps named the Rail Service De-Nationalization Act, which would contain the following provisions:

1. *Repeal existing laws.* The Rail Service De-Nationalization Act would substitute for or repeal provisions of the Rail Passenger Service Act, the law that created Amtrak and gave Amtrak its statutory monopoly. The new statute should also repeal the Swift High Speed Rail Development Act, a law that channels capital funding to questionable Amtrak projects. A search for needed changes in other statutes is also in order. Congress should avoid creating confusion as it did when it closed the U.S. Bureau of Mines but left references to the bureau's responsibilities in 158 laws.

2. *Create an Amtrak Transition Board (ATB).* As previously described, this board would hold broad powers to manage the privatization and regionalization of intercity rail passenger service and the sale or transfer of Amtrak's fixed and rolling assets to appropriate interests. It should have the same protections (or stronger ones) that the military base–closing commission had against political interference.

3. *Set "sunset" dates.* The law should establish a deadline by which Amtrak shall be dissolved as an entity. To allow time for asset sales and other obligations to be completed, the sunset date of the ATB would follow that of Amtrak's, probably by several years.

4. *Name the ATB as Amtrak's successor agency.* The act should specify that the ATB assume liabilities that remain after Amtrak is dissolved. Examples would be claims and legal actions

that arose in Amtrak's ordinary course of business, such as injury claims by its employees and third parties.

5. *Continue Northeast Corridor capital funding as presently planned.* The Northeast Corridor is America's most important rail passenger line, and its continued development is vital to the future of post-Amtrak rail service.

6. *Impose a moratorium on most other capital funding.* All federal capital financing for Amtrak outside the Northeast should cease, except as required to ensure safe operations or as part of matching funds when states are upgrading facilities for regional service likely to survive Amtrak's demise.

7. *Limit operating funds.* Caps should be set on operating subsidies for rail passenger service. States should be permitted to have limited access to such funds, perhaps based on train-miles to be operated, to assist in the transition to regional train service. Subsidies should scale downward to eventual termination.

8. *Pre-authorize interstate compacts.* The law should pre-authorize creation of an interstate compact composed of the eight northeastern states and the District of Columbia for the purpose of facilitating Northeast Corridor rail service in a post-Amtrak era. Further, it should authorize "any and all" future compacts that states may wish to form for rail passenger service, without the need for further federal legislation.

9. *Establish a "post-Amtrak employee" category of worker.* If Congress fails to repeal the costly and unwieldy Railway Labor Act, Federal Employers' Liability Act, Railroad Retirement Act, and Railroad Unemployment Insurance Act, then Congress should at least establish in law a new category of worker, perhaps named the "post-Amtrak employee," who is exempt from those laws. Putting such employees under mainstream laws such as Social Security and the National Labor

Relations Act will be vital to induce investment, create jobs, and foster rail service to places that otherwise would be without such service.

10. *Create equitable funding mechanisms.* Congress should create an Intercity Public Transportation Fund and modify the Intermodal Surface Transportation Efficiency Act to permit states to utilize funds without perpetuating one mode of transportation over another. Amtrak should be excluded from receiving such funding.

There it is—a ten-point plan that would forever change the nature of passenger train service in the United States.

This plan will be called "provocative" or worse by dissenters, those who refuse to see the Amtrak experiment as a failed one. Objections and protests are sure to be heard from vested interests who gain from the status quo. Arguments are sure to be made to preserve Amtrak, but a close scrutiny of those arguments will reveal them to be holdovers from the 1970s and early 1980s, when it seemed Amtrak might have a chance.

One argument sure to be heard is that Congress should just put Amtrak through a massive "re-engineering," change related laws, and let Amtrak continue as a "more efficient operator." The problem is, it won't work.

Look elsewhere in the world, and the lesson is that an enterprise with a zero or negative net worth has sunk so low that it isn't worth saving. Robert Poole has examined public-asset sales worldwide and explained, "The reality is that over the years these enterprises have been saddled with all kinds of directives and controls that constrain them from operating as true businesses. Our counterparts in England, France, Italy, Germany, Australia, New Zealand, and elsewhere have all found that it is much easier to make these enterprises efficient and profitable by privatizing them than by attempting to reform them within the government. . . . The debates in these countries have passed beyond whether to privatize and focus instead on how best to do the job."

New Trains on the Horizon

T he United States can do this job. Rail passenger service is changing in many diverse nations as significant railroad restructurings are implemented. It is only a matter of time before Amtrak takes its turn in a long line of historic railroad changes.

If we take the proper steps—like enacting laws to reflect conditions as we expect them to be in the year 2001, not as they were in 1901—passenger trains will run in America for a long time to come. Despite Amtrak's dissolution, the basic requirement for train transportation will remain in the markets where trains are useful and needed.

Will Americans continue to be served by commuter trains? Yes, and the numbers of these trains will increase.

Regional trains? Yes, and eventually with augmented frequency.

Land-cruise trains? Yes, and they will offer amenities unseen on Amtrak trains today.

Auto-trains? Yes, and more than the single frequency operating on only one line today.

High-speed trains? In the Northeast, yes. Other corridors with exceptionally high travel demand? Yes, someday.

Tomorrow's non-Amtrak environment will offer trains of interest to America's rail visionaries, rail incrementalists, and rail passengers.

Participants on all sides of the Amtrak debate will probably agree that travel by train can be a thoroughly pleasurable and memorable experience. That lure will remain a part of American trains, nurtured by those who will step forward and run tomorrow's rail services.

We have an inkling of that in the *American Orient Express* brochure, which creates the urge to climb aboard a train:

Travel through the dramatic Columbia River Gorge, pass towering cliffs and cascading waterfalls. . . . Marvel at Yellowstone's famous geysers and watch for elk, moose, bison, and bears. . . . It is also a journey back in time to the romantic days of railroading. In vintage carriages glistening with mahogany and polished brass, we enjoy the pleasures of gourmet meals and attentive service, the camaraderie of fellow travelers, and the classic experience of exploring our country the way people did more than half-a-century ago. . . . It is a sentimental journey through some of the country's most spectacular landscapes aboard the deluxe *American Orient Express*—and a celebration of American history and culture and the rich legacy of our nation's railroads.

Nearly every accommodation on these private-sector trains will be sold out. That kind of entrepreneurship can spread throughout the United States if only we give it a chance.

ACKNOWLEDGMENTS

M any people in many countries responded to my request for assistance, including some who went out of their way to locate historical data. I appreciate the help I have received from them all. They are:

In the North American railroad industry, Kathy Deppen, assistant to the treasurer, Conrail; Gail Dever, Public Relations, Canadian National Railway; Bruce M. Flohr, chief executive officer, RailTex; William A. Frederick, president, Arizona & California Railroad Co.; M. J. Furtney, public relations director, Union Pacific; Jim Sabourin, general director—Media Relations, Burlington Northern Santa Fe; Kathy

Simpson, Public Relations, Kansas City Southern Railway; and Ann G. Thomas, corporate relations officer, Illinois Central.

In the commuter rail field, Marjorie Anders, Public Relations, Metro-North; Carole Foster, commuter rail assistant, Dallas Area Rapid Transit; Jack R. Gilstrap, executive vice president (retired), American Public Transit Association; Jeff Maclin, director of public information, New Jersey Transit; Janet McGovern, public information specialist, Peninsula Corridor Joint Powers Board; Susan McGowan, Media Relations, Long Island Rail Road; Philip A. Pagano, executive director, Metra; and Nanci Philips, public relations manager, Maryland Mass Transit Administration.

Others involved in rail service, Julia Andrick, Grand Canyon Railway; Eric Bélanger, Public Relations, Rocky Mountaineer Railtours; Ken Bird, president, Illinois Rail; Vicki Brems, Marketing, American Orient Express; Anthony Haswell, founder, National Association of Railroad Passengers; Marcia Pilgeram, Operations, Montana Rockies Rail Tours; Alfred Runte, author of *Trains of Discovery: Western Railroads and the National Parks;* David H. Rush, board member, First American Railways; and Eugene K. Garfield, founder, Florida Bee Line Rail.

In the privatization community, Pamela Arruda-Lambo, press secretary to Congressman Scott Klug; Michael D. LaFaive, research assistant, Mackinac Center for Public Policy; Robert W. Poole, Jr., president, Reason Foundation; and Sonja Wilmink, business development manager, BAA USA.

In government, Peter Necheles, Finance Policy Office, U.S. Department of the Treasury; John H. Anderson, Jr., and Richard Jorgensen, U.S. General Accounting Office; and Lee Grissom, director of the Governor's Office of Planning and Research, Sacramento.

In the media, I'm indebted to Murray Hughes, editor of *Railway Gazette International.* This is an appropriate place to mention that reviewing several years' worth of that publication, along with *International Railway Journal, Passenger Train Journal* (now known as *Rail News*), *Progressive Railroading, Railway Age,* and *Trains* provided information that was indispensable to this effort. They are excellent magazines.

The scope of this book broadened after I had the benefit of conducting exhaustive interviews on foreign railroad privatization and new technological developments. In the overseas rail community, I thank Jacques Balause, International Relations Department, French National Railways; Manual Diaz del Rio, International Department, Spanish National Railways; Peter Häfner, international vice president (retired), and Frank-Matthias Ludwig, Policy Department, German Rail. Also assisting were Dominique Desjardins, GEC Alsthom Transport, Paris; Marie Dooling, Public Affairs, Virgin CrossCountry, Birmingham, England; Andy Lazarus and Rose Morgan of A. J. Lazarus Associates, Inc., New York, on behalf of Rail Europe; Thierry Marechal and P. Debaix, International Union of Public Transport, Brussels; and Charles Croce, Monica Provenzano, and Joseph Zucker (retired), Public Relations, Lufthansa German Airlines.

In Japan I met with executives of numerous organizations. For the time, effort, and sharing of information, I am indebted to quite a number of people.

JR East: Massayuki Saitoh, director general; Ryuji Sakamoto, general manager and Shinichiro Asano, assistant manager—International Department; Kozo Yoshida, managing director and director-general, Corporate Planning; and Chojiro Watanabe, manager-Sendai Shinkansen Rolling Stock Base.

JR Central: Kaoru Umemoto and Toru Fukushima, managers—International Section; Tatsushi Morishita, International Section; Kazuhisa Matsuda, director—Linear Express Development Division; Takeshi Nagai, assistant manager, Marketing, all in Japan; and Shin-Ichi Kondo, Hiroshi Kanai and Yukio Homma, general managers, and Meredith Naranjo, research coordinator, Los Angeles.

JR West: Masayuki Sakata, general manager—Corporate Planning; Hideto Hidaka, director and deputy general manager, Corporate Planning; Eiji Yagi, deputy manager, Corporate Planning; and Hiromichi Umayahara, deputy manager, Foreign Affairs.

Japan Freight Railway Company: Yasushi Tanahashi, president.

Railway Technical Research Institute: Masanori Ozeki, president; Toshiaki Sasaki, director; Yasuo Sato, general manager—Planning; Masayuki Miyamoto, general manager—Rolling Stock Research Division; Shin-Ichi Tanaka, executive director; Hisashi Tanaka, chief engineer; Shohiko Miyata, director general—Maglev Development; Nobuyuki Kokubun, senior engineer—Maglev System Development; Nobuyuki Matsumoto, chief researcher; and Koichi Ichinohe, manager—Miyazaki Maglev Test Center.

Japan Railway Technical Service: Hiroshi Okada, president, and Masao Saitoh, consultant.

Ministry of Transport: Hideaki Mukaiyama, vice minister—International Affairs; Minoru Ekuni, deputy director—International Affairs; Jun Sawada, deputy director-general for Engineering Affairs, Railway Bureau; and Katsuhiko Hara, senior officer—International Affairs, Railway Bureau.

Japan Transport Economics Research Center in Tokyo: Yasuo Wakuda, president; Hikoshirou Matsumoto, director—International Affairs Division; Hiroshi Ugai, director for research; Akihiko Yamane, senior researcher; and Ayako Tomite, International Affairs Division. Helping from the Washington, D.C., office were Osamu Matsumoto, senior representative, and Toshiki Sakurai, deputy representative.

Japan Railways Group in New York: Akio Kambara, executive director; Akiyoshi Yamamoto, deputy director; Shiro Katsurai, director; and John Tedford.

Teramura International, Inc.: Keiko Nishimoto, vice president.

HSST Development Corporation: Tatsuo Doi, Tokyo.

I'm grateful for the help of Stuart Carroll, my attorney in Los Angeles, for his assistance.

Finally, I wish to acknowledge Jim Fitzgerald, my editor at St. Martin's, who liked my first book enough to give me a chance on my second. I am blessed to find support at such a fine publishing house.

Thank you, all.

BIBLIOGRAPHY

| | |

RAIL SERVICE

Alaska Railroad Historical Summary. Anchorage: Alaska Railroad, n.d.
———. *Background on Amtrak.* Washington, D.C.: Amtrak, September 1978.
Barriger, John Walker, III. *Super-Railroads for a Dynamic American Economy.* New York: Simmons-Boardman Publishing Corp., 1956.
Carpenter, T. G. *The Environmental Impact of Railways.* New York: John Wiley & Sons, 1994.
Cupper, Dan. *Crossroads of Commerce: The Pennsylvania Railroad Calendar Art of Grif Teller.* Richmond, Vt.: Great Eastern Publishing, 1992.
Daughen, Joseph R. and Peter Binzen. *The Wreck of the Penn Central.* Boston: Little, Brown, 1971.
Federal Subsidies for Rail Passenger Service: An Assessment of Amtrak. Washington, D.C.: Congressional Budget Office, July 1982.

First American Railways, Inc., Registration Statement with U.S. Securities and Exchange Commission, September 1, 1995.

High-Speed Rail Summary Report and Action Plan (Final Report). Sacramento: California Intercity High-Speed Rail Commission, December 1996.

Hilton, George W. *Amtrak: The National Railroad Passenger Corporation.* Washington, D.C.: American Enterprise Institute for Public Policy Research, 1980.

Hughes, Murray. *Rail 300: The World High Speed Train Race.* North Pomfret, Vt.: David & Charles, 1988.

In Pursuit of Speed: New Options for Intercity Passenger Transport. Special Report No. 233. Washington, D.C.: Transportation Research Board, 1991.

Itzkoff, Donald M. *Off the Track: The Decline of the Intercity Passenger Train in the United States.* Westport, Conn.: Greenwood Press, 1985.

Jensen, Oliver. *The American Heritage History of Railroads in America.* New York: American Heritage, 1975.

Keeping Track: Preliminary 1997 Program and Budget. Chicago: Metra, October 1996.

Kisor, Henry. *Zephyr: Tracking a Dream Across America.* New York: Times Books, 1994.

Martin, Albro. *Railroads Triumphant.* New York: Oxford University Press, 1992.

Middleton, William D. *North American Commuter Rail 1994.* Pasadena, Calif.: Pentrex, 1994.

Monthly Management Report (June 1996) and *FY96 in Review.* Boston, Mass.: Massachusetts Bay Transportation Authority.

Ogburn, Charlton and James A. Sugar. *Railroads: The Great American Adventure.* Washington, D.C.: National Geographic Society, 1977.

Pell, Claiborne. *Megalopolis Unbound: The Supercity and the Transportation of Tomorrow.* New York: Frederick A. Praeger, 1966.

Recent Issues in Rail Research. Transportation Research Record No. 1381. Washington, D.C.: Transportation Research Board, 1993.

Runte, Alfred. *Trains of Discovery: Western Railroads and the National Parks.* Niwot, Colo.: Roberts Rinehart Publishers, 1994.

Salk International Airport Transit Guide. Sunset Beach, Calif.: Salk International, 1995.

Strohl, Mitchell P. *Europe's High Speed Trains: A Study in Geo-Economics.* Westport, Conn.: Praeger Publishers, 1993.

Thomas Cook European Timetable (September 24–October 31, 1995). Peterborough, England: Thomas Cook Publishing.

Thomas Cook Overseas Timetable (September–October 1995). Peterborough, England: Thomas Cook Publishing.

Thompson, Gregory Lee. *The Passenger Train in the Motor Age: California's Rail and Bus Industries, 1910–1941*. Columbus, Ohio: Ohio State University Press, 1993.

GOVERNMENT

Amtrak's Current Situation. Hearings before the Subcommittee on Railroads, Committee on Transportation and Infrastructure, February 7, 10, and 13, 1995. Washington, D.C.: U.S. House of Representatives.

Budget of the United States Government, 1996. Washington, D.C.: U.S. Government Printing Office, 1995.

Final Report on Basic National Rail Passenger Service. U.S. Department of Transportation, Washington, D.C., January 28, 1971.

Creating a Government That Works Better & Costs Less (also known as "The Gore Report on Reinventing Government" and "Report of the National Performance Review"). New York: Times Books, 1993.

Kennedy, William R., Jr. and Robert W. Lee. *A Taxpayer Survey of the Grace Commission Report*. Ottawa, Ill.: Jameson Books, 1984.

MacNeil, Neil and Harold W. Metz. *The Hoover Report 1953–1955: What It Means to You as Citizen and Taxpayer*. New York: Macmillan, 1956.

Phillips, Kevin. *Arrogant Capital: Washington, Wall Street, and the Frustration of American Politics*. Boston: Little, Brown, 1994.

Rauch, Jonathan. *Demosclerosis: The Silent Killer of American Government*. New York: Times Books. 1994.

U.S. Senate. *The Doyle Report: National Transportation Policy*. Washington, D.C.: U.S. Government Printing Office, 1961.

Woodward, Bob. *The Agenda: Inside the Clinton White House*. New York: Simon & Schuster, 1994.

PRIVATIZATION

Aslund, Anders, ed. *Economic Transportation in Russia*. New York: St. Martin's Press, 1994.

Financing the Future: Report of the Commission to Promote Investment in America's Infrastructure. Washington, D.C.: U.S. Department of Transportation, 1993.

Fukui, Koichiro. *Japanese National Railways Privatization Study*. Washington, D.C.: World Bank, 1992.

Galal, Ahmed and Mary Shirley. *Does Privatization Deliver? Highlights from a World Bank Conference*. Washington, D.C.: World Bank, 1994.

Gibbon, Henry. *A Guide for Divesting Government-Owned Enterprises.* Los Angeles: Reason Foundation, 1996.

Gómez-Ibáñez, Jose A. and John R. Meyer. *Going Private: The International Experience with Transport Privatization.* Washington, D.C.: Brookings Institution, 1993.

Hilke, John. *Cost Savings from Privatization: A Compilation of Study Findings.* Los Angeles: Reason Foundation, 1993.

Holt, Jane. *Transport Strategies for the Russian Federation.* Washington, D.C.: World Bank, 1993.

Hudgins, Edward L., ed. *The Last Monopoly: Privatizing the Postal Service for the Information Age.* Washington, D.C.: Cato Institute, 1996.

Issues and Achievements in the Five Years Since the Japan National Railway Reform. Tokyo: Japan Transport Economics Research Center, October 1992.

Kikeri, Sunita, John Nellis, and Mary Shirley. *Privatization: The Lessons of Experience.* Washington, D.C.: World Bank, 1992.

Linowes, David F. *Privatization: Toward More Effective Government.* Report of the President's Commission on Privatization. Urbana, Ill.: University of Illinois Press, 1988.

Love, Jean, Wendell Cox, and Stephen Moore. *Amtrak at Twenty-Five: End of the Line for Taxpayer Subsidies.* Policy Analysis No. 266. Washington, D.C.: Cato Institute, December 1996.

O'Leary, John and William D. Eggers. *Privatization and Public Employees: Guidelines for Fair Treatment.* Los Angeles: Reason Foundation, 1993.

Osborne, David and Ted Gaebler. *Reinventing Government: How the Entrepreneurial Spirit Is Transforming the Public Sector.* New York: Plume, 1993.

Poole, Robert W., Jr. *A Federal Privatization Agenda.* Testimony presented to the U.S. Senate Budget Committee, June 29, 1995. Los Angeles: Reason Foundation.

Poole, Robert W., Jr. *Guidelines for Airport Privatization.* Los Angeles: Reason Foundation, 1994.

Privatization 1996: Tenth Annual Report on Privatization. Los Angeles: Reason Foundation, 1996.

Ridley, Tony M. and Francis R. Terry. *International Review of Railway Privatisation and Major Investment Projects.* University of London, Centre for Transport Studies, October 1992.

Savas, Emanuel S. *Privatization: The Key to Better Government.* Chatham, N.J.: Chatham House Publishers, 1987.

Weicher, John C., ed. *Private Innovations in Public Transit.* Washington, D.C.: American Enterprise Institute for Public Policy Research, 1988.

INDEX

Aerolineas Argentinas, 189
*Agenda: Inside the Clinton White House,
    The* (Woodward), 164–65
Air France, 185
Airlines:
    high-speed train operations and,
        123–26
    myth about influence at Amtrak of,
        128–29
Airports, 101
    privatization of, 178
    -rail cooperation, 126–27
Air Transport Association, 59
Air travel, 15, 51, 52, 101
    overseas, 60–61

safety of, 21, 52–53
subsidies for, 41–42
Alaska Railroad, 64, 121, 159, 171
Alitalia Airlines, 123, 124
Allen, Michael, 224
Allen, Ron, 177
American Airlines, 123, 125–26
American High Speed Rail Corporation
    (AHSRC), 85
American Orient Express, 64–65, 69
American Orient Express (AOE), 30–31,
    122, 146, 151, 241–42
Amtrak:
    accidents, 17–22, 149–50
    annual reports, 20–21, 43–44, 45, 46

Amtrak *(continued)*
  Auto Train, 4, 67
  board members, 33
  Chicago operations, 9–12
  as commuter train contractor, 111–14
  comparison with Third World train
    systems, 10–11
  creation of, ix, 2, 28, 76
  discontinued trains, 7, 22–26, 54–55,
    168–70
  dissolution of, *see* Dissolution and
    transition plan, Amtrak
  financial performance of, 36–41, 95, 210
  food service, 5, 16–17, 25
  high-speed trains, 74–116
  long-distance trains, 49–67, 72–73
  maglev and, *see* Maglev (magnetic
    levitation) trains
  maintenance of tracks, 21, 148–49, 204
  marketing efforts, 3, 4, 23, 43, 128
  as monopoly, 28–31, 43
  Northeast Corridor, *see* Northeast
    Corridor
  on-time performance, 5–6, 7–9
  politics and, *see* Politics and Amtrak
  privatization of, 156, 158–59, 172–73,
    203–207, 211, 212
  public agency status, 32–34
  reorganization at, 43
  ridership projections, 34–35
  safety, 17–22, 52, 149–50
  schedule deterioration, 11–14
  schedule improvement, 12–15
  state ownership, transfer of assets to, 159
  stock of, 33, 203–204
  structural problems, 27–47
  subsidies, *see* Subsidies for Amtrak
  terminals, 4–5
  track ownership, 8, 109, 145
  unsanitary conditions on, 15–17
Amtrak Transition Board (ATB),
    proposed, xii, 214–16, 219, 223,
    238–39
Ansco Corporation, 120
Argentina, xii, 180, 189–91
Armstrong, Peter, 65
Arrogant Capital (Phillips), 162
Associated Press, 5, 24, 82

Association of American Railroads, 102, 228
ATE Management & Service Company,
    133
Australia, 193, 240
Austria, 187
Auto-ferry service, 72, 73, 133, 241
  Amtrak *Auto Train,* 4, 67
Automobile travel, 21, 50–51, 61–62
  overseas, 60
  see also Highways
Auto-Train company, 29
Aviation Daily, 92
Aviation Week, 101, 123, 185
Ayling, Robert, 94

BAA, 126, 183
Bagby, Milton, 70
Barriger, John W., III, 44, 146
Barton, Joe, 213, 225–26, 227
Bayh, Birch, 54
BC Rail, 66
Beggs, James M., 171
Belden, Tom, 85
Berriger, John, 153
Bezilla, Mike, 24
Biaggini, Benjamin F., 28
Binzer, Peter, 77
Bird, Ken, 26, 233
Blanc, Christian, 185
Blaszak, Michael W., 150
Bombardier Incorporated, 83–84, 98
Boyd, Alan S., 8, 85
Branson, Richard, 123, 181
Brazil, 191
Breaux, John, 179
British Rail, 181
Brown, Robert Clarke, 123
Build-operate-transfer (BOT), 234–35
Burkhardt, Edward A., 192
Burlington Northern Santa Fe (BNSF),
    18, 48–49, 110, 120, 121, 122, 133,
    136, 140, 190
Buses, 21, 51, 60, 122, 170–71
Bush, George, 174
Business Week, 26

California, 99–100, 132
CalTrain, 111–12

Canadian National Railway, 141, 201–202, 232
Cane, Mark S., 30
Carmichael, Gilbert, 231, 235
Carol, David, 81
Carpenter, A. R. "Pete," 144, 147
Carr, Bob, 90, 93
Car travel, *see* Automobile travel
Cato Institute, 61
China, 193–94, 204
Claytor, W. Graham, Jr., 8, 25, 86–87, 90–93, 94, 96, 103
Cleary, Patrick J., 227–28
Clinton, Bill, and Clinton administration, 31, 144–45, 162–66, 174, 209
Colodny, Ed, 125
Comarco, Inc., 175–76
Commuter trains, x, 28, 104–16, 241
   Amtrak as commuter rail contractor, 111–14
   dissolution of Amtrak, effect of, 114, 115–16
   facility sharing and joint operations with Amtrak, 114
   freight railroads and, 117–21
   growth in ridership, 104
   non-Amtrak, 106–10
Condé Naste Traveler, 7
Congress, U.S.:
   politics and Amtrak, *see* Politics and Amtrak
   subsidies for Amtrak, *see* Subsidies, federal
Congressional Budget Office, 42
Conrail, 19–20, 100–101, 109, 138–39, 143, 150, 171, 221, 232
   creation of, 137
   privatization of, 158
   success of, 158–59, 218
Conte, Christopher, 157
Continental Airlines, 16
CP Rail, 121, 141
Crandall, Bob, 126
Crossroads of Commerce (Cupper), 129
CSX, 121, 134–35, 143–44, 149–50, 159
Cupper, Dan, 24, 84, 129, 233

Daughen, Joseph R., 77
DeLibero, Shirley A., 116

Delta Air Lines, 123, 125, 135
Demosclerosis: The Silent Killer of American Government (Rauch), 159–60
Denmark, 187
Dissolution and transition plan, Amtrak, xiii, 208–42
   Amtrak Transition Board (ATB), proposed, xii, 214–17, 219, 223, 238–39
   commuter systems, effect on, 114, 115–16
   Congressional action plan, 237–41
   labor laws and, 224–31, 239–40
   liquidation questions, 212–14
   market demand issues, 217–19
   passenger trains, 224–35
   rolling stock disposition, 222–23
Douglas, Roger, 180
Downs, Thomas M., x, 5, 8, 22, 27, 35, 43, 47, 57, 83, 157–58, 172, 203, 209–10
Doyle Report, 55
Drucker, Peter F., 173
Duncombe, Ted, 24

Earth in the Balance (Gore), 163
Eastern Europe, 61, 187–89
East-West Airlines, 124
Economist, The, 174
Eggers, William D., 231–32
Europe's High Speed Trains: A Study in Geo-Economics (Strohl), 95
Eurotunnel, 184–85

Federal Aviation Administration (FAA), 15, 51, 177–78
Federal Employer's Liability Act (FELA), 228–29, 230–31, 239
Federal Railroad Administration (FRA), 18–19, 20, 40, 80, 88, 163–66, 213–14
Federal Transit Administration, 81
Federal trust funds, 236–37
Ferrocarriles Afgentinoos (FA), 189–91
Field, David, 94
Financial Times, 123
Financial World, 126
Fink, Jonann, 130

First American Railways, 133, 150
Florida Fun Train, 68–69, 134–35, 150
Florida Overland Express (FOX), 98–99
Food and Drug Administration (FDA),
    15–17
Forbes, 209
Foulke, Judith, 16
France, privatization in, 185–86, 240
Freight railroads, 9, 73, 107, 118, 136–54
    delays, costs of, 147–48
    future of, 152–53
    intercity passenger trains and, 121–22
    interference with passenger service, 143–
        45
    liability exposure from passenger train
        accidents, 149–50
    need for more track, 139–41
    passenger train business and, 118–22,
        134–35
    passenger train costs on, 145–47
    in post-Amtrak environment, 151
    rolling stock advances, 141–43
    success of, 44, 136–38
    track-maintenance costs, 148–49
French National Railway, 185
French TGV, 8, 18, 21, 60, 74, 87, 90,
    95–96, 102, 125, 185–86
Fukui, Koichiro, 196, 215–16

Gaebler, Ted, 44–45
Garibotto, Enrique, 191
GEC Alsthom, 83–84, 98
Geist, Richard A., 31
Gelleflint, 189
General Accounting Office (GAO), U.S.,
    34–35, 38, 39, 41, 46, 71, 89, 111,
    145, 218
German railway system, 46, 165, 186–87,
    240
    ICE train, 18, 60, 83, 88–89, 96, 102
Gertz, Dwight, 139–40
Gibbon, Henry, 220
Gilliam, Reginald E., Jr., 102
Gilson, Lawrence D., 95
Glickman, Dan, 95
*Going Private: The International Experience
    with Transport Privatization* (Gómez-
    Ibáñez and Meyer), 178

Goldin, Daniel, 176
Gómez-Ibáñez, Jose A., 178
Gonzalez, Felipe, 180
Gore, Al, 83, 163, 165
Gore Report on Reinventing Government,
    155–56
Grace Commission Report, 156, 176, 179
Great Britain, privatization in, xii, 181–
    84, 218, 221, 240
Greyhound Lines, 3, 51, 122
*Guide for Divesting Government-Owned
    Enterprises, A* (Gibbon), 220

Hannigan, Tom, 132
Harper, Edwin L., 102
Harrison, E. Hunter, 228
Hartke, Vance, 54
Hartley, Scott, 108
Haswell, Anthony, 1–2, 8–9, 11, 26, 35–
    36, 42, 57, 59, 63, 130, 131, 160–
    61, 218, 221, 237
Hatfield, Robert S., Jr., 121
Hefley, Joel, 166, 225, 226
Herzog Transit Services, Inc., 110, 133
High Speed Rail Association (HSRA), x,
    87, 96
High-speed trains, x, 28, 61, 162–65, 233–
    35, 241
    airlines and, 123–26
    American Flyers, 83–85, 91
    growth in passenger traffic, 60
    Los Angeles–San Diego fiasco, 85
    maglev, *see* Maglev (magnetic levitation)
        trains
    Northeast Corridor programs, 76–85
    profitable, 94–96
    redefinition by Amtrak, 86–90, 97
    safety of, 21
    Texas TGV, death of, 90–94, 126, 163–
        64
    visionaries versus incrementalists, 74–
        76, 80, 82, 88, 97–101, 102–103,
        163
    see also individual systems
Highways, 15
    subsidies for, 42, 105
    see also Automobile travel
Hilke, John C., 175

Hilton, George W., 35
Hinson, David R., 101, 177–78
Holland America Westours, 64
Hughes, Murray, 80, 188

Illinois Regional Transportation Authority
(RTA), 131
Ingles, J. David, 102
In Search of Excellence (Peters and
Waterman), 45, 89
Institute for Transport Studies, 62
Intercity passenger trains, 121–22
Interest groups, 159–62
Intermodal Surface Transportation
Efficiency Act, 105–106, 236, 237,
240
International Air Transport Association
(IATA), 127
International Rail-Air Organization, 126
International Railway Gazette, 194
International Railway Journal, 18, 98, 197
Interstate Commerce Commission (ICC),
12, 49, 102, 118, 137
Interstate compacts, 130, 239
Italy, 187
Itzkoff, Don, 78

Japan Air Lines, 123, 125
*Japanese National Railways Privatization
Study,* 196, 215
Japan rail system, 46, 172, 203, 207
Bullet Trains, 18, 21, 75, 78, 87, 95, 218
maglev and, 165
privatization of, xii, 194–201
Japan Railway and Transport Review, 189
Japan Transport Economics Research
Center, 198
J. B. Hunt Company, 122
Jeannoit, Pierre, 127
Johnson, Lyndon B., 77
Jordan, Ed, 100
Jorgenson, Timothy R., 50, 130
Journal of Commerce, 143
Judge, Tom, 232

Kansas City Southern Railroad, 192, 203
Karr, Albert R., 166–67
Katopodis, John, 69

Kaye, Steven D., 20
Keefe, Kevin P., 5
Kelleher, Herb, 90, 92
Kelley, David, 132
Kerasiotes, James J., 111, 116, 178
Kiley, Robert, 31
Kirzner, Jerry, 112
Kisor, Henry, 9–10
Klug, Scott, 166
Knappen, Theodore, 170–71
Knutton, Mike, 18, 182, 194
Kogan, Jorge H., 189, 190
Kopp, Quentin, 132
Kramer, Gene, 82

Labor laws, 224–31, 239–40
Ladd, Jeffrey R., 109
Land-cruise trains, 30, 64–67, 73, 124,
151, 224
Lewis, Roger, 8, 34, 78
Liability insurance, 150
Lind, William S., 25
Lindley, William, 31, 161
London & Continental Railways, 124,
183–74
Long-distance passenger trains, 28, 48–67
common-carrier service, 49–53, 62, 72,
73
demographics of users of, 51–52, 57
future of, 72–73, 133
myths about, dispelling, 55–56
overseas, 59–63
politics and, 53–56
rerouted trains, 58–59
smaller communities and, 56–57
tour trains, 63–67
Long Island Rail Road (LIRR), 81, 107,
108, 114, 116
Loomis, Richard C., 176
Lufthansa Airlines, 123, 124, 125
Lukov, Boris E., 187–88

Machalaba, Daniel, 157
Mack, Connie, 213
Maglev (magnetic levitation) trains, 46–
47, 87, 124–25, 132, 165–66, 187
Maglev Consortium Inc., 125
Maglev Incorporated, 125

Malone, Frank, 119
Mansfield, Mike, 53, 54
Martin, Albro, 78–79, 144
Maryland Rail Commuter (MARC)
    agency, 113–14
Massachusetts Bay Transportation Authority
    (MBTA), 111, 114, 116, 150
Matsuda, Masatake, 200
Matthews, Anna Wilde, 210
Mead, Kenneth M., 34, 35, 40, 41, 46,
    111, 218
Menem, Carlos Saul, 180, 189
Messer, John, 32
Metra commuter rail system, Chicago,
    109–10, 116, 119, 132, 133
Metrolink, Southern California, 112–13,
    119
Metro-North, 107–108, 109, 114, 116
Mexico, 202–203, 223
Meyer, John R., 178
Mica, John L., 154, 222
Middleton, William D., 118
Midwest Express, 126
Miller, Dan, 213
Miller, Luther, 152, 202
Minge, David, 213
Molinari, Susan, 167, 209, 212
Molitoris, Jolene M., 163–66
Moynihan, Daniel Patrick, 166

Nakasone, Yasuhiro, 194, 216
Nall, Stephanie, 47
National Aeronautics and Space
    Administration (NASA), 176
National Association of Railroad
    Passengers (NARP), 1, 2, 90, 160–
    62, 173
National Maglev Initiative (NMI), 46–47
National parks, train travel to, 48, 63–65,
    66, 122
National Safety Council, 21
National Transportation Safety Board
    (NTSB), 19, 20, 142
Nelson, Donald N., 116
Netherlands, 187
New Jersey Transit (NJT), 81, 108–109,
    114, 116
Newman, Barry, 61

New York & Atlantic Railway Co., 107
New York Central Railroad, 12, 108
New York Times, The, 83, 162, 208
New Zealand, xiii, 180, 192, 203, 207, 240
Nordwall, Bruce D., 123
Norfolk Southern Railroad, 143, 159
Norman, James R., 209
Northeast Corridor, 35, 89, 166, 167,
    204–205, 211, 212
    future of, 219–22, 239, 241
    high-speed trains, 76–85
    sale of, 219–21
Northeast Corridor Improvement Project
    (NECIP), 78, 79, 81
Northeast High-Speed Rail Improvement
    Project (NHRIP), 79

Office of Management and Budget
    (OMB), U.S., 38
Office of Technology Assessment, 60
Off the Track (Itzkoff), 78
O'Leary, John, 231–32
Olympic Games, 1996 Atlanta Summer,
    69–70
"Operator-service provider" teams, 122
Osborne, David, 44–45

Pagano, Philip A., 109, 116
Passenger Train Journal, 26, 42, 79, 85, 209
Pell, Claiborne, 77
Peña, Federico, 52, 83, 177, 212
Peninsula Corridor Joint Powers Board, 120
Penn Central, 78, 108, 128, 137
Pennsylvania Railroad, 77
Peters, Thomas, 45, 47, 89
Peters, Tom, 162
Pettigrew, Andrew, 89
Phillips, Don, 84, 140, 156–57
Phillips, Edward H., 101
Phillips, Kevin, 162
Politics and Amtrak, 25, 154–71, 209
    call to kill Amtrak, 157–58
    Clinton's promises, 162–63
    interest groups, 159–62
    irrelevancy of Amtrak to voters, 168–71
    Republicans' role in preserving Amtrak,
        166–68
    retention of routes and, 53–56, 57

Poole, Robert W., Jr., 175, 180, 234, 235, 240
Princess Tours, 64
Private-sector contractors, 133
Privatization, xii, xiii
  of Amtrak, 156, 158–59, 172–73, 203–207, 211, 212
  definition of, 173
  federal agency, 176–79
  international developments, 179–203, 240–41
  of railroads, examples of, 180
  in the United States, 173–76
Privatization: The Key to Better Government (Savas), 174, 224–25
Profit sharing, 231–32
Progressive Railroading, 119, 139–40, 191, 219, 228, 232
Prouty, Winston L., 53
Public-private partnerships for high-speed rail development, 233–34

Railroad Retirement Act (RRA), 229–31, 239
Railroads Triumphant, 144
Railroad Unemployment Insurance Act (RUIA), 230–31, 239
RailTex, 139, 191
Railtrack, 183, 203, 221
Rail Travel News, 7
Railway Age, 118, 138, 152, 210, 219
Railway Gazette International, 8, 57, 59–60, 80, 188, 189, 191, 192
Railway Labor Act, 225–28, 227–28, 230–31, 239
Railway Technical Research Institute (RTRI), 198
Rauch, Jonathan, 159–60
Read, Brendan, 98
Reagan, Ronald, 86, 156, 157
Reason Foundation, 174–75, 231, 234
Reed, John, 9
Regional trains, x, 28, 241
  operated by state and regional authorities, 129–32, 224, 236
  state-developed, 70–71
Reinhardt, William G., 164

Reinventing Government (Osborne and Gaebler), 44–45
Reistrup, Paul H., 8, 35
Resor, Randolph R., 147–48, 149
Rice, Richard, 77
Richter, Frank, 191
Ridge, Tom, 167
Ridley, Tony, 8, 34, 195, 196
Rights-of-way, 120–21, 235
Riley, John, 117, 123
Robert, Gilbert M., 110
Roberts, Stephen T., 113
Roberts, William L., 47
Rocky Mountaineer Railtours, 65–66
Roth, Bill, 161
Rubin, Robert, 203
Runte, Alfred, 63, 64, 66, 73
Russia, 187–89
Russian High Speed Railways Shareholding Company, 188

Safety, 17–22, 52–53, 142, 149–50
Salci, Larry, 93–94, 95, 236–37
Samuelson, Robert J., x, 52, 155
San Diego & Imperial Valley Railroad, 133
San Diego Northern Railway, 113
Santa Fe Railway, 9, 63, 129
Savas, E. S. "Steve," 173–74, 178, 208, 224–25, 232, 236
Schmid, Randolph E., 24
Scott, Steve, 67
Sharp, Andrew, 126
Short-distance leisure-style trains, 67–70, 134–35, 150
Shuster, Bud, 167, 209, 212
South American rail systems, 59, 189–92, 223
Southeastern Pennsylvania Transportation Authority (SEPTA), 109, 131–32
Southern California Regional Rail Authority (SCRRA), 112–13, 119
Southern Pacific Railroad, 32, 58, 120, 128, 140–41
Southwest Airlines, 16, 90, 92, 93, 94
Spain, 180, 187
Sparaco, Pierre, 185
Staggers, Harley O., 53–54

Stanger, Richard, 112
State rail passenger corporations
  ("Babytracks"), 130
Stockman, David, 157
Strohl, Mitchell, 95
Subsidies for Amtrak, 73, 211
  comparison to other transportation
    system subsidies, 41–42
  federal, 26, 27, 32, 36–37, 42, 57, 154–
    55, 171, 205, 210
  from state and local governments, 32,
    36–38, 72
Sullivan, Dennis F., 17
Superelevation of tracks, 148–49
Super-Railroads for a Dynamic Economy
  (Barriger), 44, 146
Swan, Christopher C., 66
Sweden, 187
Swedish X2000, 82–83
Swift Rail Development Act, 31, 164, 238
Swissair, 123, 124, 125

Tanahashi, Yasushi, 200
Tellier, Paul M., 201, 202
Terry, Francis, 8, 34, 195, 196
Thatcher, Margaret, 181
Thompson, Louis S., 189
Tour trains, 63–67
Traffic World, 31
Trains, 5, 24, 26, 50, 84, 102, 108, 130,
  140, 150, 156–57, 233
Trains of Discovery (Runte), 63, 64
Transit Realty Associates, 111
Translinks 21, 57
Transportation Research Board, 148
Travel Industry Association of America
  (TIAA), 50–51
Tri-County Commuter Rail Authority,
  South Florida, 110
TurboTrain, 82–83, 84

Union Pacific Railroad, 48, 63–64, 104,
  110, 118–19, 122, 129, 133, 140–
  41, 146
United Airlines, 126
United Parcel Service, 140, 153
U.S. Railway Association, 137

USAirways, 123, 125
USA Today, 6, 94
U.S. News & World Report, 34

Vantuono, William C., 210, 219
VIA Rail, 202
Virgin Atlantic Airways, 123–24, 135
Virginia Railway Express, 113
Virgin Rail Group, 181
Volpe, John, 78

Wald, Matthew L., 83
Walker, Robert, 166–67
Wallop, Malcolm, 29
Wall Street Journal, 25, 35, 61, 157, 166,
  210, 224
Warner, David C., 79
Washingtonian, 20
Washington Post, 33, 157
Waterman, Robert, Jr., 45, 47, 89
Watson, Rip, 143
Watts, Ben, 98, 227
Watts, John, 183
Weicker, Lowell, Jr., 78
Weight system average cost model
  (WSAC), 149
Welty, Gus, 138, 152
Weyrich, Paul, 105
Wilson, Craig, 6
Wilson, Pete, 132
Windmuller, Thomas Stephen, 127
Wisconsin Central Railroad, 110, 120,
  133, 139, 183
Wise, Dean, 139–40
Wolf, Frank, 167, 213
Woodward, Bob, 164–65
Wreck of the Penn Central, The (Daughen
  and Binzen), 77
Wright, Michael, 7

Yamanouchi, Shuichiro, 172
Yardley, Jonathan, 157
Yeltsin, Boris, 188

Zephyr: Tracking a Dream Across America
  (Kisor), 9–10
Zeta-Tech, 147, 148, 149